Table of Contents

S0-CWW-129

MAP LEGEND

HIGHWAY TYPES — PRIMARY — TOLL HIGHWAYS — SECONDARY — CONNECTING — NEARING COMPLETION — UNDER CONSTRUCTION — ROUTE NUMBERS

CONTROLLED ACCESS

Multi-Lane Divided
Ⓡ Rest Area with Rest Rooms
▲ Rest Area without Rest Rooms
⏚ Principal Ski Area
81 · 81 · 690 · 40 U.S. Interstate · Provincial Autoroute

50 — Interchange and Exit Number
Interchange

2 & 3 Lane Undivided
National · State and Provincial Capitals · County Seat · ✈ Passenger Service Airport
1 · 301 · 57 U.S. Federal · Mexico Federal

Paved Divided
Distances between diamonds and outlined cities:
MILES in U.S. - KILOMETERS in Canada and Mexico.
3 · 24 · 177 State and Provincial · Trans-Canada

OTHER HIGHWAY CLASSIFICATIONS

Paved Undivided
City
Campground in Area (Check CampBook)
AAA Designated Scenic Byway
Town

Gravel
Customs Station · Ghost Town
Auto & Passenger Ferries
Trail
1 · 610 · A Indian · County and Local · County Boundary

Earth
Passenger Only
Coral Reef · Rocks
Time Line

AAA-recommended lodgings and/or restaurants are located in those communities printed in red on state and provincial maps. AAA members should consult the appropriate TourBook® for detailed listings.

Index Population Figures (2,755) Reflect Official United States and Canadian Census.

Photographs
Cover and inside pages © Digital Archives

©2003 HealthForum, LLC

Canadian population figures - Statistics Canada's 2002 GeoSuite, by permission of Canadian Minister of Industry.

Printed in Peru
Library of Congress 85-117512
AAA Stock #2804

Index – U.S. Counties

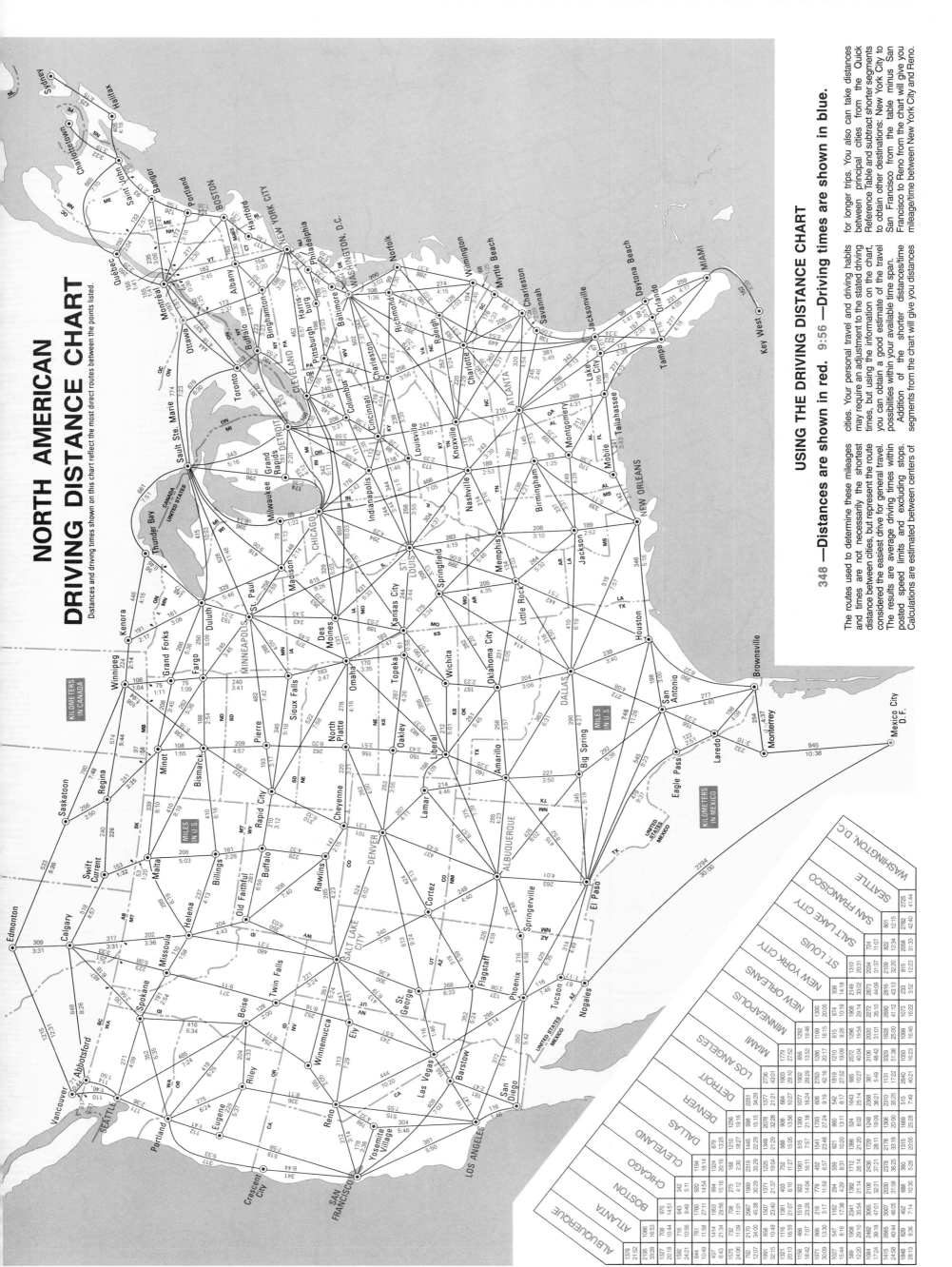

NORTH AMERICAN DRIVING DISTANCE CHART

Distances and driving times shown on this chart reflect the most direct routes between the points listed.

USING THE DRIVING DISTANCE CHART

348 —Distances are shown in red.   **9:56 —Driving times are shown in blue.**

The routes used to determine these mileages and times are not necessarily the shortest distance between cities, but represent the route considered the easiest drive for general travel. The results are average driving times within posted speed limits and excluding stops. Calculations are estimated between centers of cities. Your personal travel and driving habits may require an adjustment to the stated driving times, but using the information on the chart, you can obtain a good estimate of the travel possibilities within your available time span. Addition of the shorter distances/time segments from the chart will give you distances for longer trips. You also can take distances between principal cities from the Quick Reference Table and subtract shorter segments to obtain other destinations: New York City to San Francisco from the table minus San Francisco to Reno from the chart will give you mileage/time between New York City and Reno.

ALASKA
Scale in Miles
0 100 200 300 400
0 100 200 300 400 Scale in Kilometers

MEXICO SEE PAGES 142-143

HAWAII
Scale in Miles
0 20 40 60 80 100
0 20 40 60 80 100 Scale in Kilometers
Hawaii-Aleutian Time Zone

UNITED STATES

NATIONAL PARKS, MONUMENTS AND
STATE CAPITAL NAMES ARE SHOWN IN RED

Scale in Miles
50   0   50   100   150   200

50   0   50   100   150   200   Scale in Kilometers

ONE INCH EQUALS APPROXIMATELY 135 MILES OR 215 KILOMETERS
SEE PAGE 144 FOR DISTANCE CHART

CANADA SEE PAGES 126-127

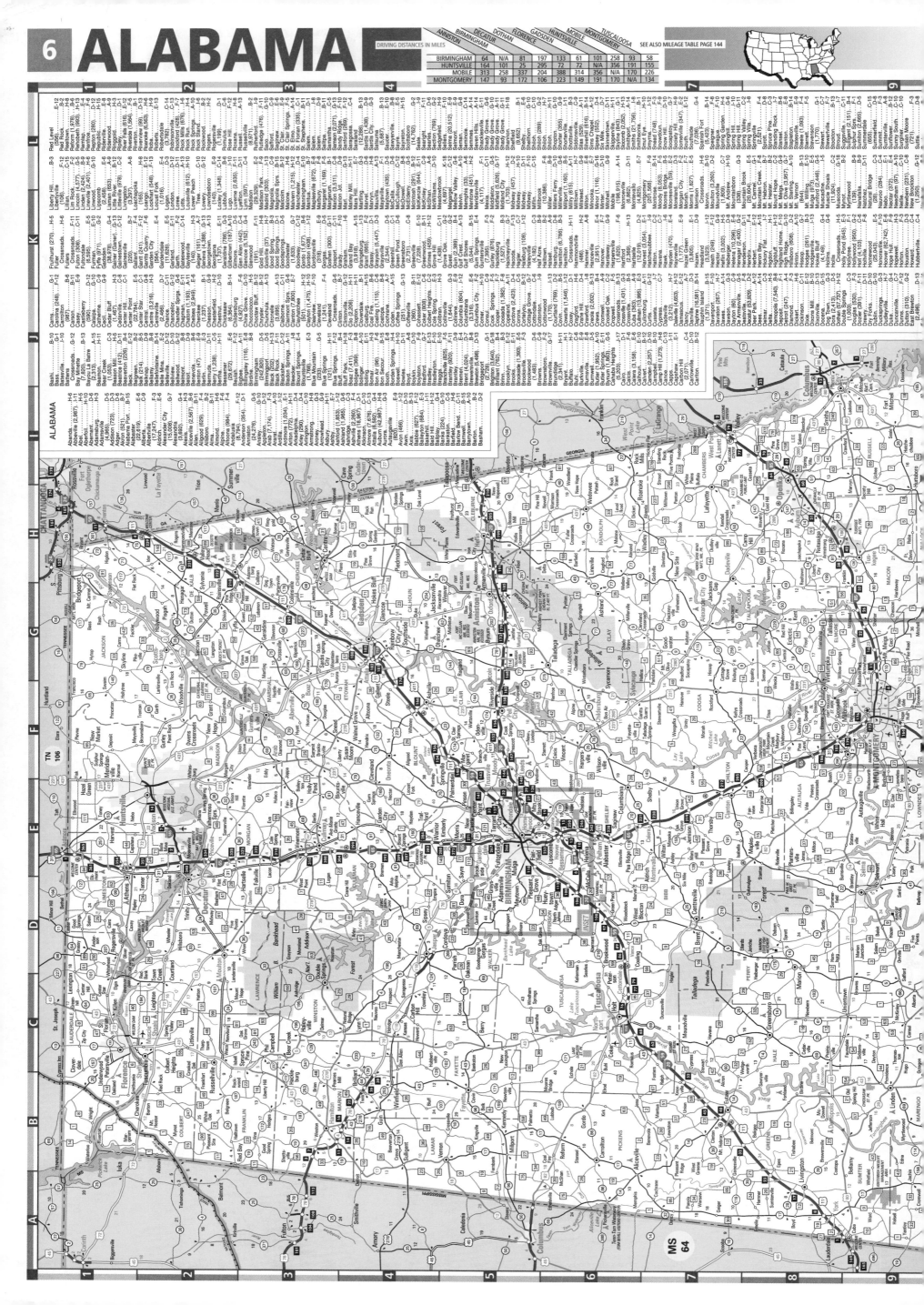

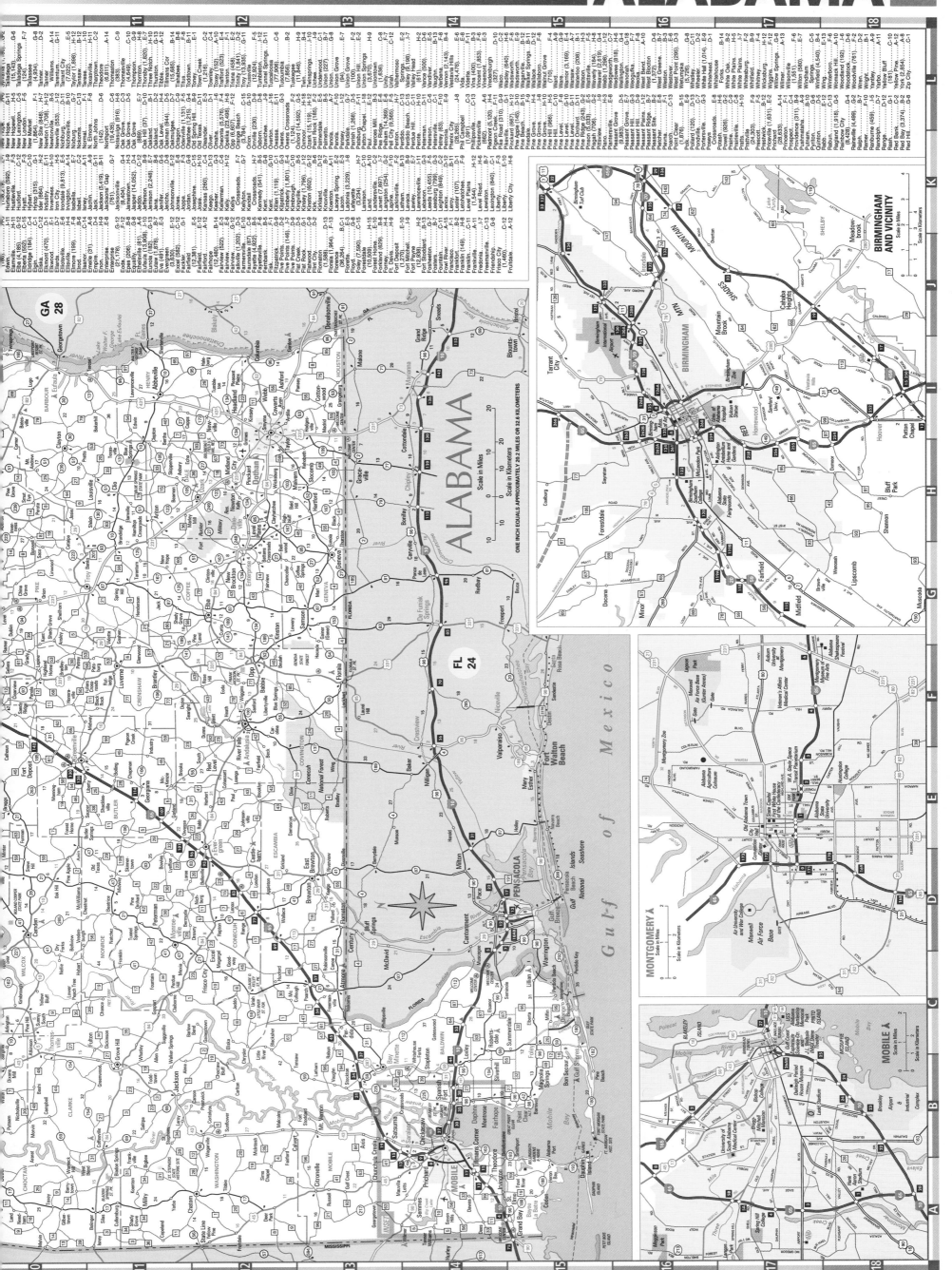

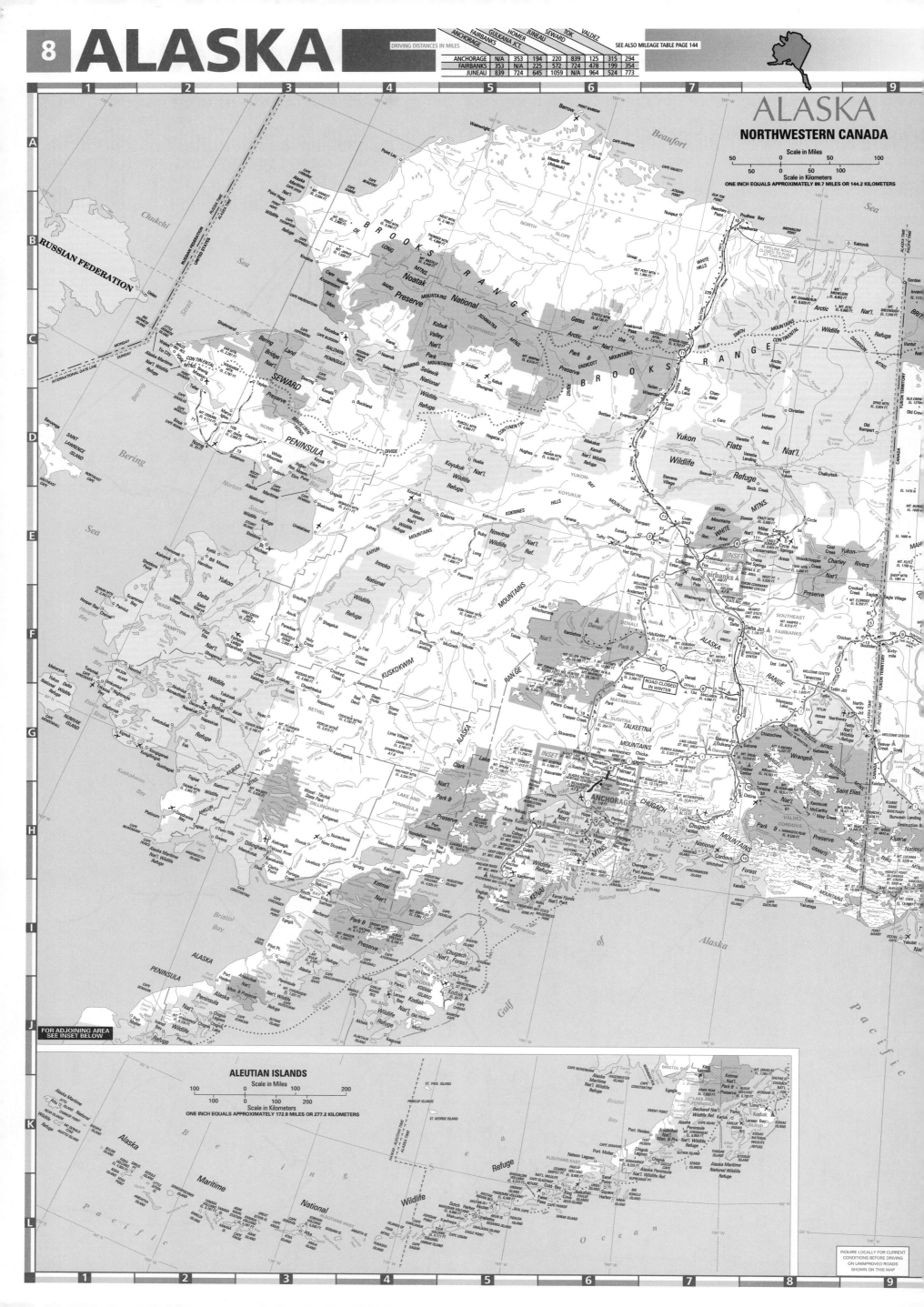

	ANCHORAGE	FAIRBANKS	GULKANA JCT.	HOMER	JUNEAU	SEWARD	TOK	VALDEZ
ANCHORAGE	N/A	353	194	220	839	125	315	294
FAIRBANKS	353	N/A	225	572	724	478	199	354
JUNEAU	839	724	645	1059	N/A	964	524	773

ALASKA
NORTHWESTERN CANADA

Scale in Miles

ONE INCH EQUALS APPROXIMATELY 89.7 MILES OR 144.2 KILOMETERS

RUSSIAN FEDERATION

BROOKS RANGE

SEWARD PENINSULA

NOME

Yukon Flats Nat'l. Wildlife Refuge

Fairbanks

ANCHORAGE

ALEUTIAN ISLANDS

Scale in Miles

ONE INCH EQUALS APPROXIMATELY 172.8 MILES OR 277.2 KILOMETERS

FOR ADJOINING AREA SEE INSET BELOW

Alaska Maritime National Wildlife Refuge

INQUIRE LOCALLY FOR CURRENT CONDITIONS BEFORE DRIVING ON UNIMPROVED ROADS SHOWN ON THIS MAP

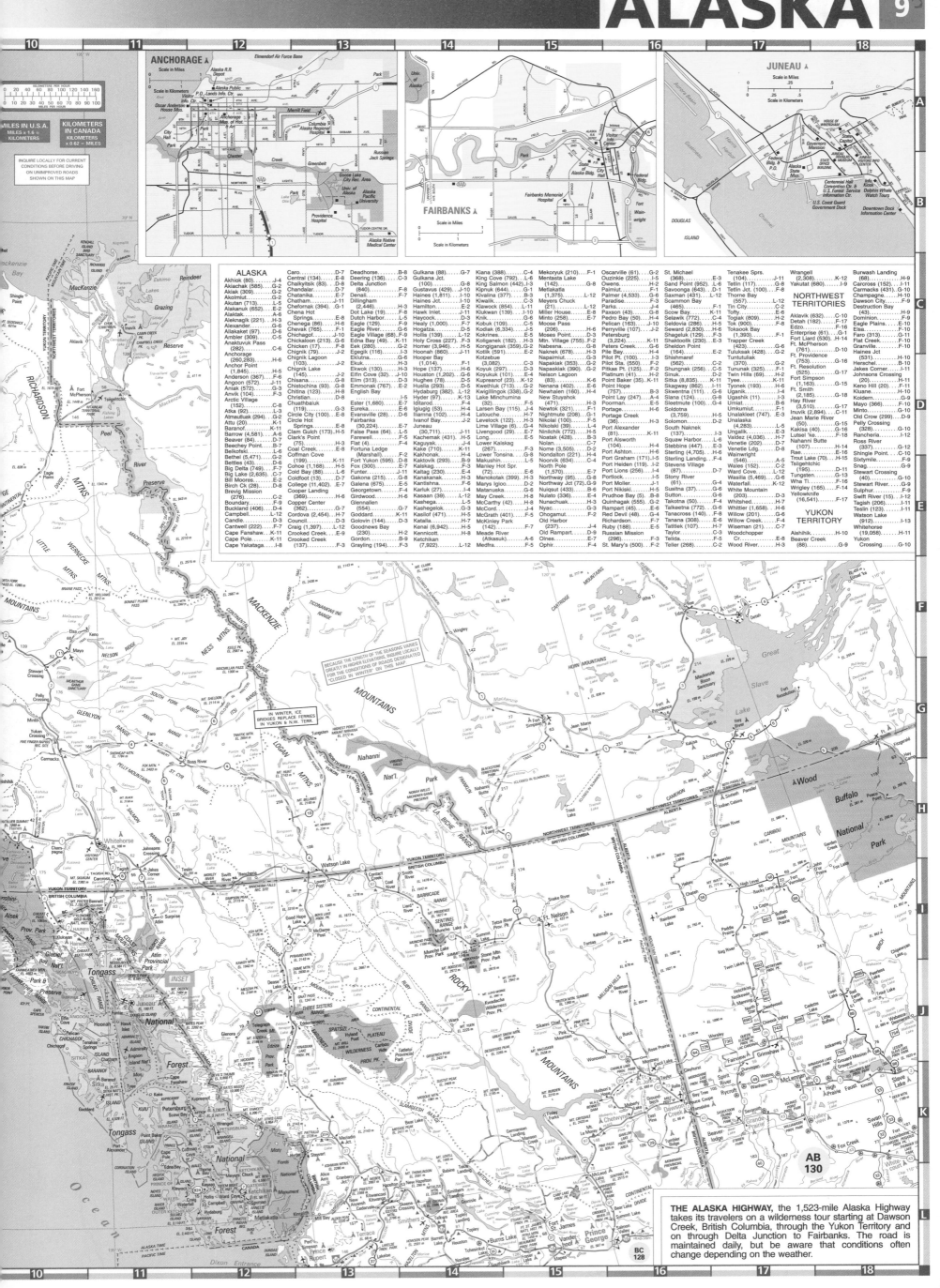

THE ALASKA HIGHWAY, the 1,523-mile Alaska Highway takes its travelers on a wilderness tour starting at Dawson Creek, British Columbia, through the Yukon Territory and on through Delta Junction to Fairbanks. The road is maintained daily, but be aware that conditions often change depending on the weather.

	CASA GRANDE	FLAGSTAFF	GRAND CANYON VILLAGE	HOLBROOK	KINGMAN	NOGALES	PHOENIX	SPRINGERVILLE	TUCSON	YUMA
FLAGSTAFF	196	N/A	90	93	148	321	137	186	255	322
GRAND CANYON VILLAGE	282	90	N/A	179	176	407	229	272	342	408
PHOENIX	53	137	229	232	184	179	N/A	216	116	184
TUCSON	67	255	342	237	297	67	116	236	N/A	237

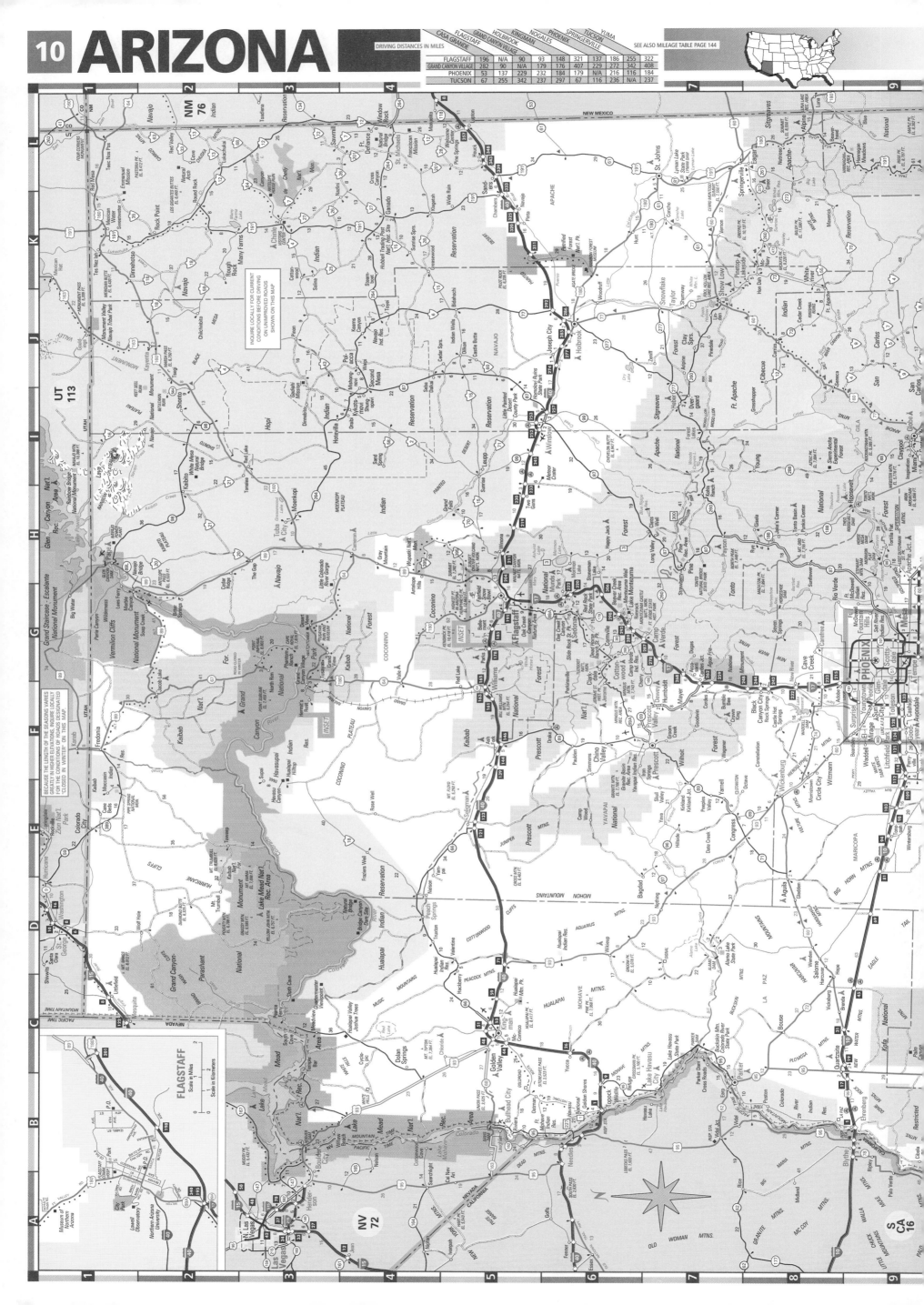

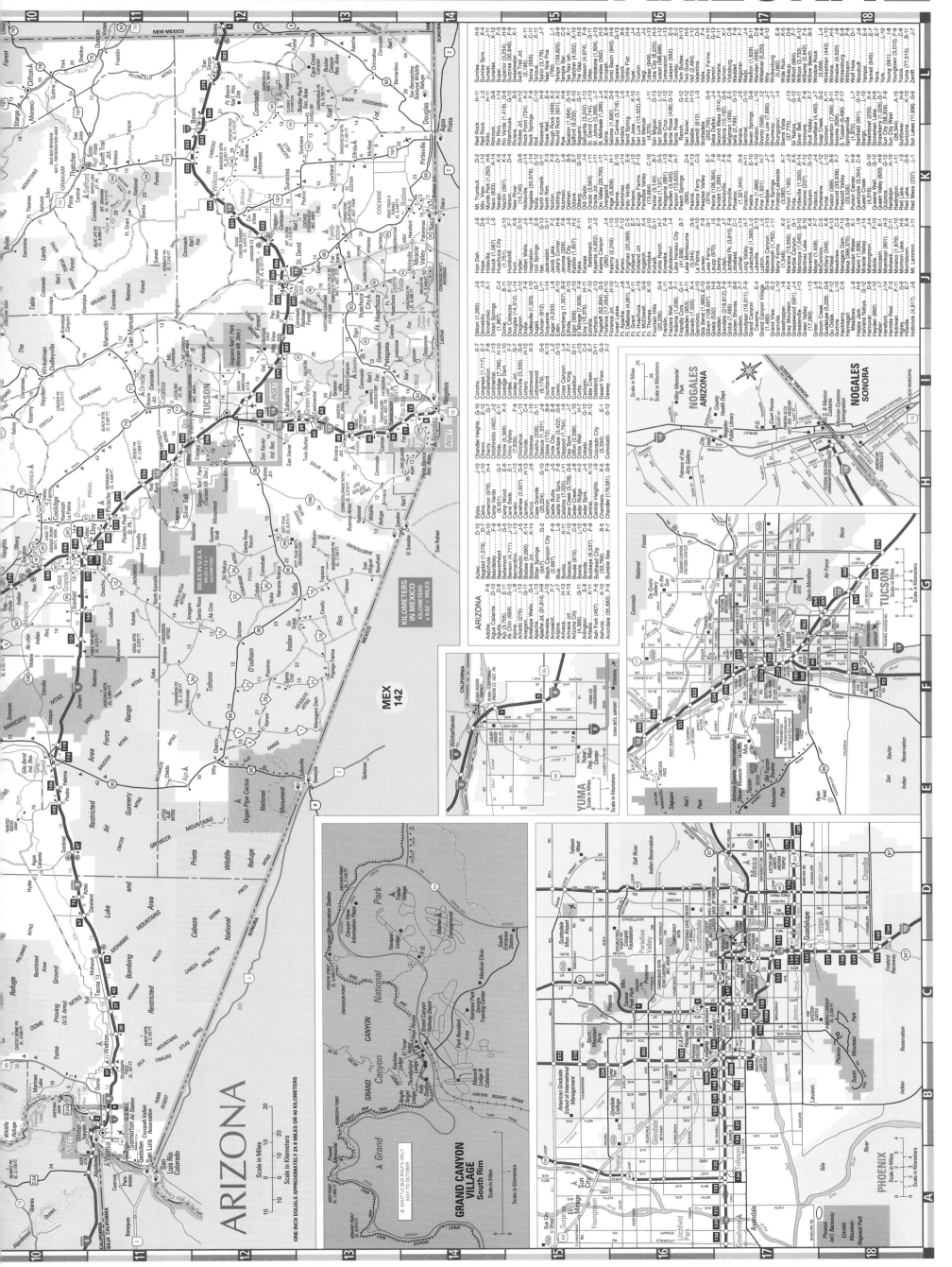

DRIVING DISTANCES IN MILES

SEE ALSO MILEAGE TABLE PAGE 144

	BRANSON, MO	EL DORADO	FAYETTEVILLE	FORT SMITH	HOT SPRINGS NAT'L PARK	JONESBORO	LITTLE ROCK	MEMPHIS, TN	PINE BLUFF	TEXARKANA
FORT SMITH	170	275	62	N/A	129	282	160	289	202	181
LITTLE ROCK	174	117	188	160	52	127	N/A	134	44	143
MEMPHIS, TN	303	250	318	289	186	71	134	N/A	177	277
TEXARKANA	310	87	324	181	113	269	143	277	181	N/A

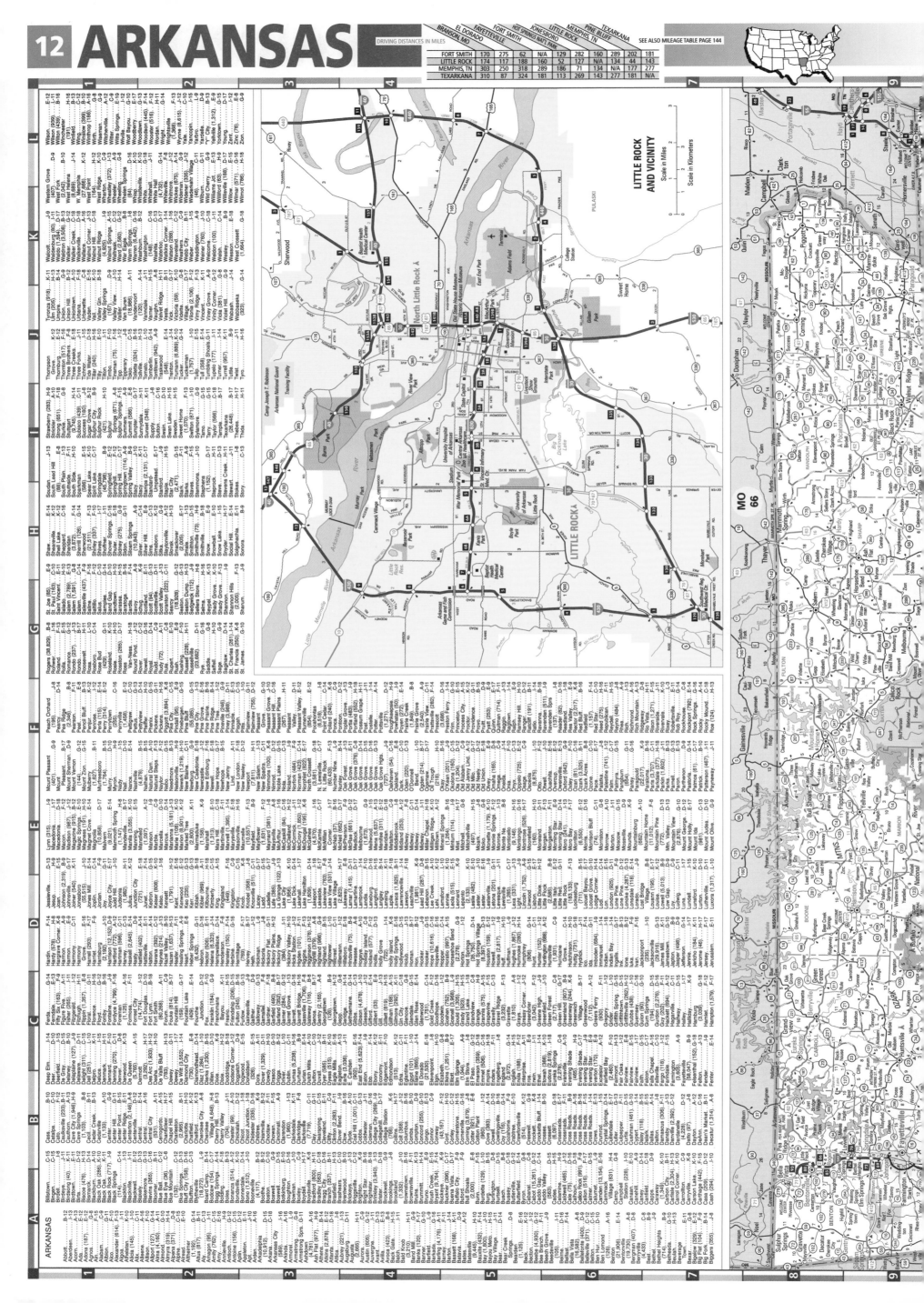

LITTLE ROCK
AND VICINITY

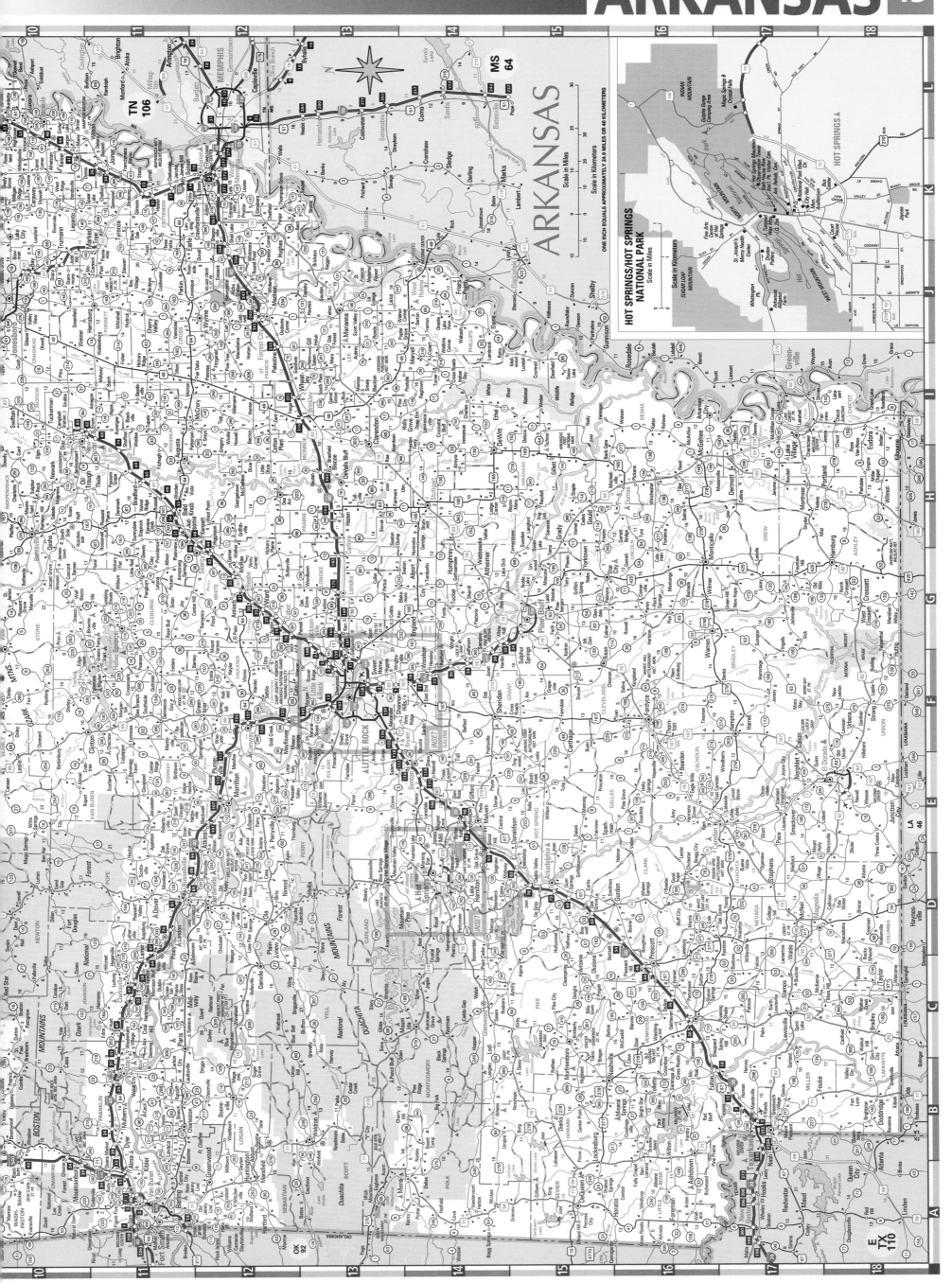

ARKANSAS

Scale in Miles

Scale in Kilometers

ONE INCH EQUALS APPROXIMATELY 24.9 MILES OR 40 KILOMETERS

HOT SPRINGS/HOT SPRINGS NATIONAL PARK

Scale in Miles

DRIVING DISTANCES IN MILES

SEE ALSO MILEAGE TABLE PAGE 144

	BAKERSFIELD	CRESCENT CITY	DEATH VALLEY	FRESNO	LOS ANGELES	SACRAMENTO	SAN BERNARDINO	SAN DIEGO	SAN FRANCISCO	SAN JOSE	SANTA BARBARA	YOSEMITE VILLAGE
LOS ANGELES	112	798	259	217	N/A	383	59	116	381	340	94	304
SACRAMENTO	275	416	550	168	383	N/A	440	501	86	123	397	192
SAN DIEGO	231	916	321	336	116	501	106	N/A	491	459	212	428
SAN FRANCISCO	282	353	567	185	381	86	437	491	N/A	46	335	178
SANTA BARBARA	178	685	352	253	94	397	152	212	335	290	N/A	374

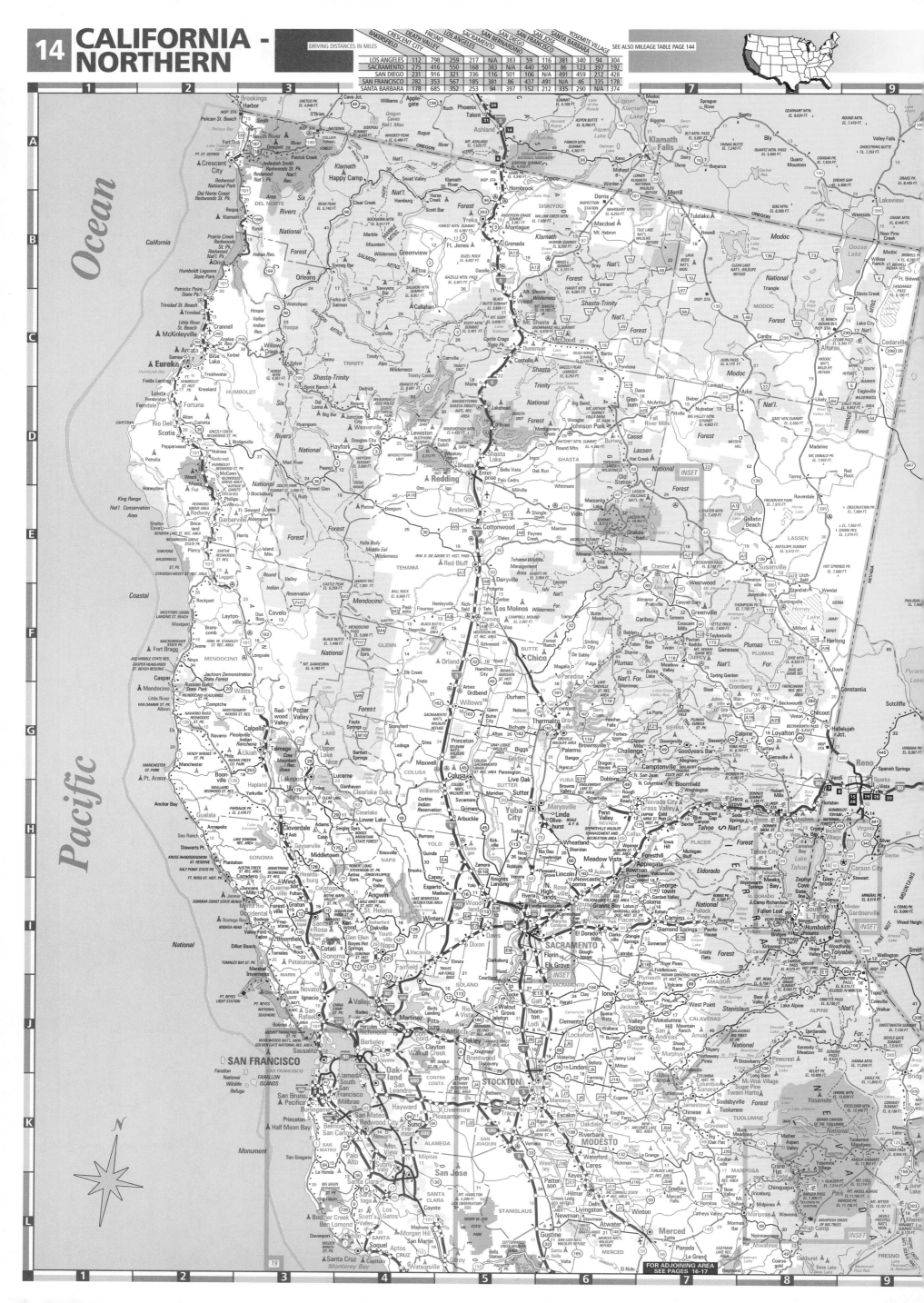

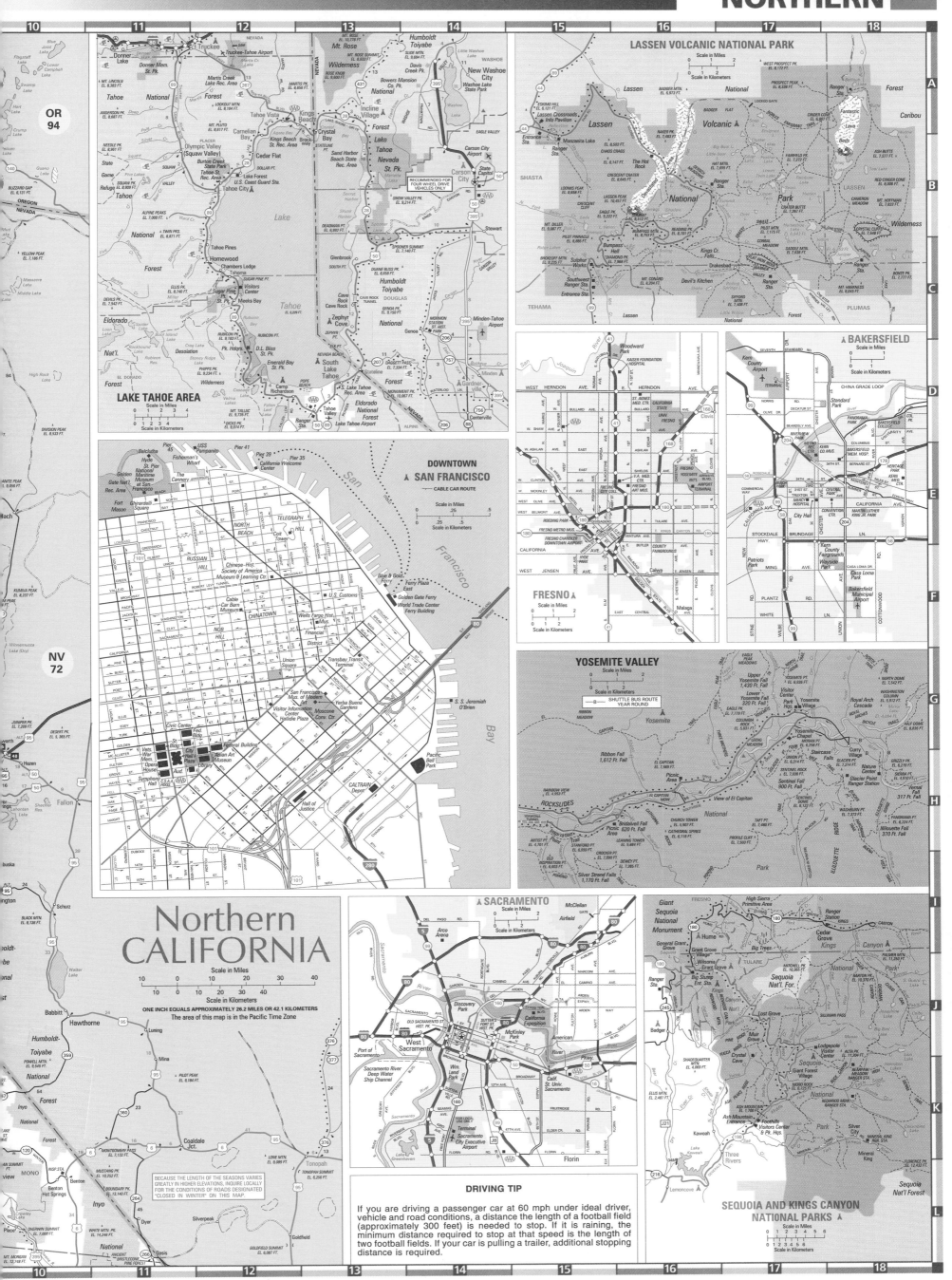

LAKE TAHOE AREA

Scale in Miles
0 1 2 3 4
Scale in Kilometers
0 1 2 3 4 5

LASSEN VOLCANIC NATIONAL PARK

Scale in Miles
Scale in Kilometers

DOWNTOWN SAN FRANCISCO

CABLE CAR ROUTE

Scale in Miles
0 .25 .5
Scale in Kilometers
0 .25 .5

FRESNO

Scale in Miles
0 1 2
Scale in Kilometers
0 1 2

BAKERSFIELD

Scale in Miles
Scale in Kilometers

YOSEMITE VALLEY

Scale in Miles
0 1 2
SHUTTLE BUS ROUTE YEAR ROUND

Northern CALIFORNIA

Scale in Miles
10 0 10 20 30 40
Scale in Kilometers
10 0 10 20 30 40

ONE INCH EQUALS APPROXIMATELY 26.2 MILES OR 42.1 KILOMETERS
The area of this map is in the Pacific Time Zone

BECAUSE THE LENGTH OF THE SEASONS VARIES GREATLY IN HIGHER ELEVATIONS, INQUIRE LOCALLY FOR THE CONDITIONS OF ROADS DESIGNATED "CLOSED IN WINTER" ON THIS MAP.

SACRAMENTO

Scale in Miles

SEQUOIA AND KINGS CANYON NATIONAL PARKS

Scale in Miles
0 1 2 3 4 5
Scale in Kilometers
0 1 2 3 4 5 6

DRIVING TIP

If you are driving a passenger car at 60 mph under ideal driver, vehicle and road conditions, a distance the length of a football field (approximately 300 feet) is needed to stop. If it is raining, the minimum distance required to stop at that speed is the length of two football fields. If your car is pulling a trailer, additional stopping distance is required.

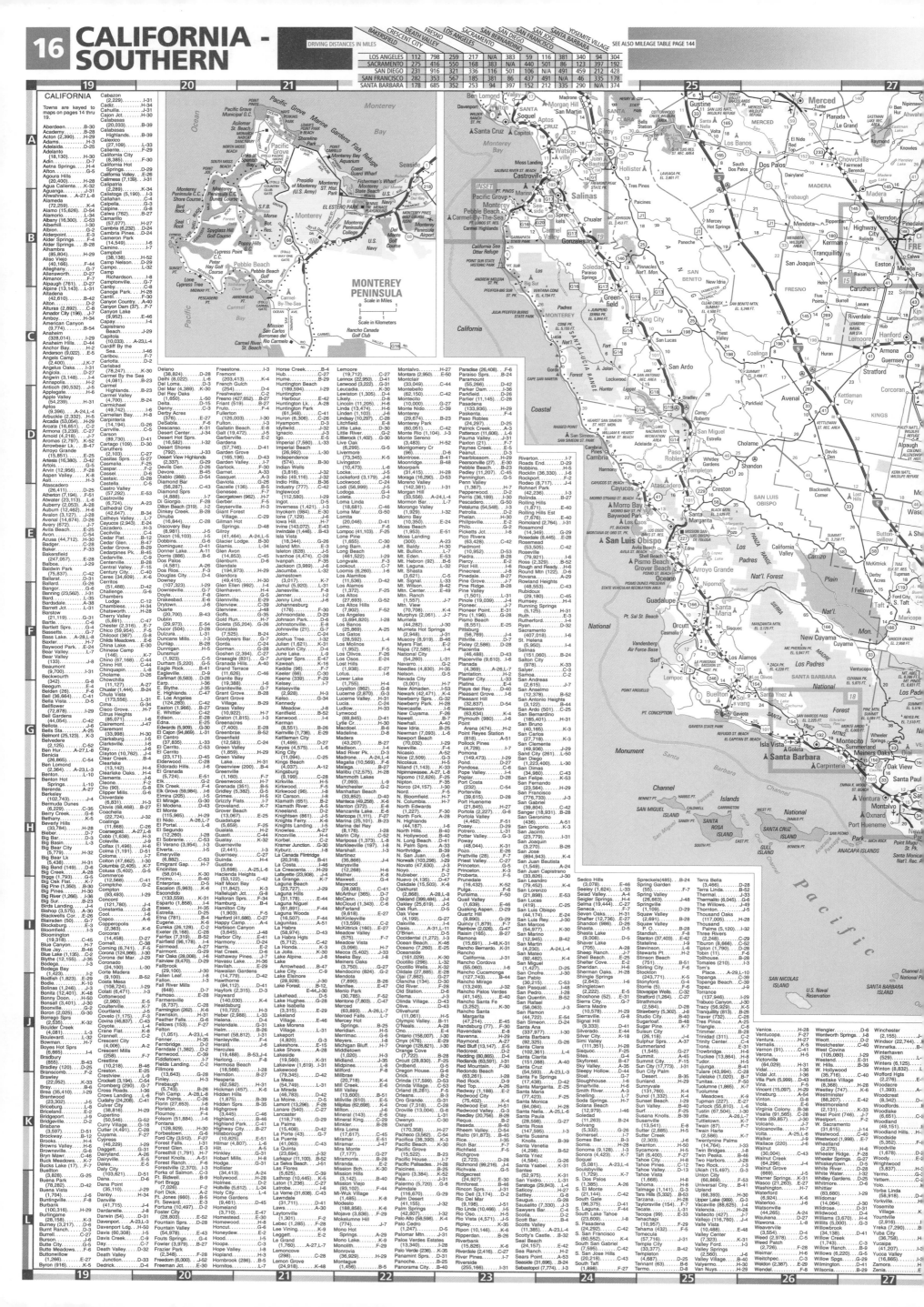

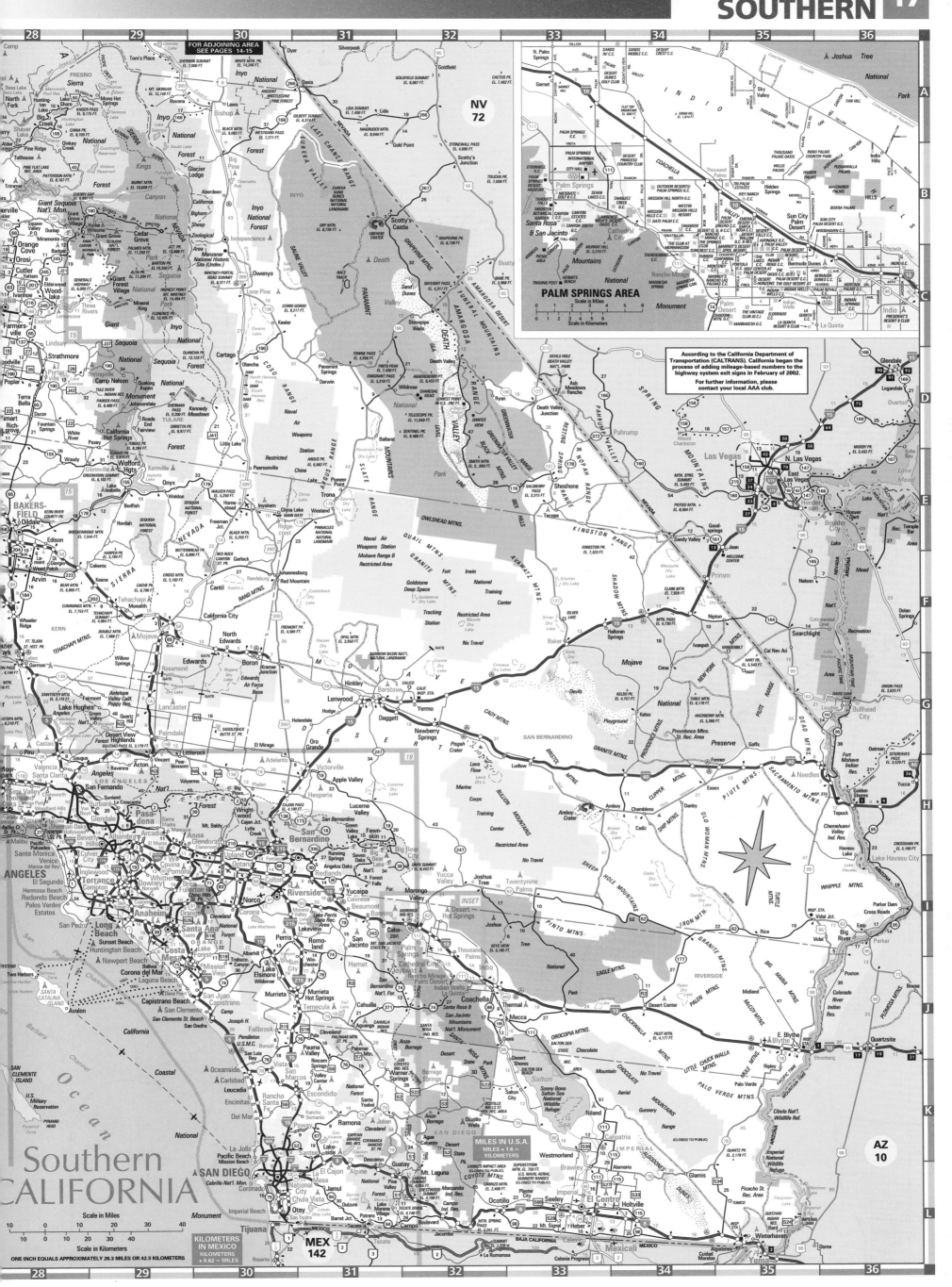

Southern CALIFORNIA

LOS ANGELES AREA

Scale in Miles

Scale in Kilometers

ONE INCH EQUALS APPROXIMATELY 10 MILES OR 16 KILOMETERS
The area of this map is in the Pacific Time Zone

SANTA BARBARA

Scale in Miles

Scale in Kilometers

VENTURA-OXNARD

Scale in Miles

Scale in Kilometers

FREEWAY SYSTEM DOWNTOWN LOS ANGELES AREA

Scale in Miles

Scale in Kilometers

DOWNTOWN SAN DIEGO

Scale in Miles

Scale in Kilometers

Major place labels

LOS ANGELES, San Diego, Santa Barbara, Ventura, Oxnard, Santa Paula, Fillmore, Piru, Moorpark, Simi Valley, Thousand Oaks, Newbury Park, Camarillo, Santa Clarita, Valencia, Newhall, San Fernando, Granada Hills, Chatsworth, Canoga Park, Winnetka, Reseda, Northridge, Van Nuys, Burbank, Glendale, Pasadena, La Cañada Flintridge, La Crescenta, Montrose, Altadena, Sierra Madre, Arcadia, Monrovia, Duarte, Bradbury, Azusa, Glendora, San Dimas, La Verne, Claremont, Upland, Montclair, Ontario, Pomona, Walnut, Diamond Bar, Chino Hills, Chino, Rancho Cucamonga, Fontana, Riverside, Norco, Corona, Home Gardens, El Cerrito

Malibu, Topanga Beach, Pacific Palisades, Santa Monica, Venice, Marina del Rey, Playa del Rey, El Segundo, Manhattan Beach, Hermosa Beach, Redondo Beach, Torrance, Palos Verdes Estates, Rolling Hills, Lomita, Harbor City, Wilmington, San Pedro, Long Beach, Signal Hill, Lakewood, Compton, Carson, Gardena, Hawthorne, Inglewood, Lennox, Lawndale, Culver City, Westchester

Huntington Park, Bell, Maywood, Vernon, Commerce, Montebello, Pico Rivera, Whittier, Downey, Paramount, Bellflower, Norwalk, Santa Fe Springs, La Mirada, La Habra, Brea, Fullerton, Buena Park, Cypress, Hawaiian Gardens, Los Alamitos, Seal Beach, Garden Grove, Westminster, Santa Ana, Anaheim, Orange, Stanton, Villa Park, Tustin, Irvine, Costa Mesa, Newport Beach, Corona del Mar, Fountain Valley, Huntington Beach, Laguna Beach, Laguna Hills, Laguna Woods, Laguna Niguel, Mission Viejo, Rancho Santa Margarita, Dana Point, San Juan Capistrano, Capistrano Beach, San Clemente, San Onofre

SAN GABRIEL MOUNTAINS, Angeles National Forest, SANTA MONICA MTNS, SANTA SUSANA MTNS, Los Padres National Forest, Cleveland National Forest

CATALINA ISLAND, Avalon, Two Harbors, Isthmus Cove, Catalina Harbor, Little Harbor, Emerald Bay

Santa Monica Bay, San Pedro Bay, Pacific Ocean, Santa Barbara Channel, Outer Santa Barbara Channel, San Pedro Channel

Downtown Los Angeles labels

Elysian Park, Dodger Stadium, Echo Park, Chinatown, El Pueblo de Los Angeles Historic Monument, Union Station, Civic Center, Music Center, Dorothy Chandler Pavilion, City Hall, Little Tokyo, Pershing Square, Staples Center, Convention Center, MacArthur Park, Lafayette Park, University of Southern California, Exposition Park, Museums, Sports Arena, Monterey Park, East Los Angeles, Lincoln Park, Hazard Park, Hollenbeck Park

Downtown San Diego labels

San Diego International Airport, Balboa Park, San Diego Zoo, Balboa Stadium, San Diego City College, U.S. Naval Hospital, Amtrak Station, Santa Fe Depot, Cruise Ship Terminal, Maritime Museum of San Diego, County Administration Center, Convention & Performing Arts Center, Seaport Village, San Diego Convention Center, Embarcadero Marina Park

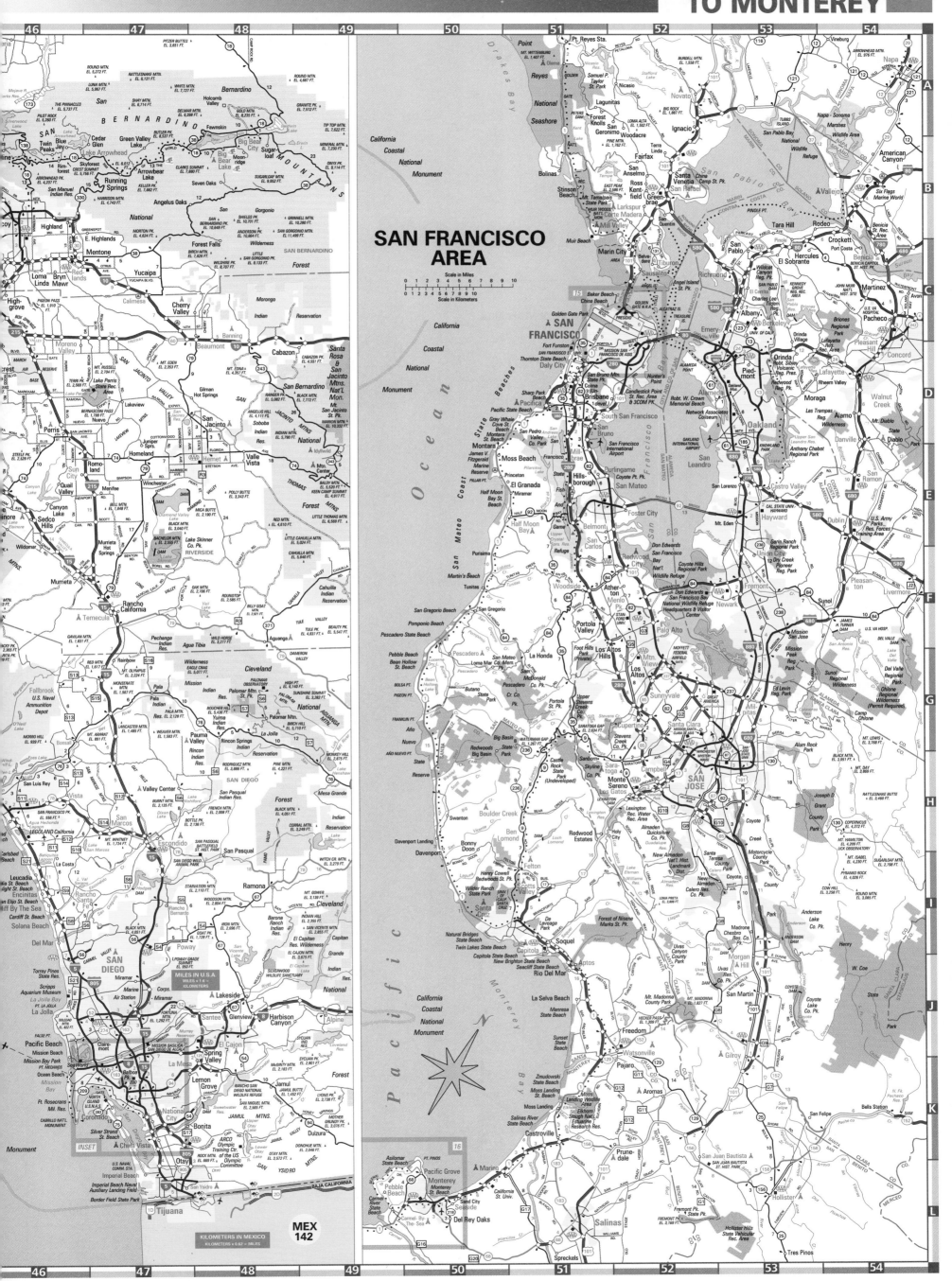

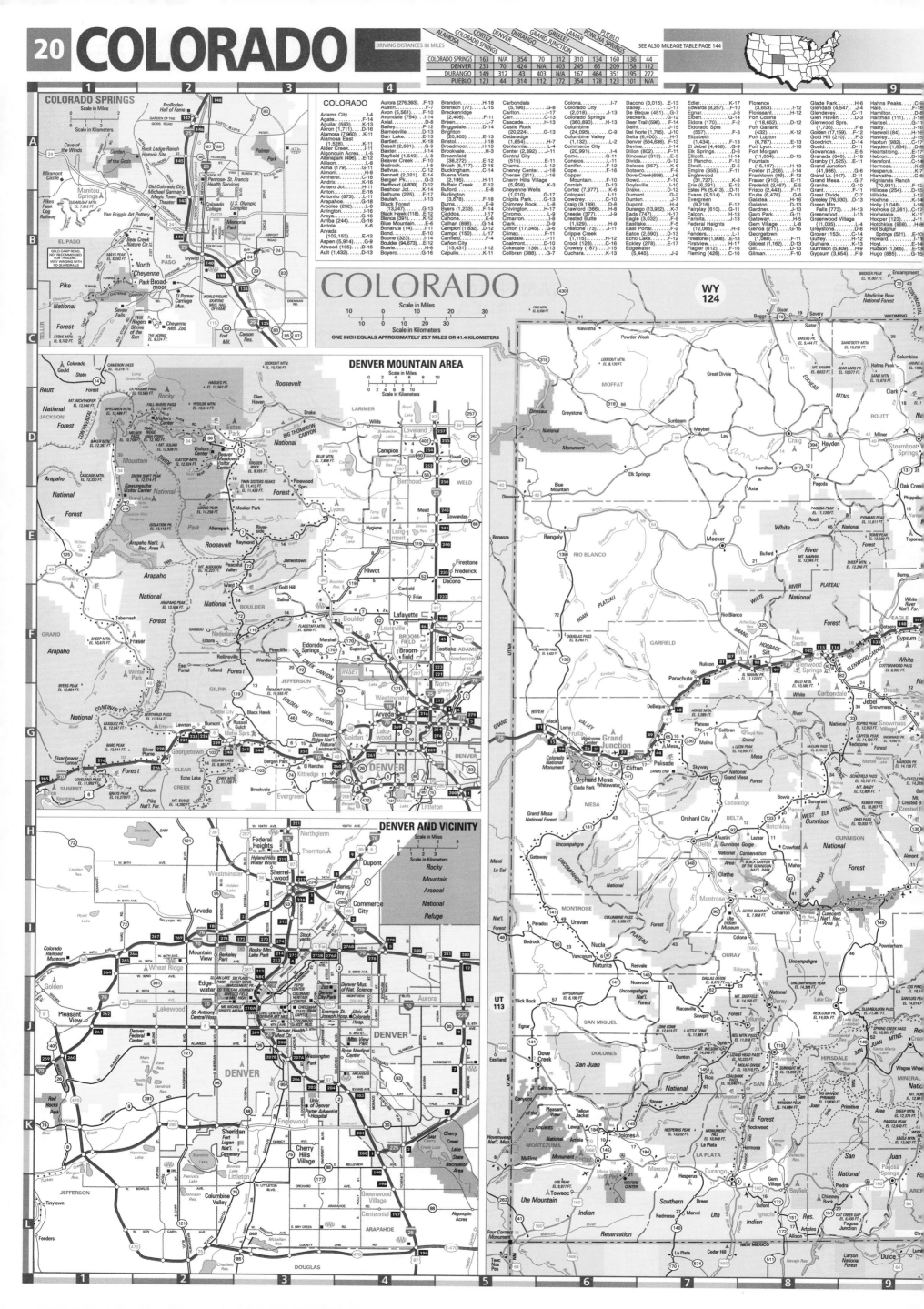

Littleton (40,340)...L-3
Livermore...C-12
Lochbuie (2,049)...I-15
Log Lane Village (1,006)...D-15
Loma...G-6
Lone Tree...L-3
Longmont (71,093)...I-12
Louisville (18,933)...I-12
Loveland (50,608)...D-12
Lycan...J-18
Lyons (1,585)...I-12
Mack...G-6
Maher...H-8
Malta...G-10
Manassa (1,042)...L-11
Mancos (1,119)...K-7

Manitou Spgs (4,980)...H-13
Manzanola (525)...J-15
Marble (105)...G-9
Marshall...F-3
Marvel...L-7
Masonville...D-7
Matheson...G-14
Maybell...C-7
McCoy...E-9
McElmo...K-6
Mead (2,017)...D-13
Meeker (2,242)...E-7
Meredith...G-9
Merino (246)...D-15
Mesa...G-7
Mesita...L-12
Milliken (2,888)...D-13
Milner...D-8
Mineral Hot Spgs...J-11
Minturn (1,068)...F-10
Model...K-14
Moffat (114)...J-11

Mogote...L-11
Monarch...H-10
Monte Vista (4,529)...K-11
Montrose (12,344)...J-8
Monument (1,971)...G-13
Monument Park...K-13
Morrison (430)...F-3
Mosca...K-11
Mountain View (569)...J-2
Mt. Crested Butte (707)...H-9
Mt. Princeton...H-10
Nathrop...H-11
Naturita (635)...J-7
Nederland...F-11
New Castle (1,984)...F-8
Ninaview...K-15
Niwot (4,160)...E-12
N. Avondale...J-14

Northglenn (31,575)...J-2
Norwood (438)...J-6
Nucla (734)...J-7
Nunn (471)...C-13
Oak Creek (849)...D-9
Ohio...H-9
Olathe (1,573)...J-8
Olney Springs (389)...J-15
Ophir (113)...J-7
Orchard...D-14
Orchard City...H-8
Orchard Mesa...G-6
Ordway (1,248)...J-15
Ouray (813)...J-8
Ovid (330)...B-17
Oxford...J-14
Padroni (97)...C-16
Pagosa...D-8
Pagosa Jct...L-9

Pagosa Springs (1,591)...L-9
Palisade (2,579)...G-7
Palmer Lake (2,179)...G-13
Paoli (42)...C-17
Paonia (1,497)...H-8
Parachute (1,006)...F-7
Paradox...H-6
Parkdale...H-11
Parker (23,558)...F-3
Parlin...H-9
Parshall...E-10
Peaceful Valley...E-11
Peckham...D-13
Penrose (4,070)...H-12
Peyton...G-13
Phippsburg...E-9
Piedra...L-9
Pierce (884)...D-13
Pine...F-12
Pine Jct...F-12

Pinecliffe...E-12
Pinewood Park...D-3
Pinon...J-14
Pitkin (124)...H-10
Placerville...J-7
Platoro...K-10
Platteville (2,370)...D-13
Plateau City...G-7
Pleasant View...K-6
Poncha Springs (466)...H-11
Portland...J-13
Poudre Park...C-12
Powderhorn...J-9
Powder Wash...C-6
Pritchett (137)...K-17
Proctor...C-16
Prospect Valley...E-13
Pryor...J-13
Pueblo (102,121)...J-13
Pueblo West (16,899)...J-13
Punkin Ctr...H-15

Purcell...C-13
Purgatory...K-7
Ramah (117)...G-14
Rand...D-10
Rangely (2,096)...D-6
Raymer (75)...E-3
Raymond...E-11
Red Cliff (289)...F-10
Red Feather Lakes (525)...C-11
Redmesa...L-7
Redvale...J-6
Red Wing...K-13
Rico (205)...J-7
Ridgway (713)...J-7
Rifle (6,784)...F-7
Rio Blanco...E-3
Riverside...E-3
Rockport...K-8
Rockwood...K-8
Rocky Ford (4,286)...J-15
Roggen...E-13
Rollinsville...E-12

Romeo (375)...L-9
Rosita...J-12
Roxborough Park (4,446)...F-12
Rulison...F-7
Rush...H-14
Russell Gulch...G-3
Rustic...C-12
Rye (202)...J-13
Saguache (578)...J-11
Salida (5,504)...H-11
Salina...J-10
San Acacio...L-11
Sanford (817)...L-11
San Francisco...L-11
San Luis (739)...L-12
San Pablo...L-11
Sapinero...J-9
Sargents...J-10
Sawpit (25)...J-7
Security...H-13
Sedalia (211)...F-13
Sedgwick (191)...B-17
Segundo...K-14

Shaw...F-16
Shawnee...F-12
Sheridan (5,600)...J-3
Sheridan Lake (66)...H-18
Sherrelwood (17,657)...J-1
Silt (1,740)...F-8
Silver Cliff (512)...J-12
Silver Plume (203)...F-11
Silverthorne (3,196)...F-10
Silverton (531)...K-8
Simla (663)...G-13
Skyway...G-6
Slater...C-8
Slick Rock...J-6
Snowmass...G-9
Snyder...D-15
Somerset...H-8
South Fork (604)...K-10

Springfield (1,562)...K-17
State Bridge...F-10
Steamboat Sprs (9,815)...D-9
Sterling (11,360)...D-15
Stoner...K-7
Stonewall...K-14
Stonington...K-18
Strasburg...F-13
Stratton (669)...F-16
Sugar City (279)...J-15
Summitville...K-10
Sunbeam...C-7
Superior (9,011)...F-14
Swink (696)...J-15
Tabernash (165)...E-11
Tarryall...G-12
Telluride (2,221)...J-7
Texas Creek...K-14

The Forks...C-12
Thornton (82,384)...J-2
Timnath...D-13
Timpas...J-15
Tinytown...L-1
Tobe...K-16
Tolland...E-11
Toonerville...K-16
Toponas...E-9
Towaoc (1,097)...L-6
Towner...H-18
Trinchera...L-15
Trinidad (9,078)...K-14
Truckton...H-14
Two Buttes (67)...J-18
Uravan...J-6
Vail (4,531)...F-10
Vancorum...J-6

Vernon...E-17
Vilas (110)...K-18
Villa Grove...J-11
Vineland...J-13
Viona (95)...F-17
Virginia Dale...C-12
Vona (833)...F-16
Wagon Wheel Gap...K-10
Walden (734)...D-10
Walsenburg (4,182)...K-13
Walsh (723)...K-18
Ward (169)...E-11
Watkins...F-13
Waunita Hot Spgs...H-10
Weldona...D-15
Wellington (2,672)...C-12
Westcliffe (417)...J-12
Westcreek...G-12

Westminster (100,940)...H-2
Weston...K-14
Wetmore...J-13
Wheat Ridge (32,913)...J-2
Whitewater...H-7
Wild Horse...H-16
Wiggins (838)...D-14
Wiley (483)...J-17
Willard...D-15
Windsor (9,896)...D-13
Winter Pk. (662)...E-11
Wolcott...F-9
Woodland Pk. (6,515)...G-13
Woodrow...E-14
Wray (2,187)...E-16
Yampa (443)...E-9
Yellow Jacket...K-7
Yoder...H-14
Yuma (3,285)...D-16

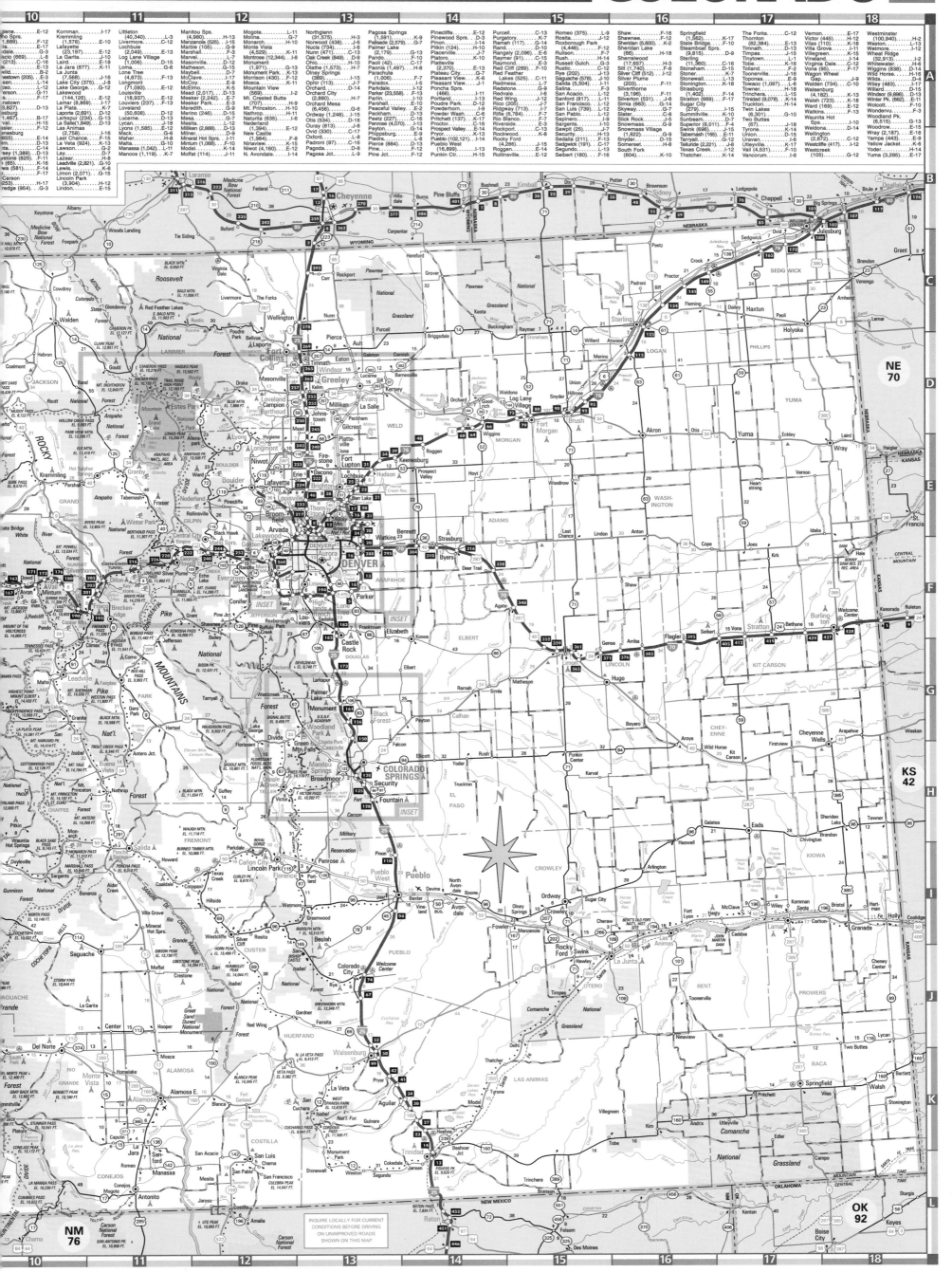

NE 70
KS 42
OK 92
NM 76

INQUIRE LOCALLY FOR CURRENT CONDITIONS BEFORE DRIVING ON UNIMPROVED ROADS SHOWN ON THIS MAP

	BRIDGEPORT	CANAAN	DANBURY	HARTFORD	NEW HAVEN	NEW LONDON	NORWALK	NORWICH	STAMFORD	WATERBURY
BRIDGEPORT	N/A	66	31	54	19	64	14	73	22	29
HARTFORD	54	42	58	N/A	39	51	67	39	76	30
NEW HAVEN	19	74	49	39	N/A	47	32	55	40	22
NEW LONDON	64	105	96	51	47	N/A	77	14	86	68

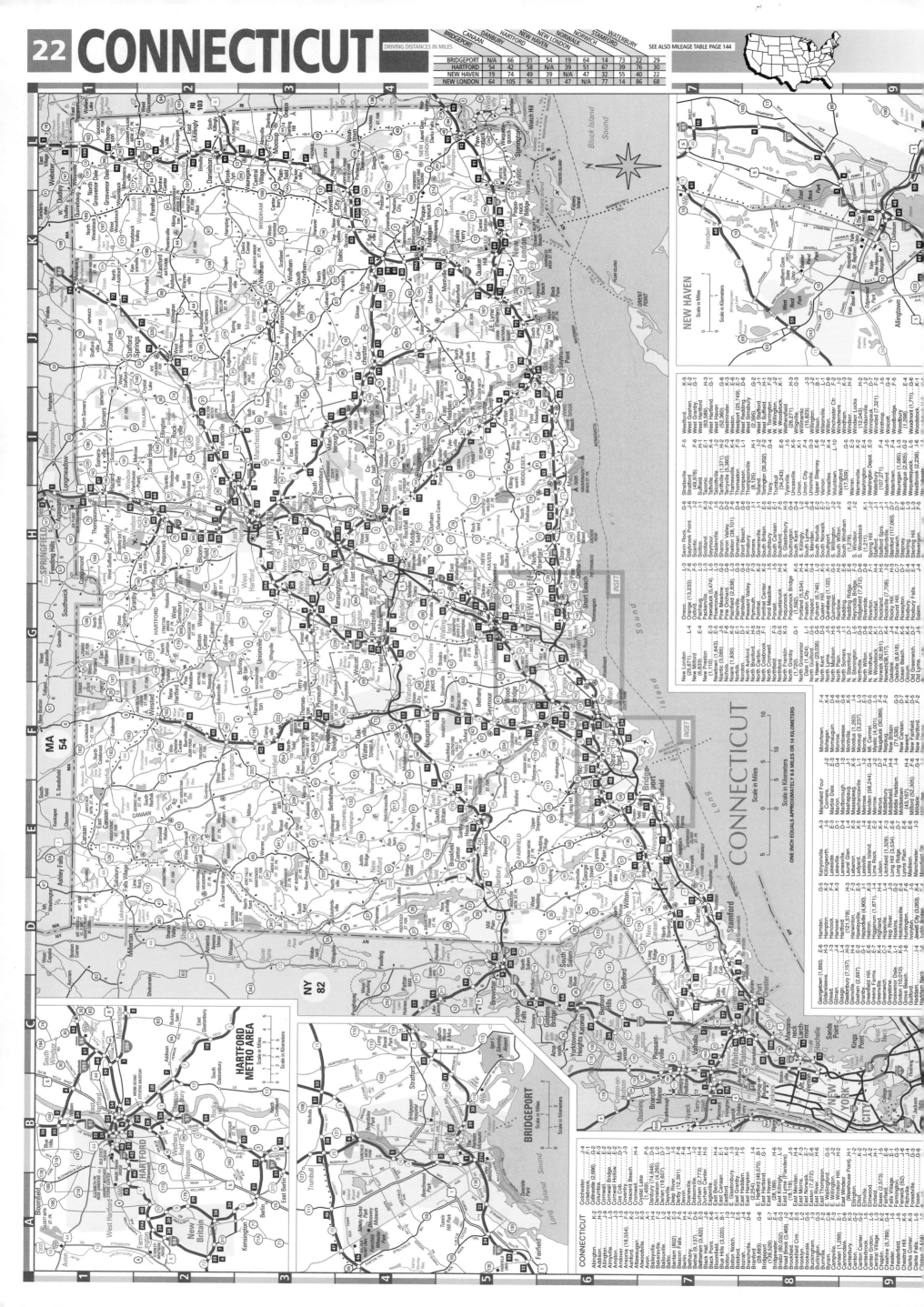

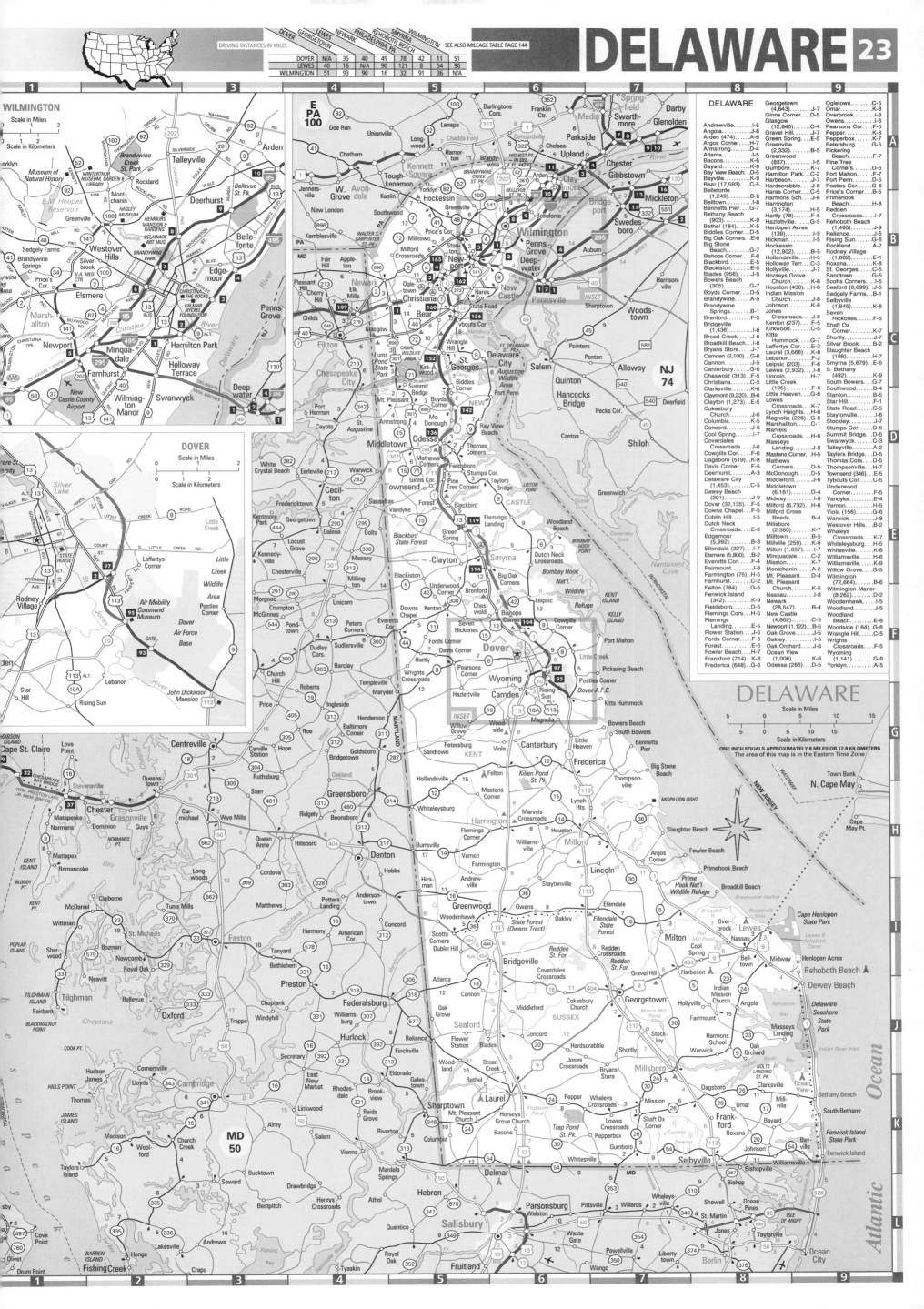

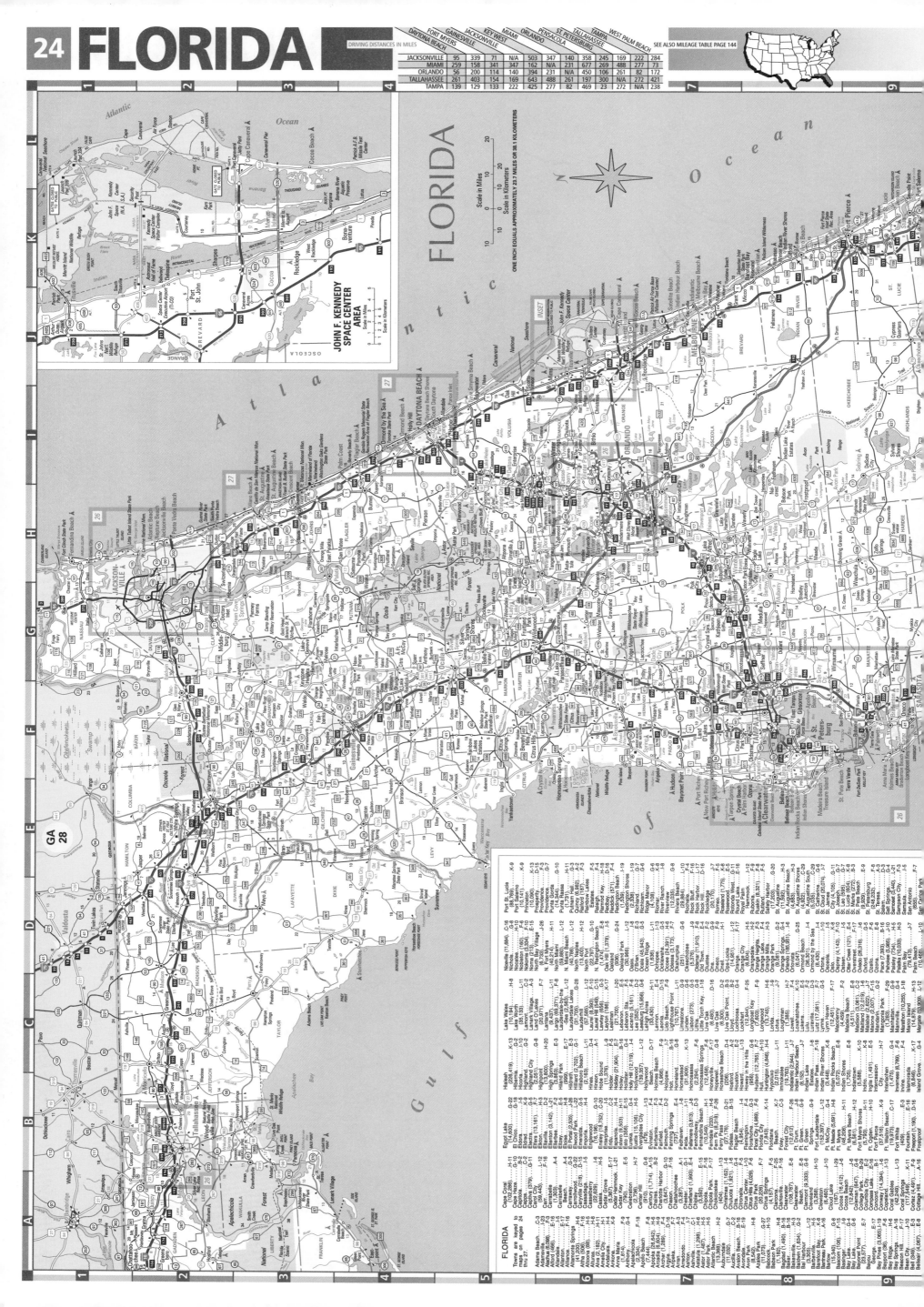

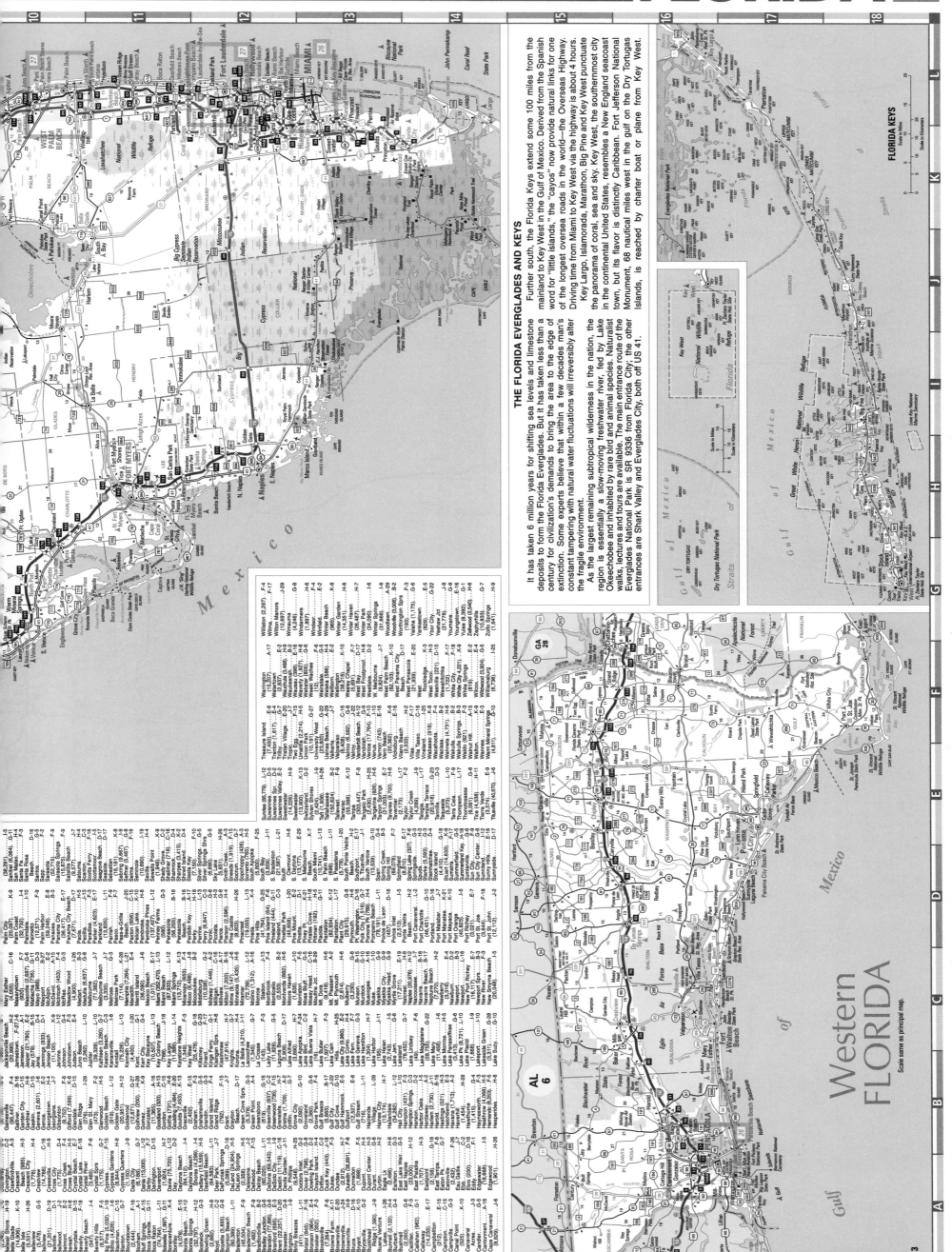

THE FLORIDA EVERGLADES AND KEYS

Further south, the Florida Keys extend some 100 miles from the mainland to Key West in the Gulf of Mexico. Derived from the Spanish word for "little islands," the "cayos" now provide natural links for one of the longest oversea roads in the world—the Overseas Highway. Driving time from Miami to Key West via the highway is about 4 hours. Key Largo, Islamorada, Marathon, Big Pine and Key West punctuate the panorama of coral, sea and sky. Key West, the southernmost city in the continental United States, resembles a New England seacoast town, but its flavor is distinctly Caribbean. Fort Jefferson National Monument, 68 nautical miles west in the gulf on the Dry Tortugas Islands, is reached by charter boat or plane from Key West.

It has taken 6 million years for shifting sea levels and limestone deposits to form the Florida Everglades. But it has taken less than a century for civilization's demands to bring the area to the edge of extinction. Some experts believe that within a few decades man's constant tampering with natural water fluctuations will irreversibly after the fragile environment.

As the largest remaining subtropical wilderness in the nation, the region is essentially a slow-moving freshwater river, fed by Lake Okeechobee and inhabited by rare bird and animal species. Naturalist walks, lectures and tours are available. The main entrance route of the Everglades National Park is SR 9336 from Florida City; the other entrances are Shark Valley and Everglades City, both off US 41.

FLORIDA KEYS

Western FLORIDA

Scale same as principal map.

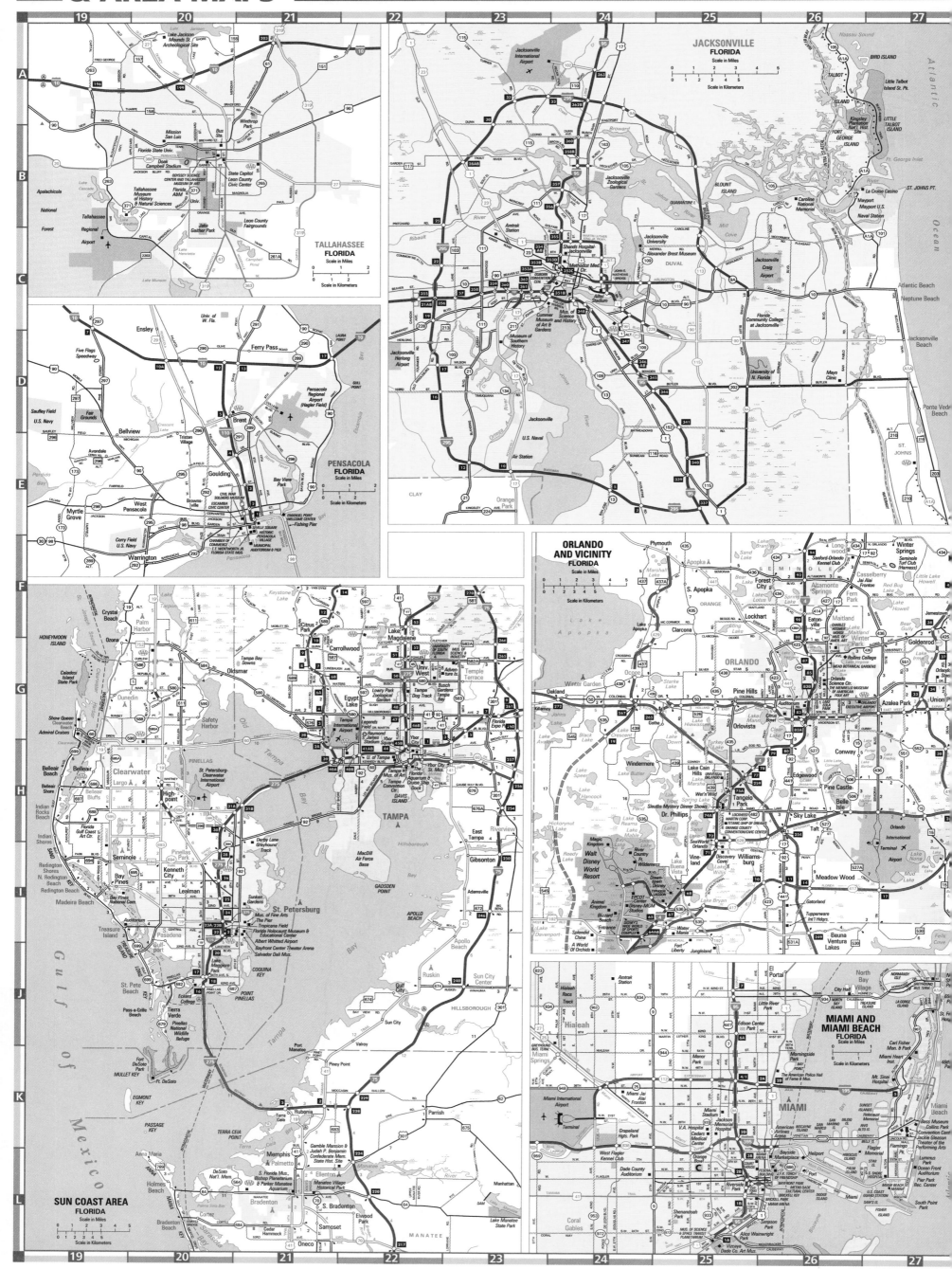

TALLAHASSEE
FLORIDA
Scale in Miles

PENSACOLA
FLORIDA
Scale in Miles

JACKSONVILLE
FLORIDA
Scale in Miles

ORLANDO
AND VICINITY
FLORIDA
Scale in Miles

SUN COAST AREA
FLORIDA
Scale in Miles

MIAMI AND
MIAMI BEACH
FLORIDA
Scale in Miles

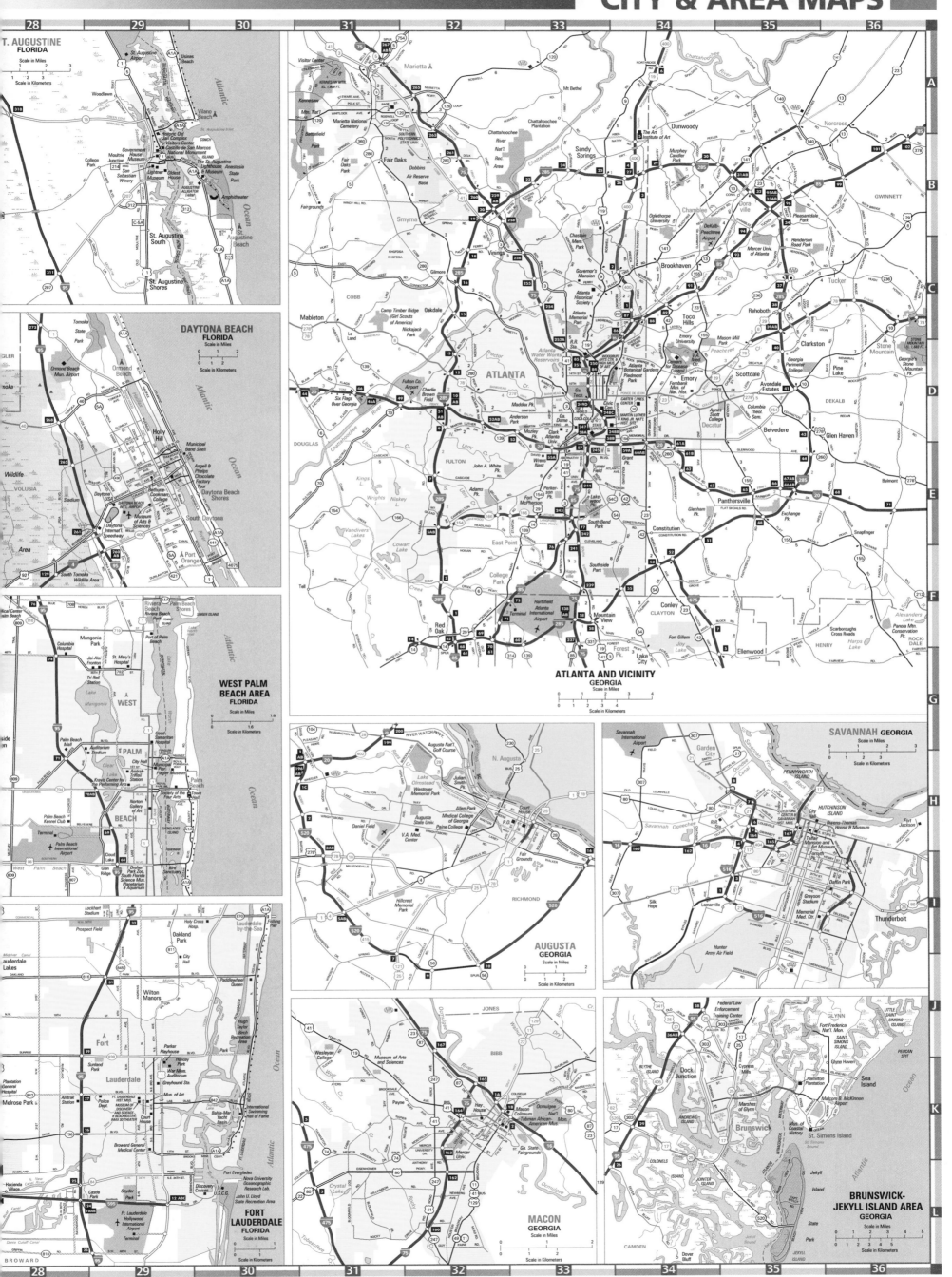

ST. AUGUSTINE
FLORIDA

DAYTONA BEACH
FLORIDA

WEST PALM
BEACH AREA
FLORIDA

FORT
LAUDERDALE
FLORIDA

ATLANTA AND VICINITY
GEORGIA

AUGUSTA
GEORGIA

SAVANNAH GEORGIA

MACON
GEORGIA

BRUNSWICK-
JEKYLL ISLAND AREA
GEORGIA

DRIVING DISTANCES IN MILES

SEE ALSO MILEAGE TABLE PAGE 144

	ALBANY	ATHENS	ATLANTA	AUGUSTA	BRUNSWICK	COLUMBUS	MACON	ROME	SAVANNAH	STATESBORO	TIFTON	VALDOSTA
ALBANY	N/A	200	184	257	173	86	107	250	251	211	41	89
ATLANTA	184	72	N/A	147	308	106	84	69	245	208	180	227
AUGUSTA	257	122	147	N/A	201	248	149	215	142	80	253	300
COLUMBUS	86	178	106	248	307	N/A	97	173	248	209	125	172
MACON	107	92	84	149	225	97	N/A	152	166	126	105	152

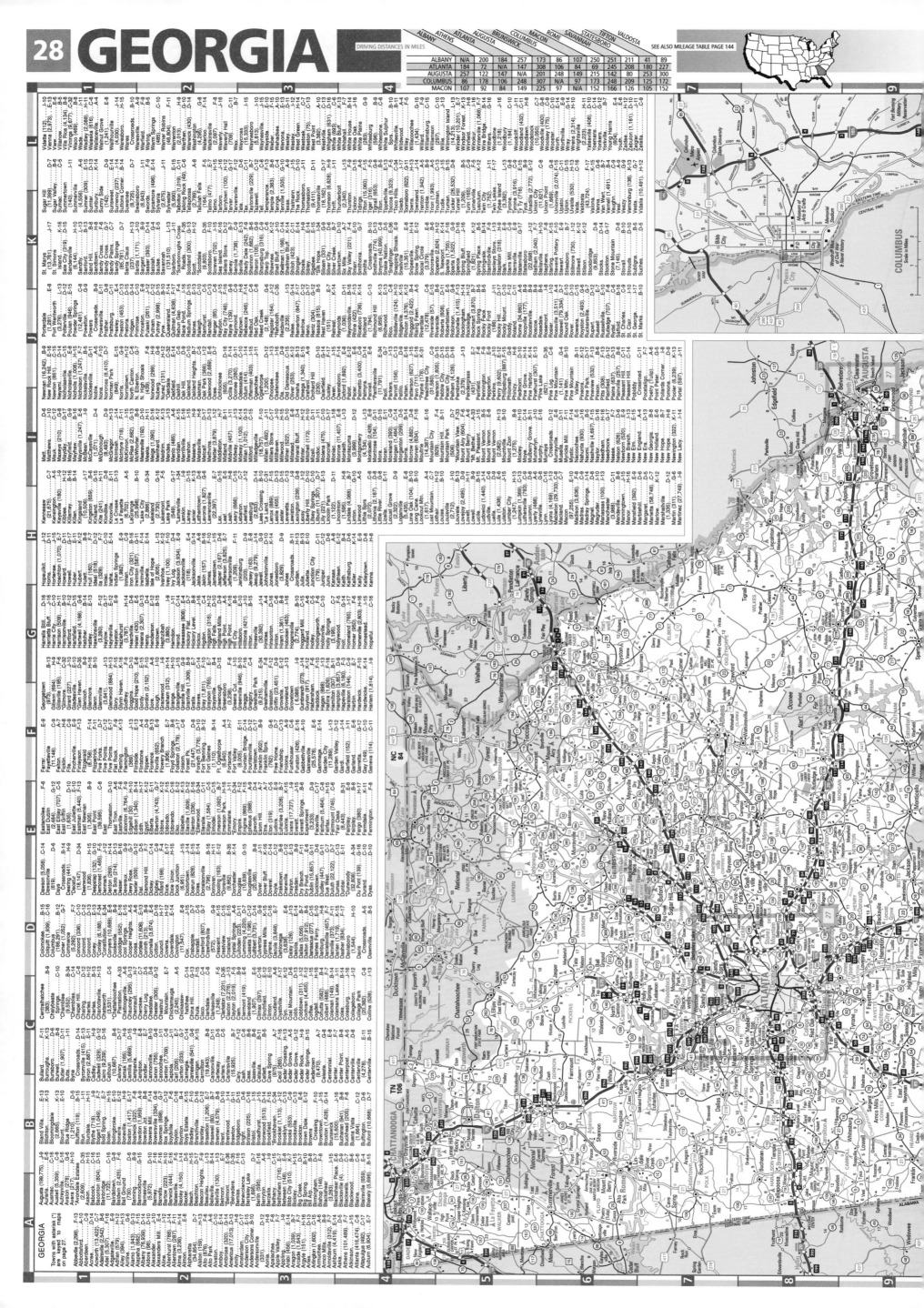

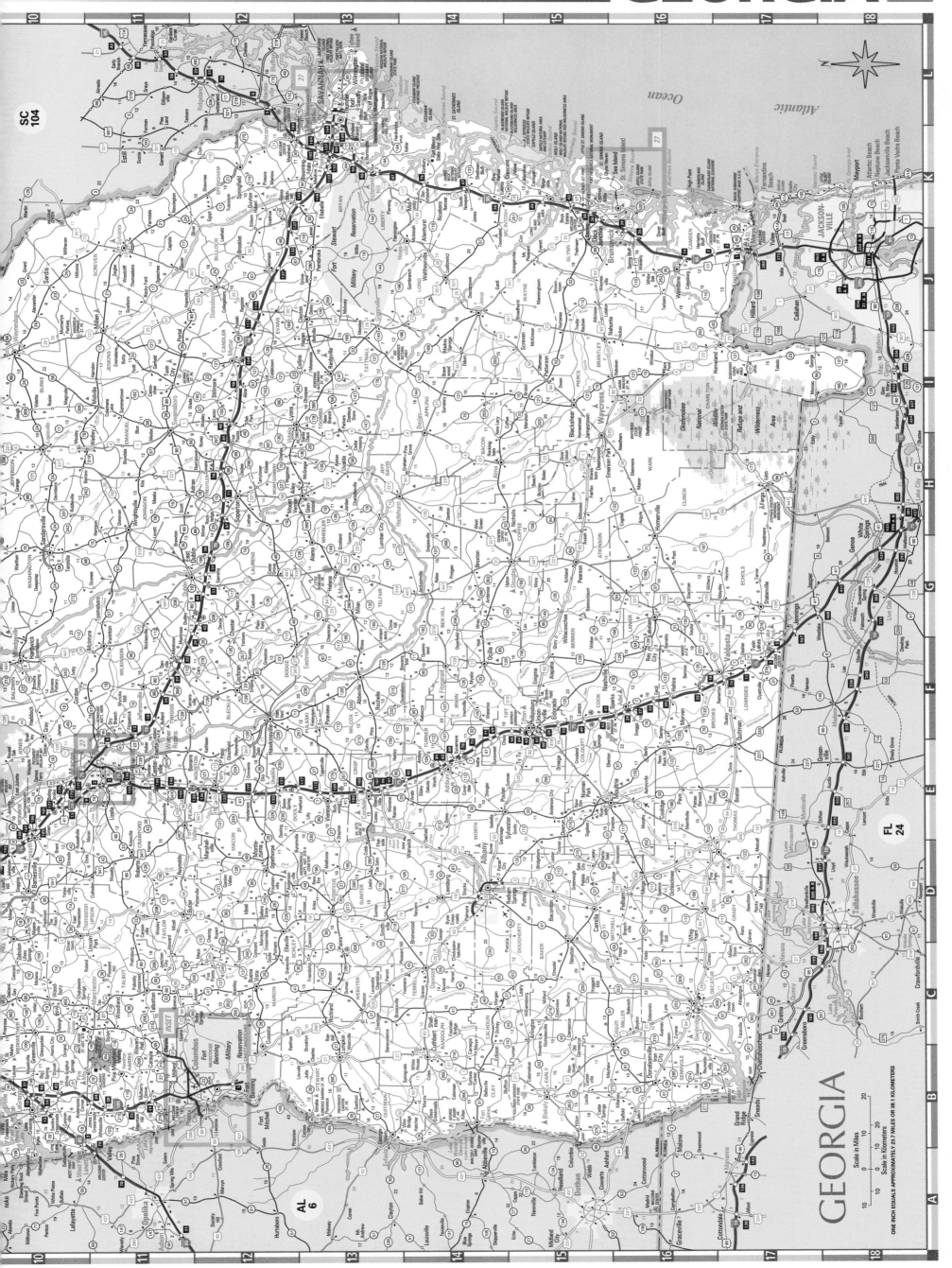

GEORGIA

Scale in Miles

Scale in Kilometers

ONE INCH EQUALS APPROXIMATELY 23.7 MILES OR 38.1 KILOMETERS

DRIVING DISTANCES IN AIR MILES

SEE ALSO MILEAGE TABLE PAGE 144

	HILO	HONOLULU	HOOLEHUA	KAHULUI	KAILUA-KONA	LANAI CITY	LIHUE	WAIMEA (KAMUELA)
HILO	N/A	216	168	121	62	156	322	45
HONOLULU	216	N/A	55	102	169	74	102	172
LIHUE	322	102	157	204	271	176	N/A	274

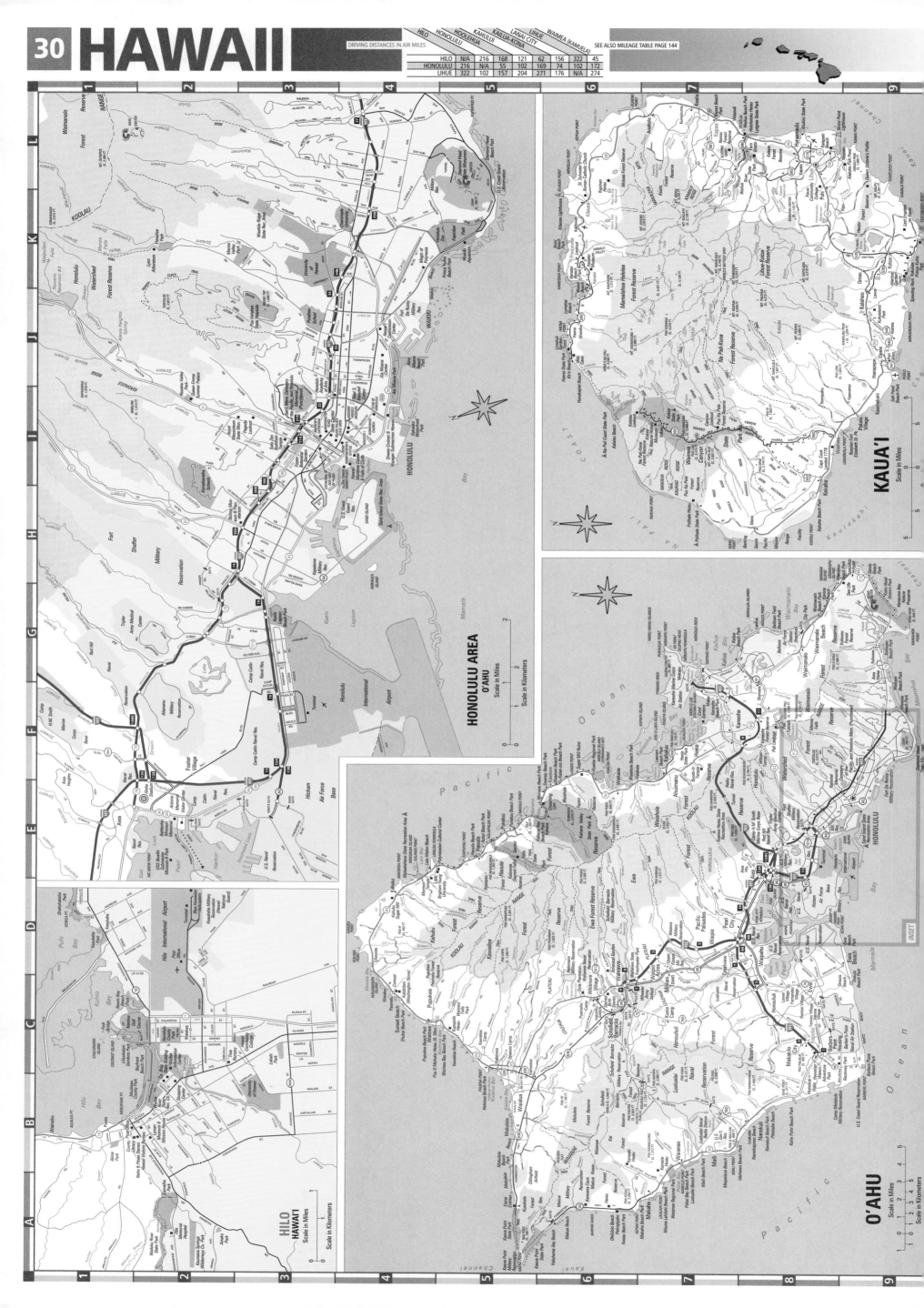

HONOLULU AREA
O'AHU
Scale in Miles
Scale in Kilometers

KAUA'I
Scale in Miles

HILO
HAWAI'I
Scale in Miles
Scale in Kilometers

O'AHU
Scale in Miles
Scale in Kilometers

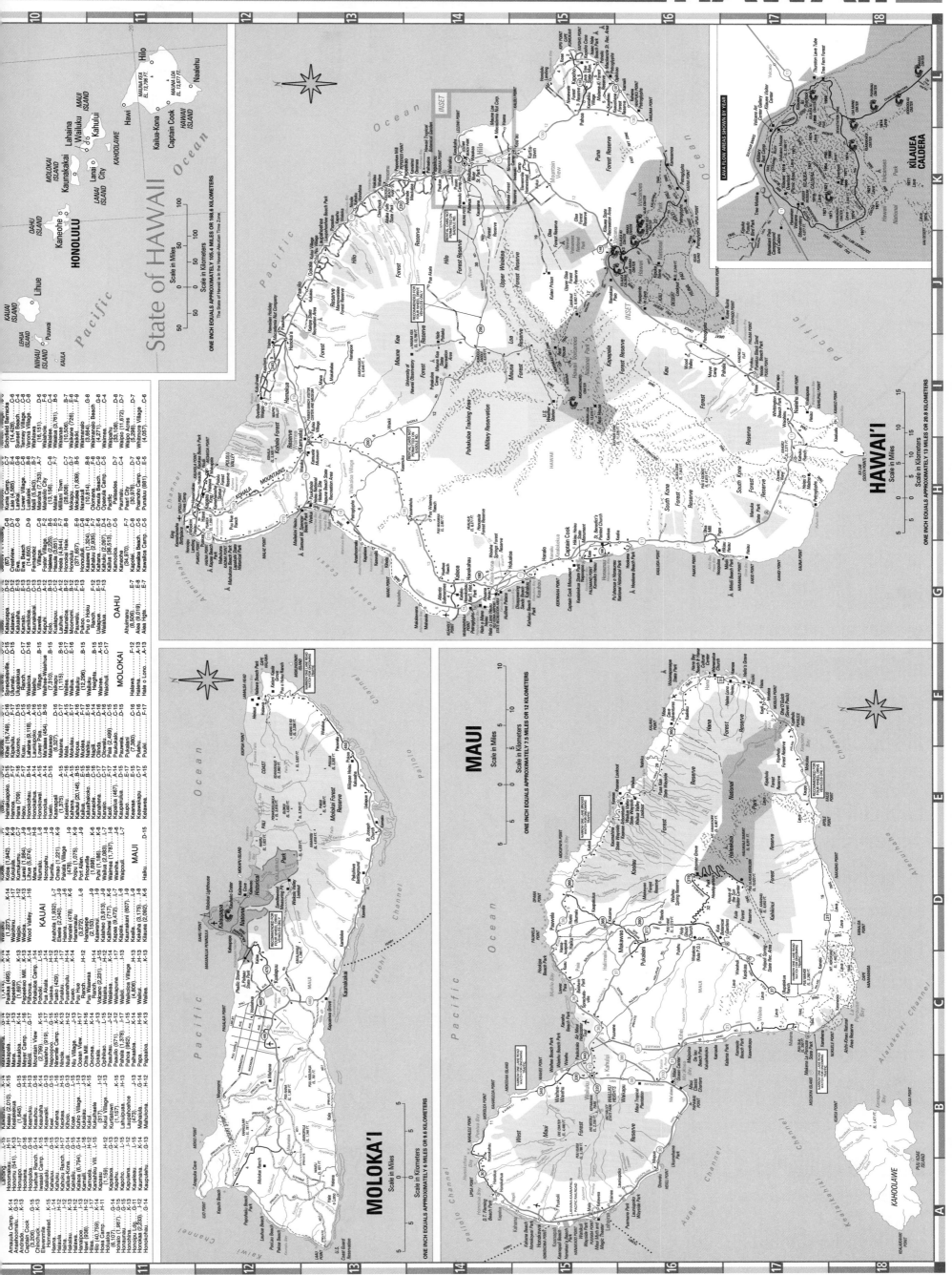

State of HAWAII

HONOLULU

MOLOKA'I

MAUI

HAWAI'I

KĪLAUEA CALDERA

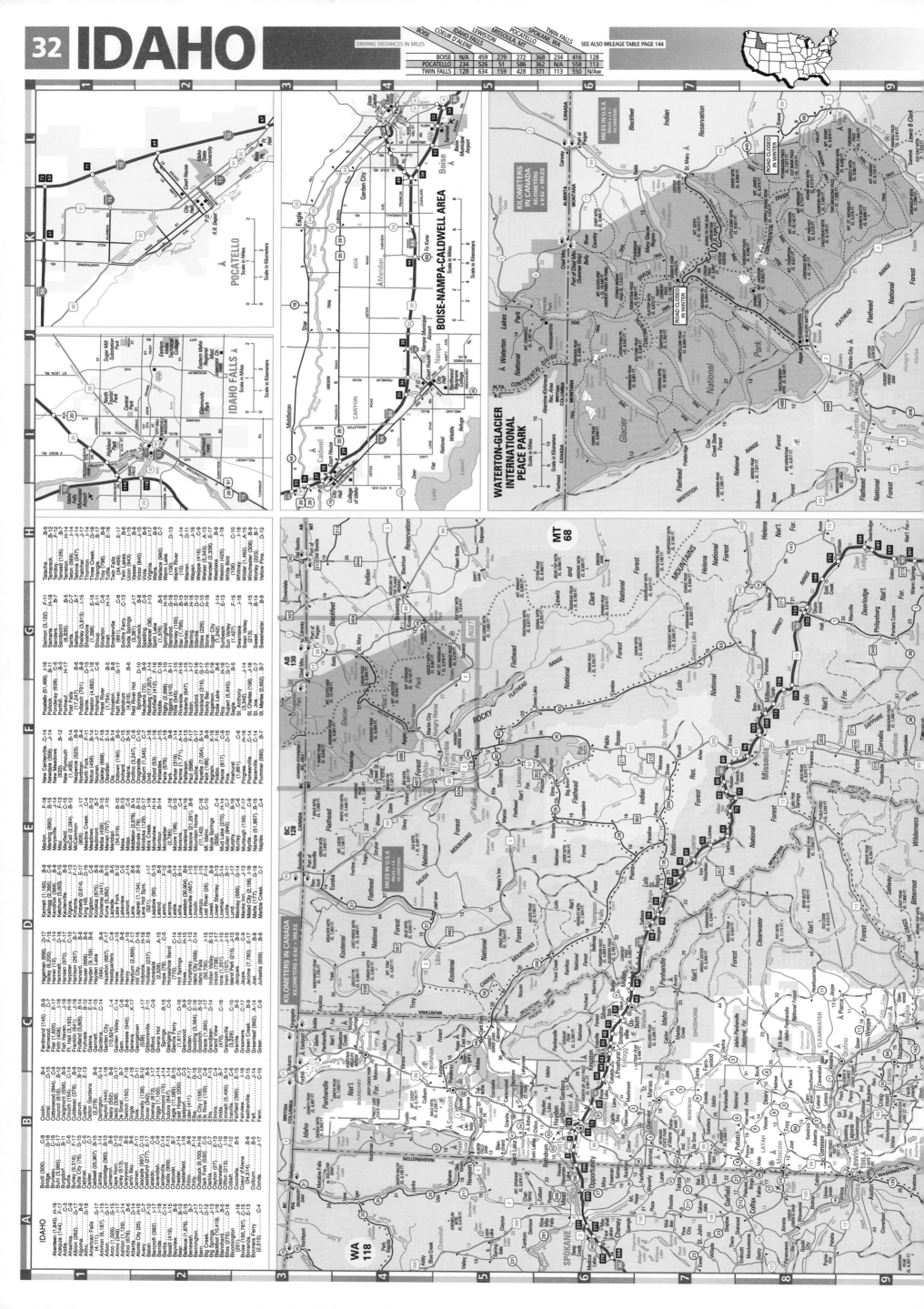

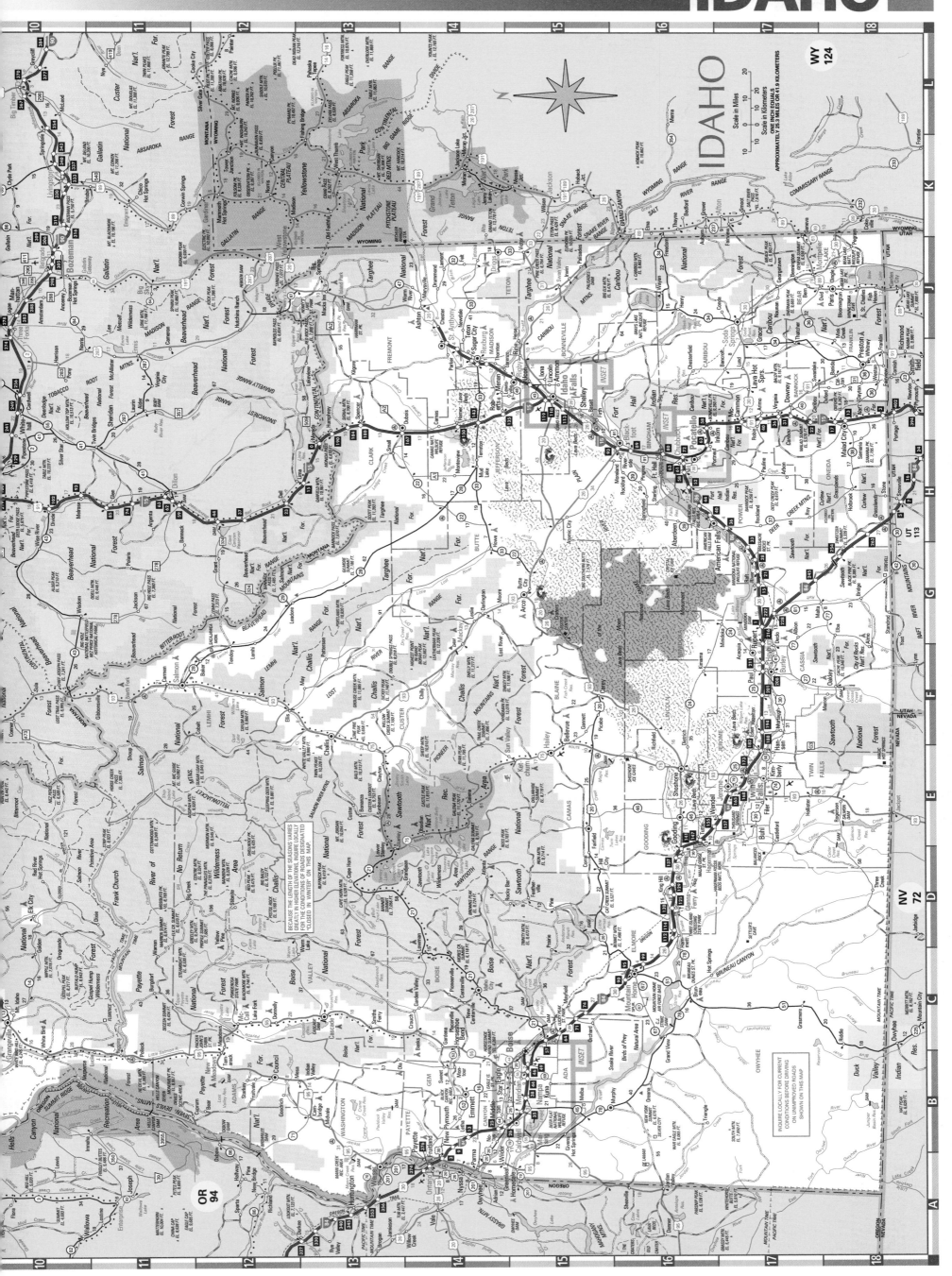

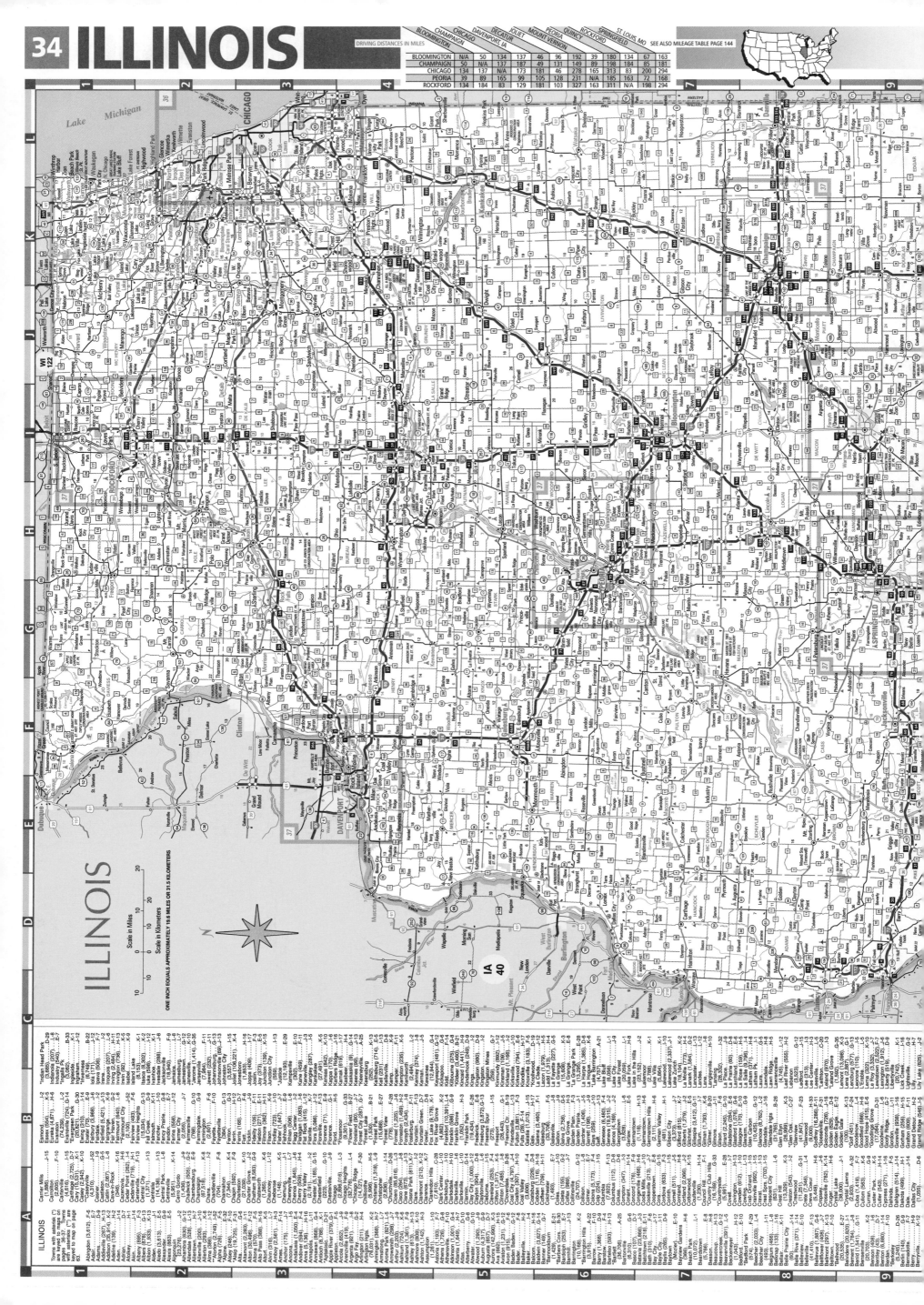

DRIVING DISTANCES IN MILES

SEE ALSO MILEAGE TABLE PAGE 144

	BLOOMINGTON	CHAMPAIGN	CHICAGO	DAVENPORT, IA	DECATUR	JOLIET	MOUNT VERNON	PEORIA	QUINCY	ROCKFORD	SPRINGFIELD	ST LOUIS, MO
BLOOMINGTON	N/A	50	134	137	46	96	192	39	180	134	67	163
CHAMPAIGN	50	N/A	137	187	49	131	149	89	198	184	85	181
CHICAGO	134	137	N/A	173	181	46	278	165	313	83	200	294
PEORIA	39	89	165	99	105	128	231	N/A	185	163	72	168
ROCKFORD	134	184	83	129	181	103	327	163	311	N/A	198	294

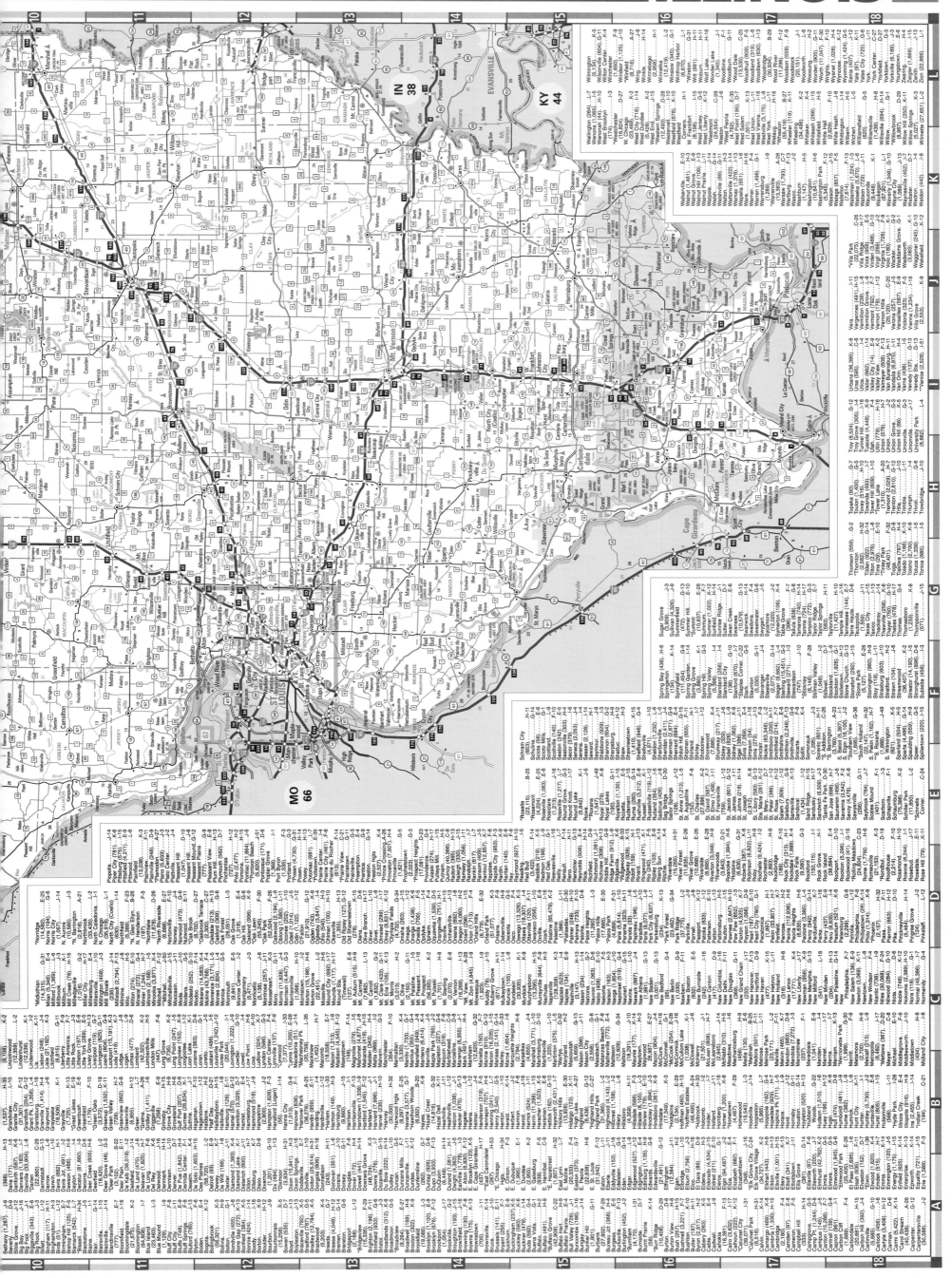

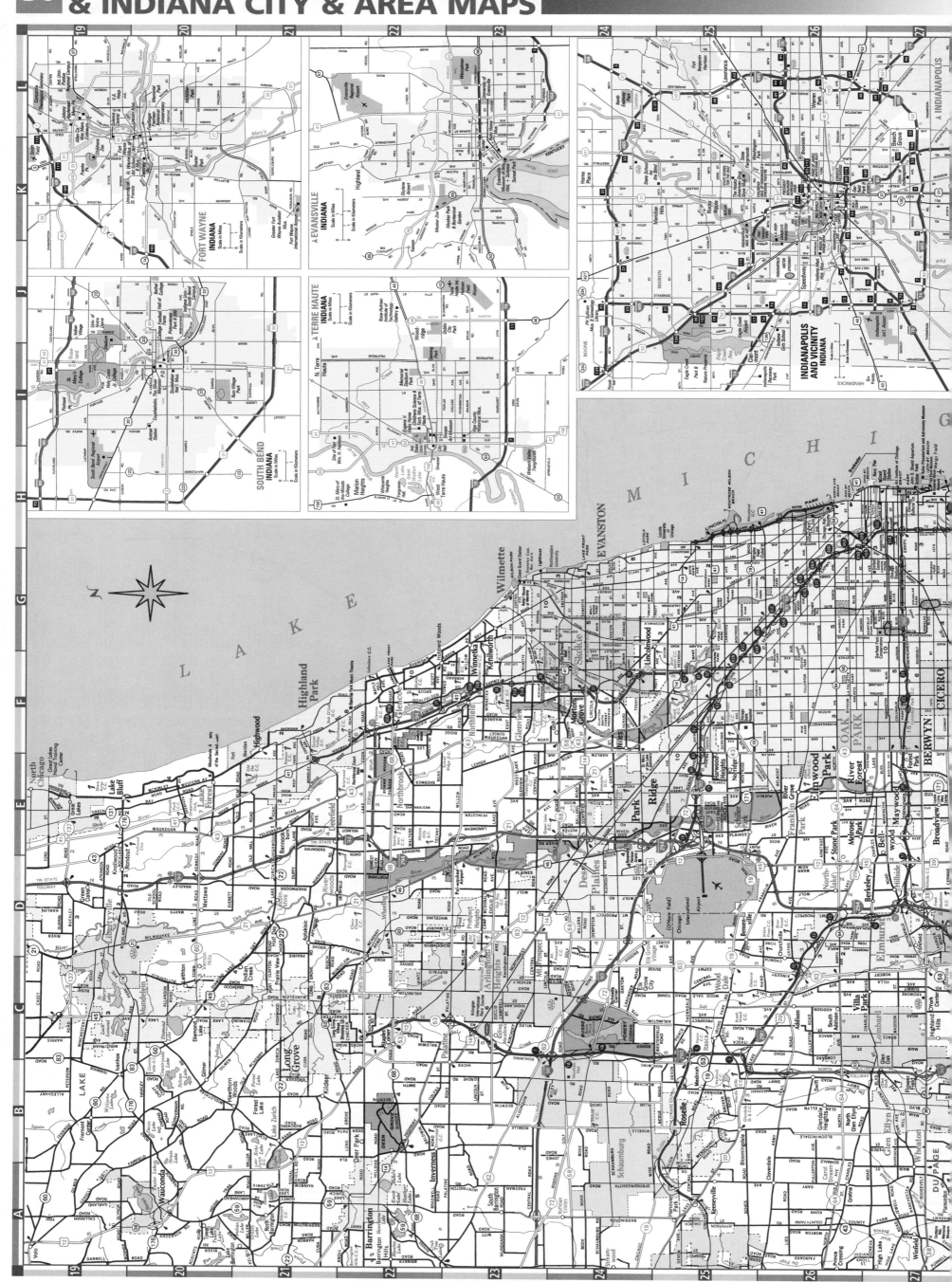

FORT WAYNE INDIANA
Scale in Miles
Scale in Kilometers

EVANSVILLE INDIANA
Scale in Miles
Scale in Kilometers

SOUTH BEND INDIANA
Scale in Miles
Scale in Kilometers

TERRE HAUTE INDIANA
Scale in Miles
Scale in Kilometers

INDIANAPOLIS AND VICINITY INDIANA
Scale in Miles
Scale in Kilometers

DRIVING DISTANCES IN MILES

	CHICAGO, IL	CINCINNATI, OH	COLUMBUS, OH	EVANSVILLE	FORT WAYNE	INDIANAPOLIS	LAFAYETTE	LOUISVILLE, KY	MICHIGAN CITY	RICHMOND	SOUTH BEND	TERRE HAUTE
FORT WAYNE	209	224	167	344	N/A	126	117	235	116	92	96	202
INDIANAPOLIS	178	112	47	220	126	N/A	125	114	175	68	141	77
MICHIGAN CITY	60	286	220	347	116	175	115	208	N/A	245	41	242
RICHMOND	253	68	114	291	92	73	134	182	245	N/A	215	149
TERRE HAUTE	251	183	117	109	202	77	102	185	242	149	279	N/A

SEE ALSO MILEAGE TABLE PAGE 144

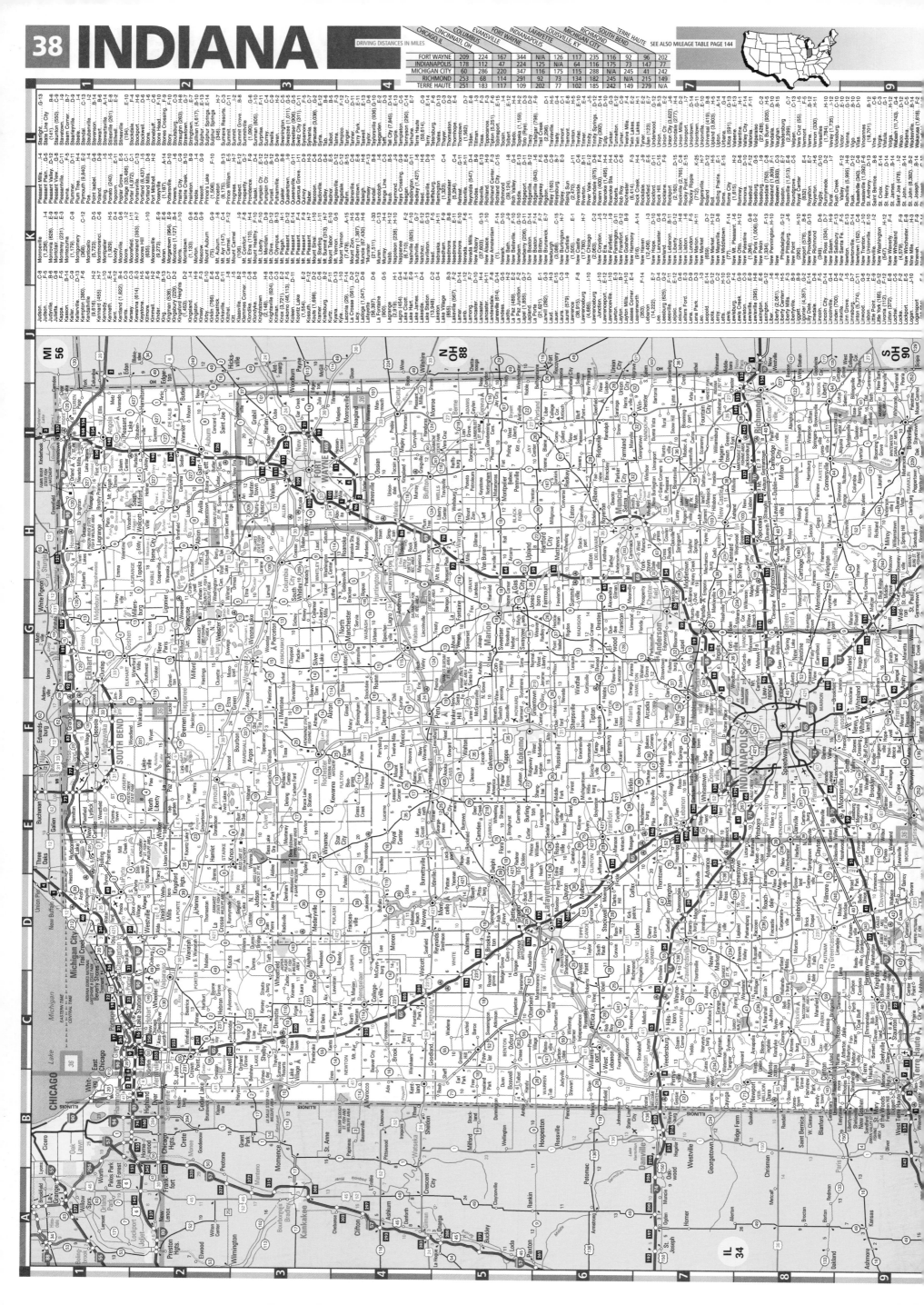

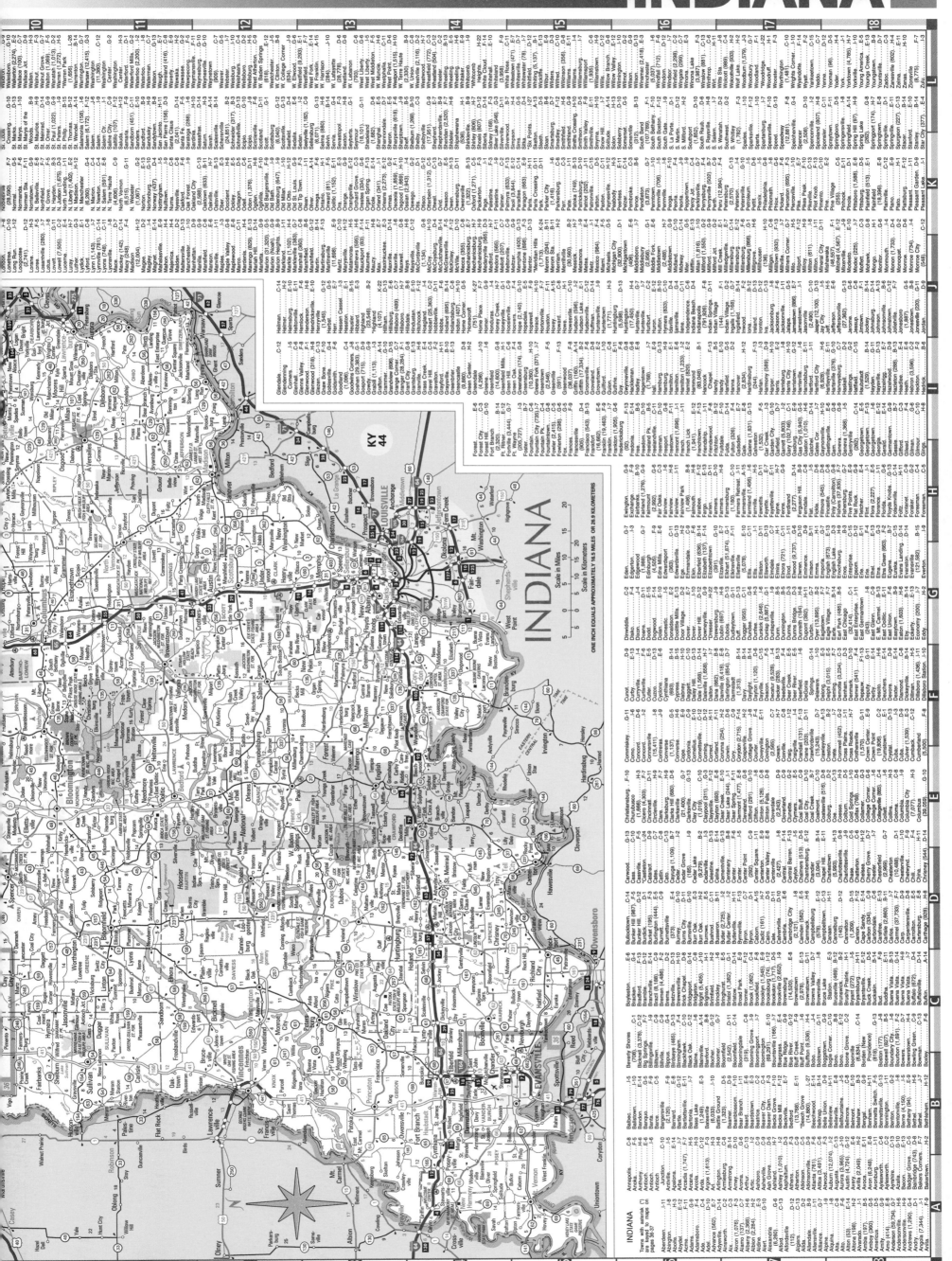

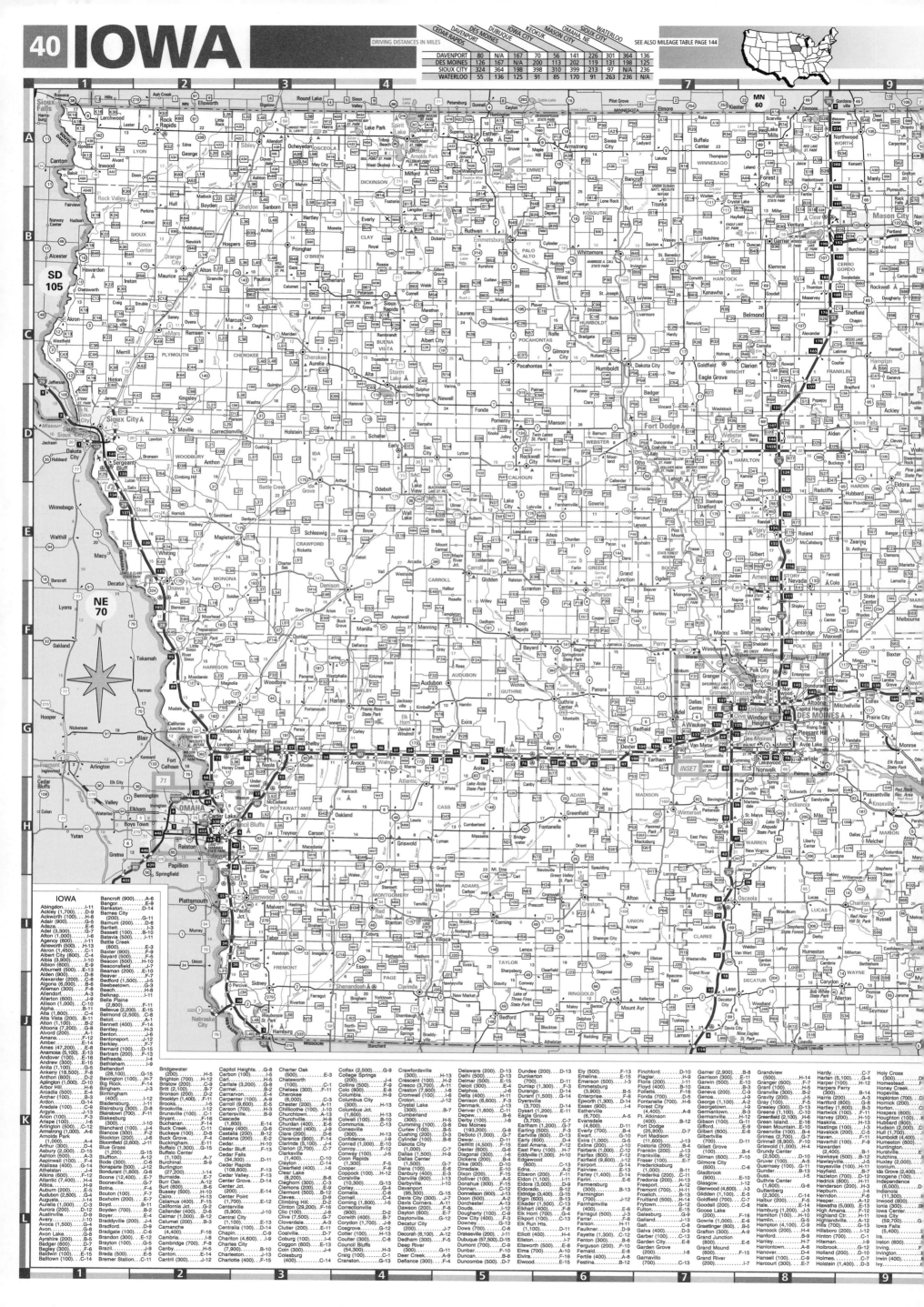

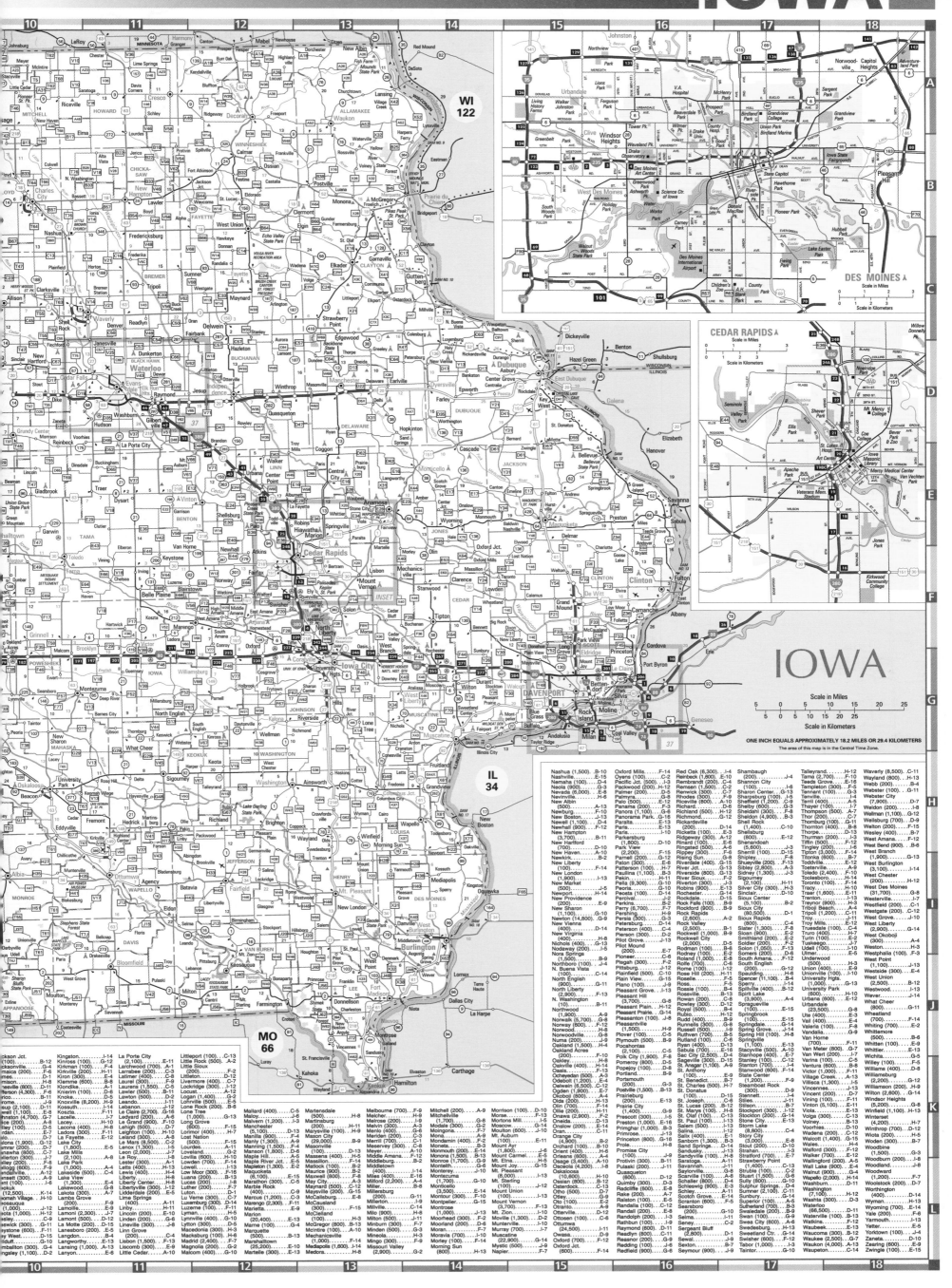

DRIVING DISTANCES IN MILES

SEE ALSO MILEAGE TABLE PAGE 144

	BELLEVILLE	DODGE CITY	FAIRVIEW	KANSAS CITY, MO	LIBERAL	OAKLEY	OBERLIN	SALINA	TOPEKA	WICHITA
LIBERAL	352	83	414	412	N/A	150	213	289	355	212
SALINA	71	202	162	175	289	182	240	N/A	111	89
TOPEKA	177	307	58	61	355	287	345	111	N/A	141
WICHITA	156	155	198	190	212	267	325	89	141	N/A

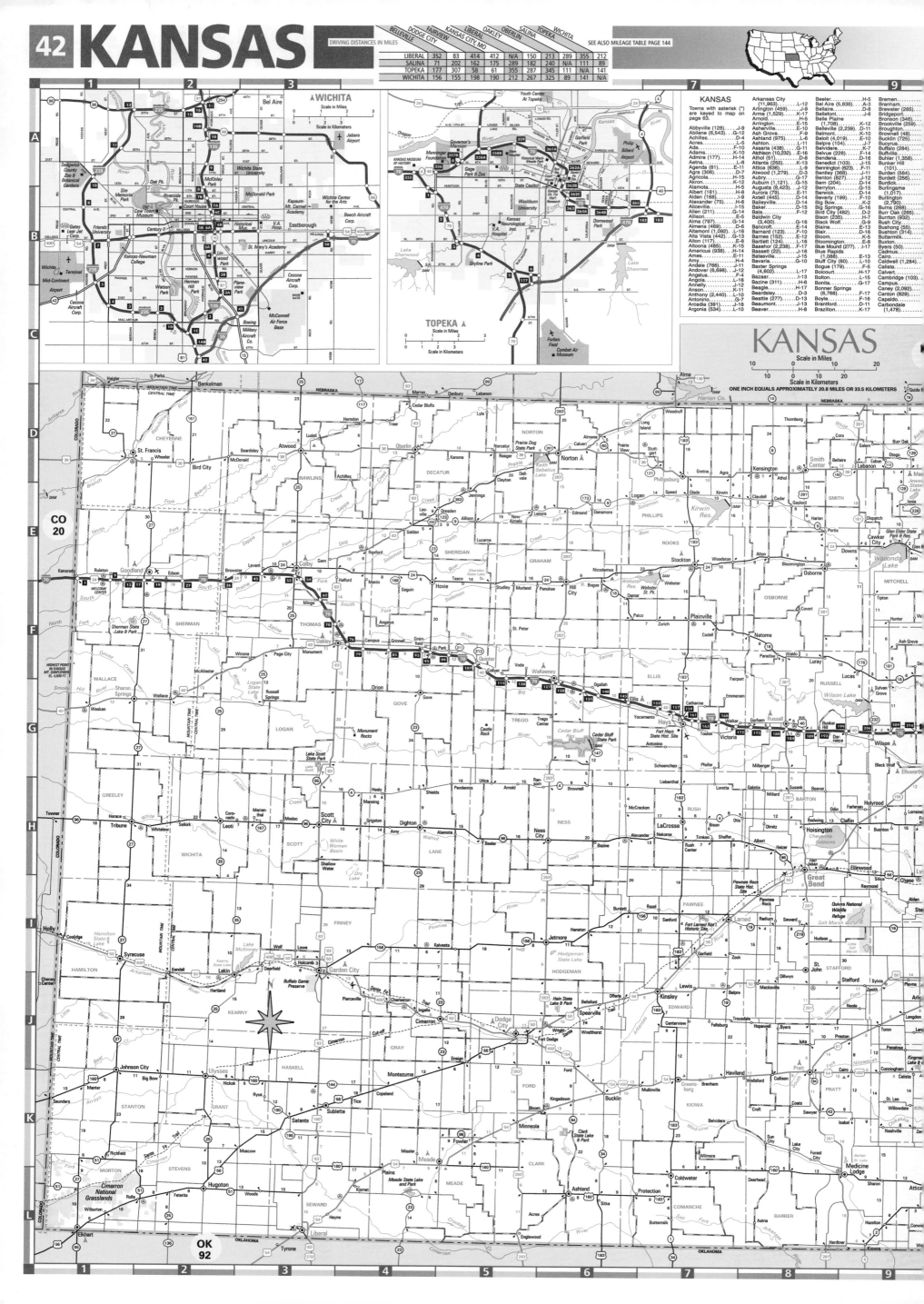

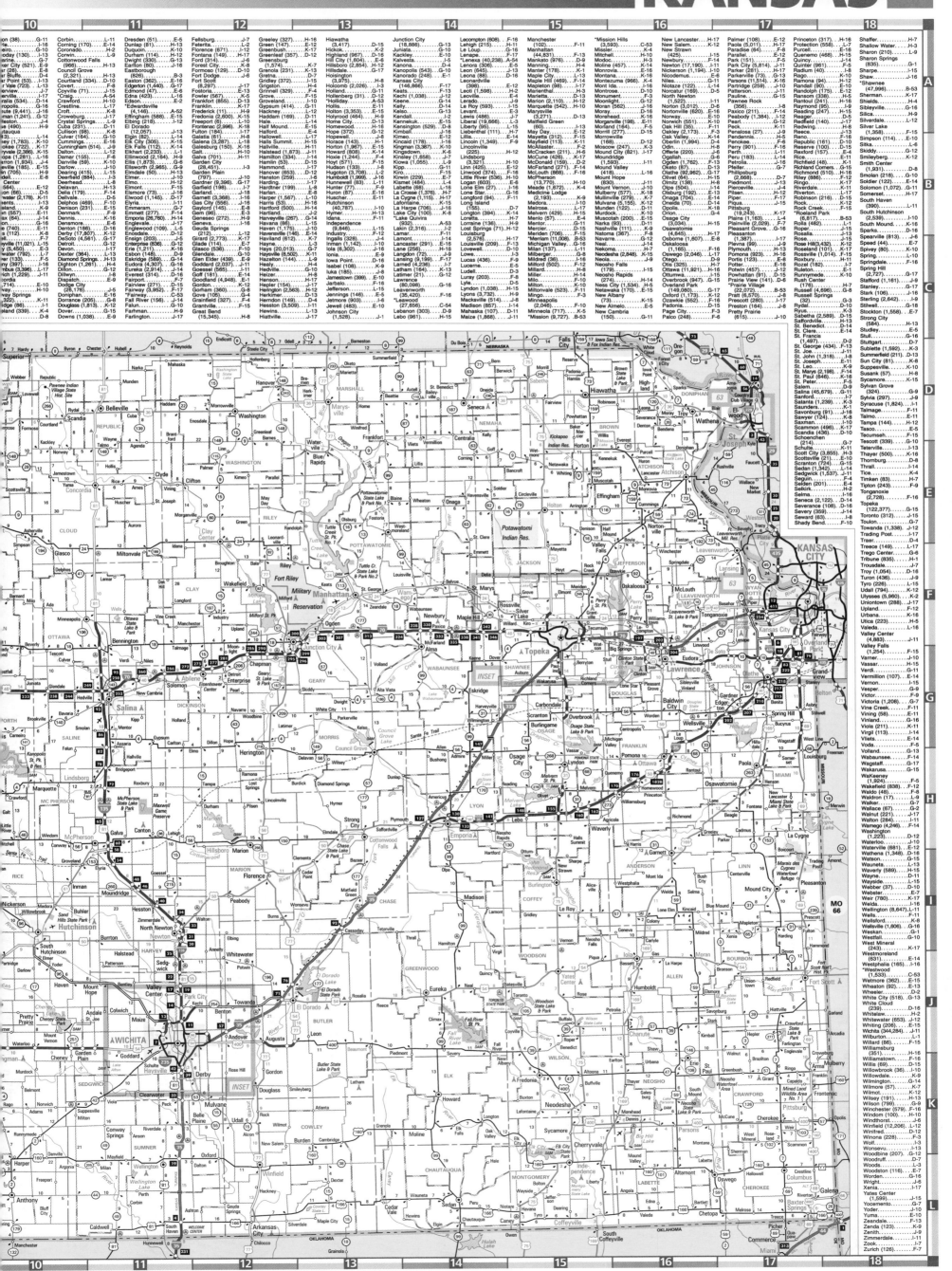

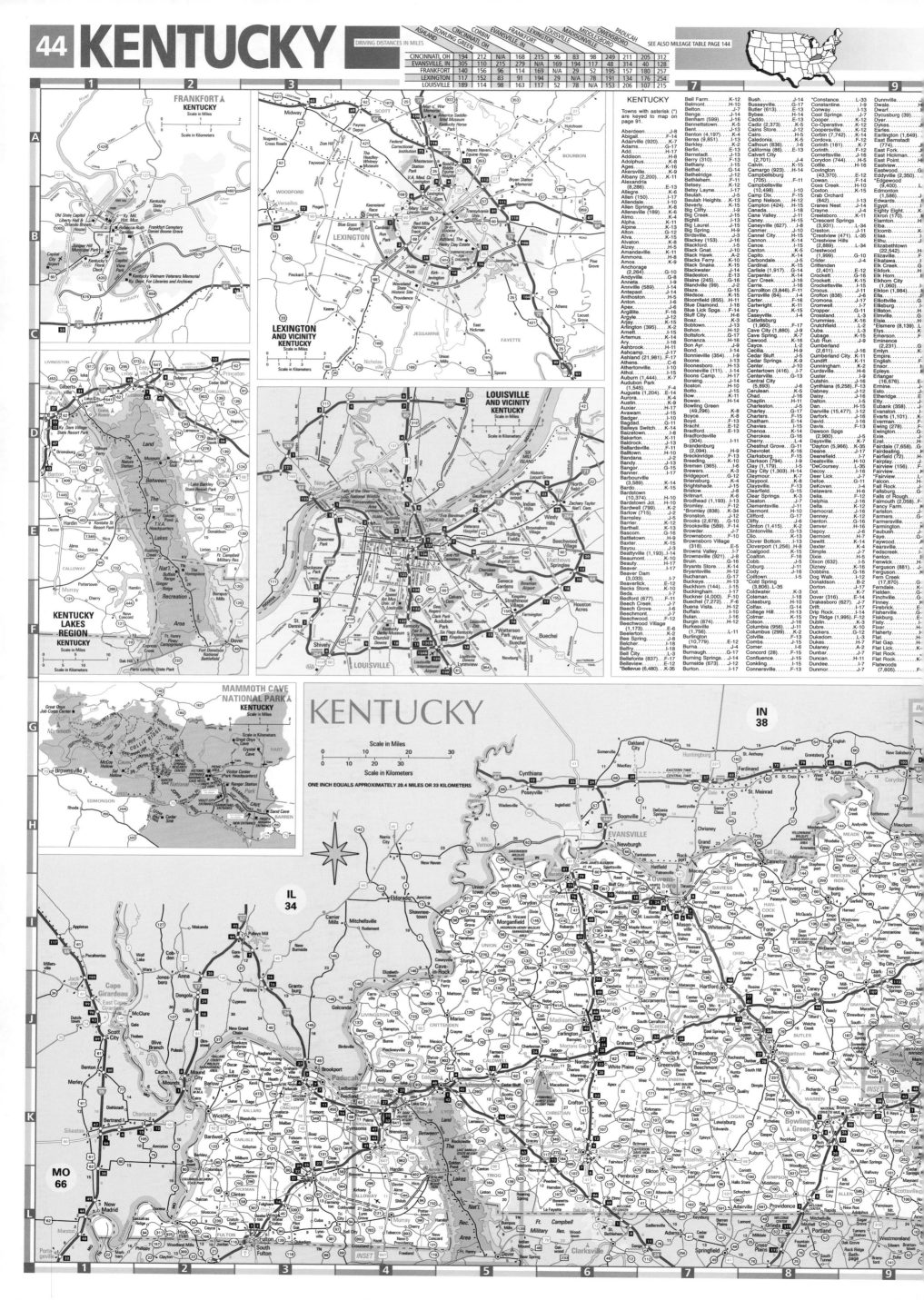

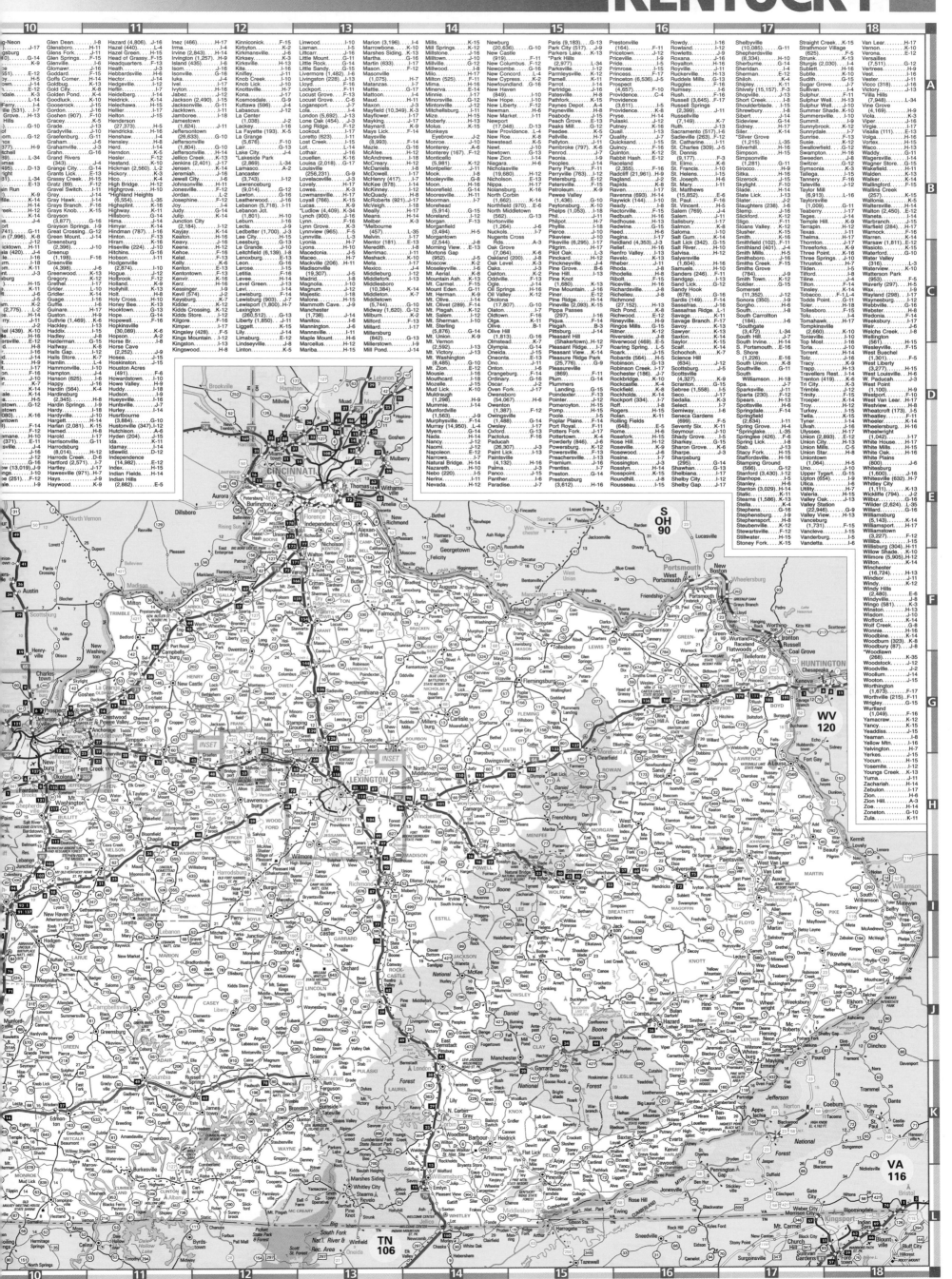

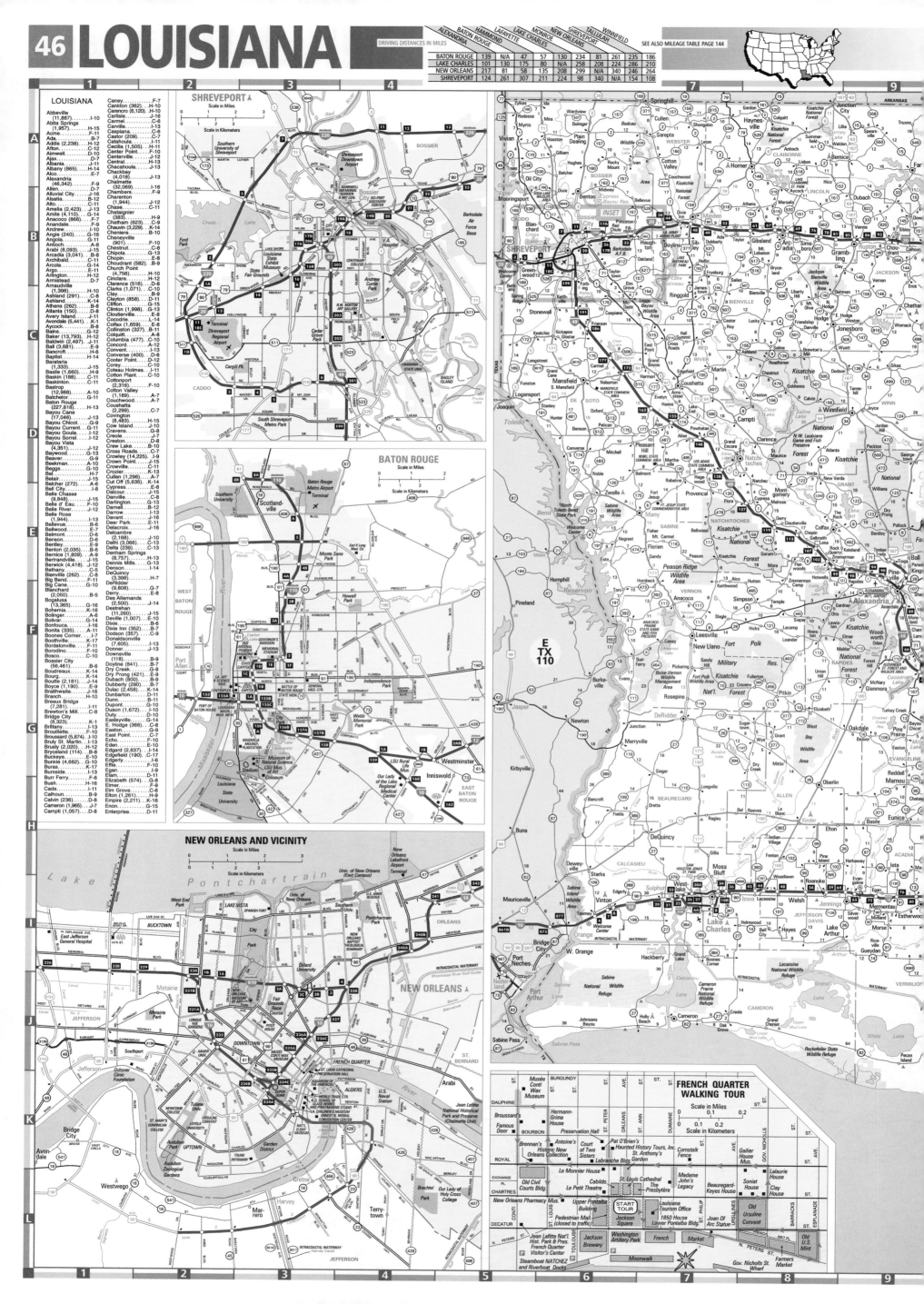

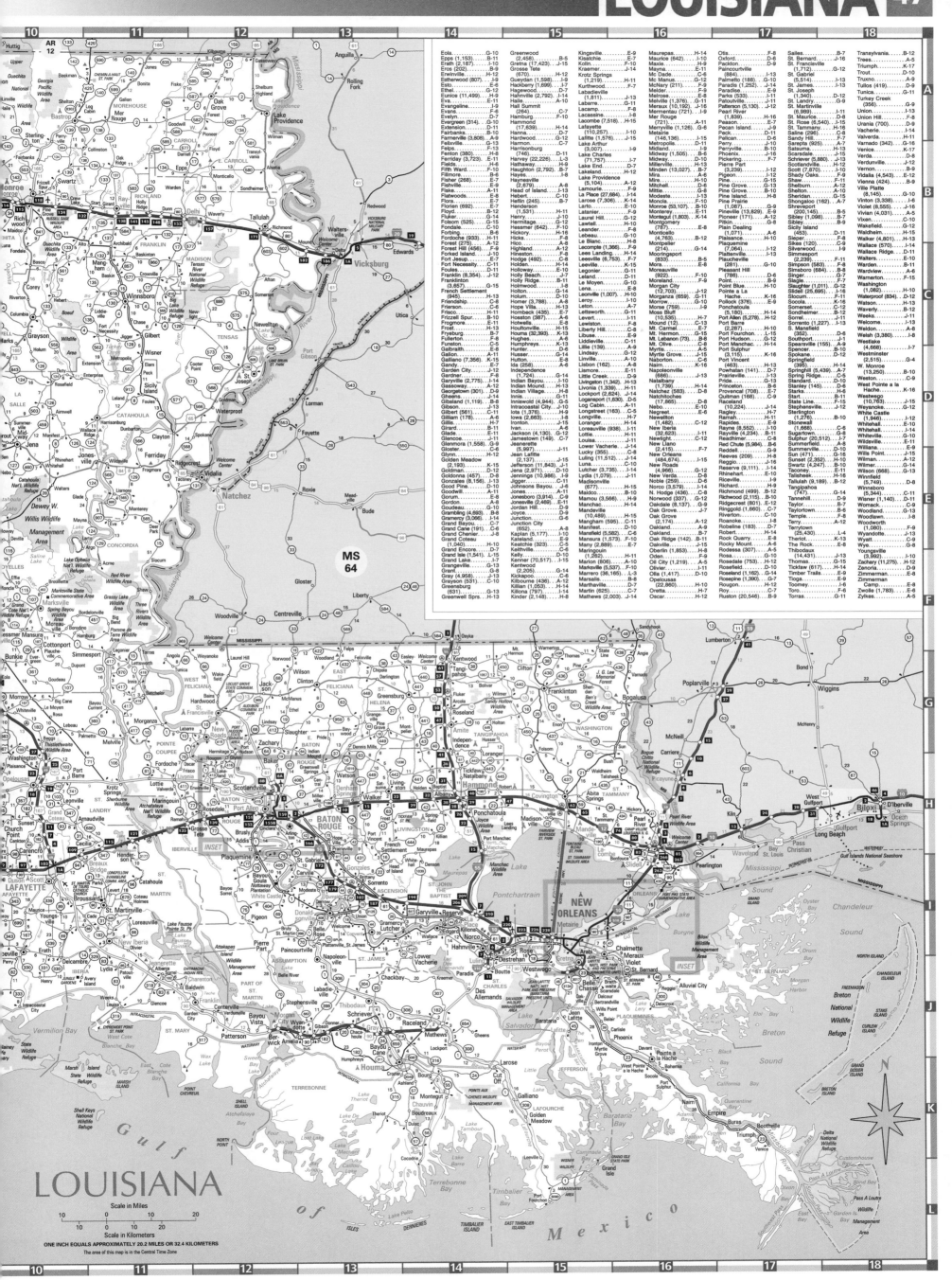

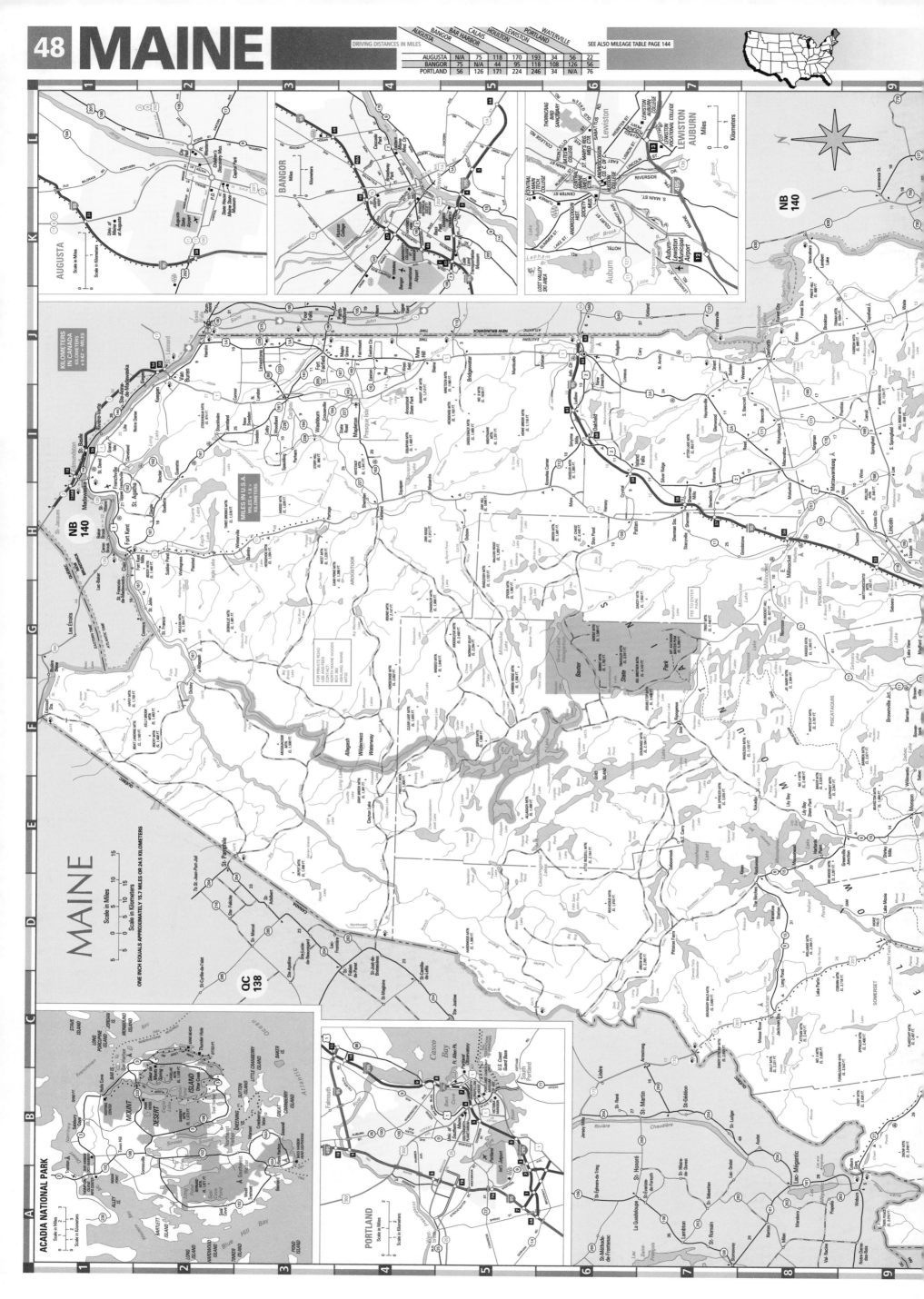

DRIVING DISTANCES IN MILES

SEE ALSO MILEAGE TABLE PAGE 144

	AUGUSTA	BANGOR	BAR HARBOR	HOULTON	LEWISTON	PORTLAND	WATERVILLE	CALAIS
AUGUSTA	N/A	75	118	170	193	34	56	22
BANGOR	75	N/A	44	95	118	108	126	56
PORTLAND	56	126	171	224	246	34	N/A	76

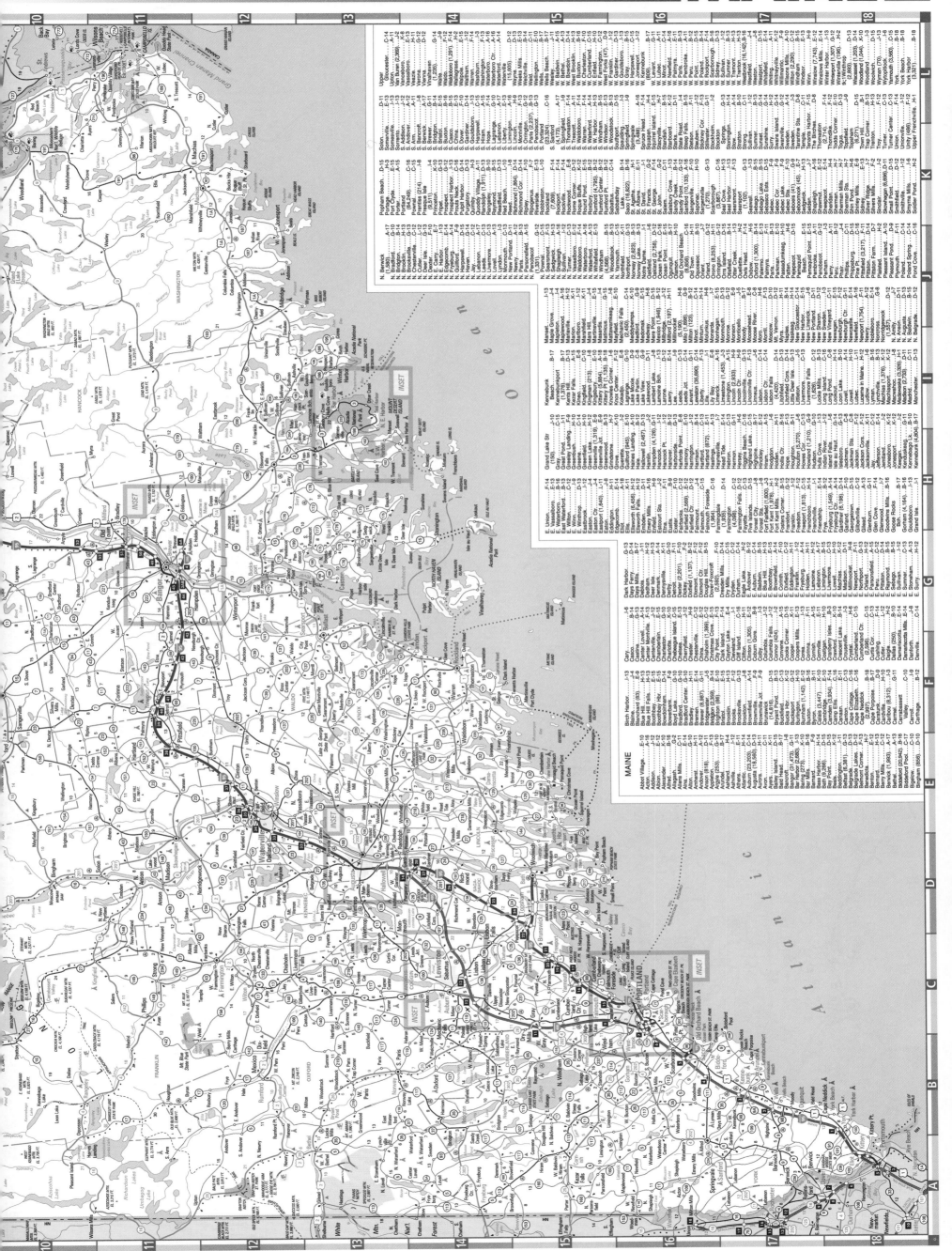

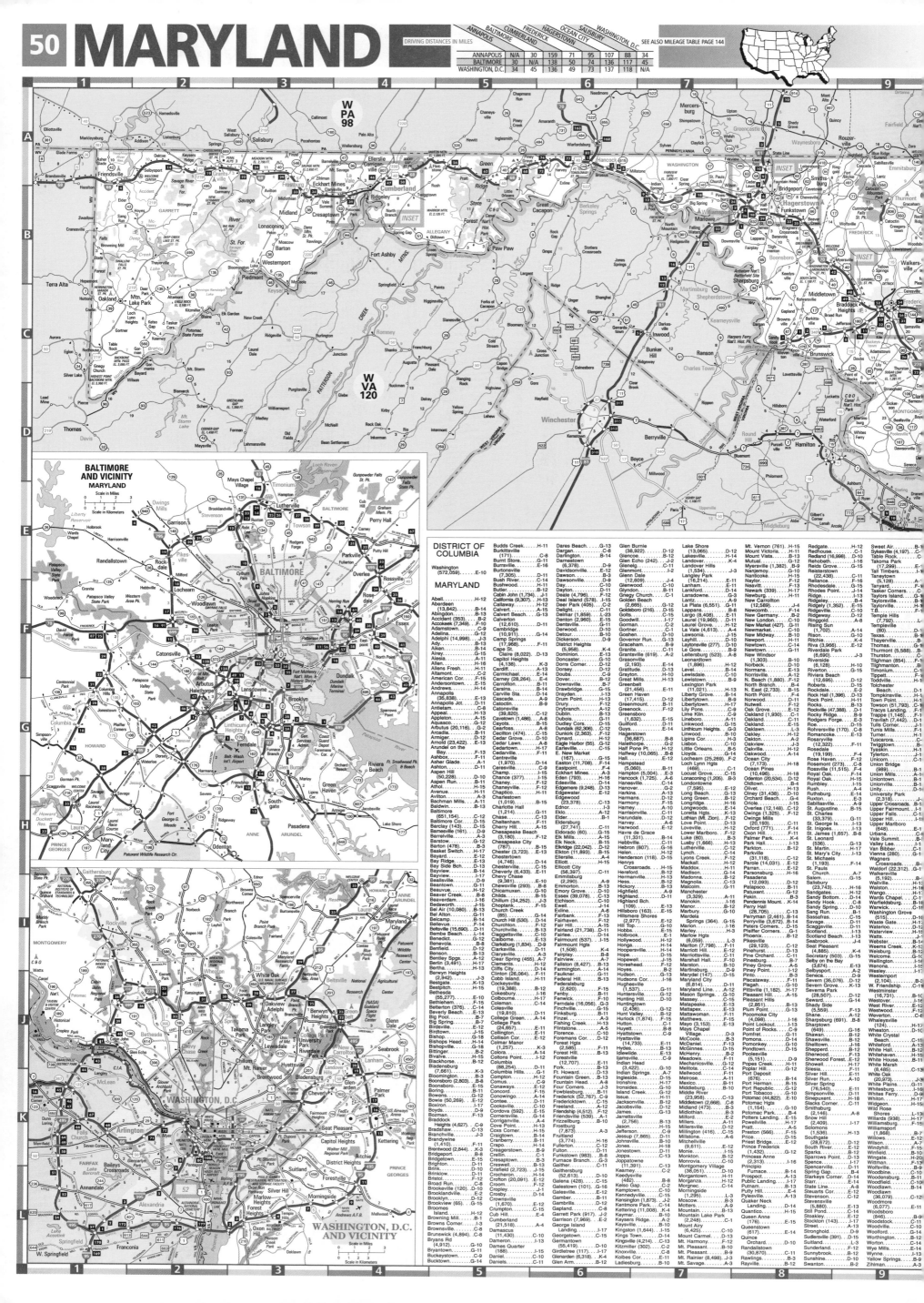

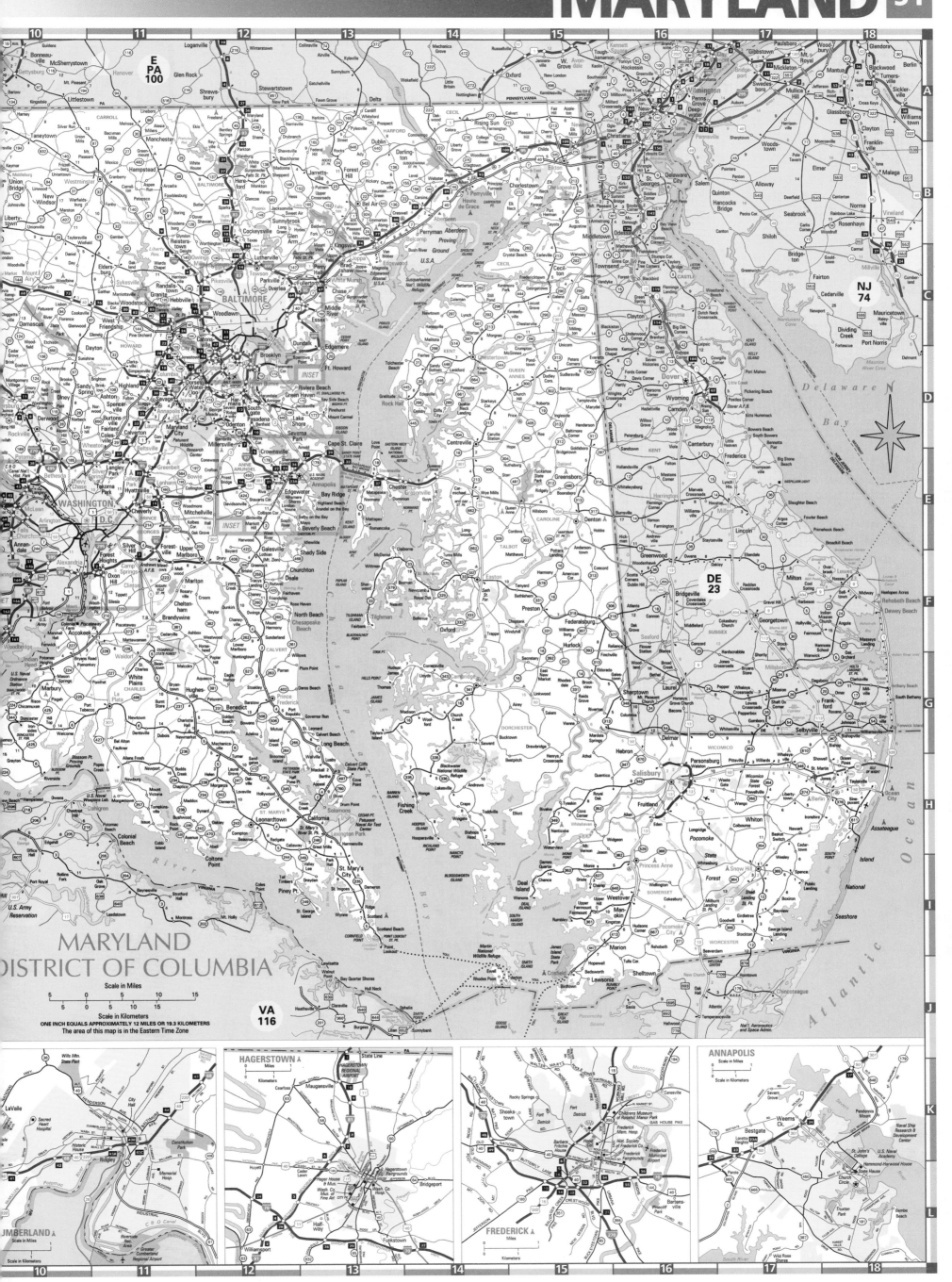

MARYLAND
DISTRICT OF COLUMBIA

Scale in Miles

Scale in Kilometers
ONE INCH EQUALS APPROXIMATELY 12 MILES OR 19.3 KILOMETERS
The area of this map is in the Eastern Time Zone

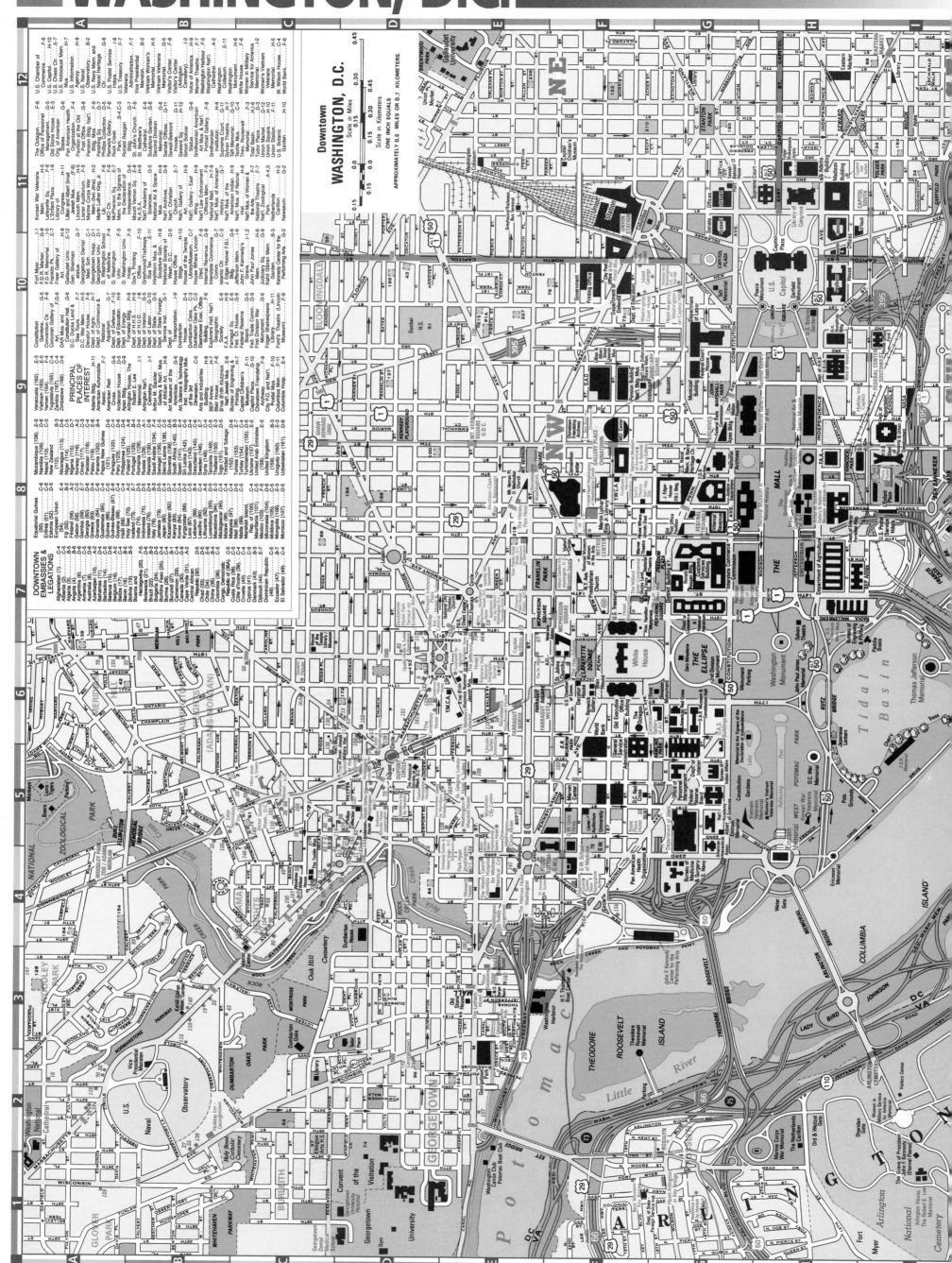

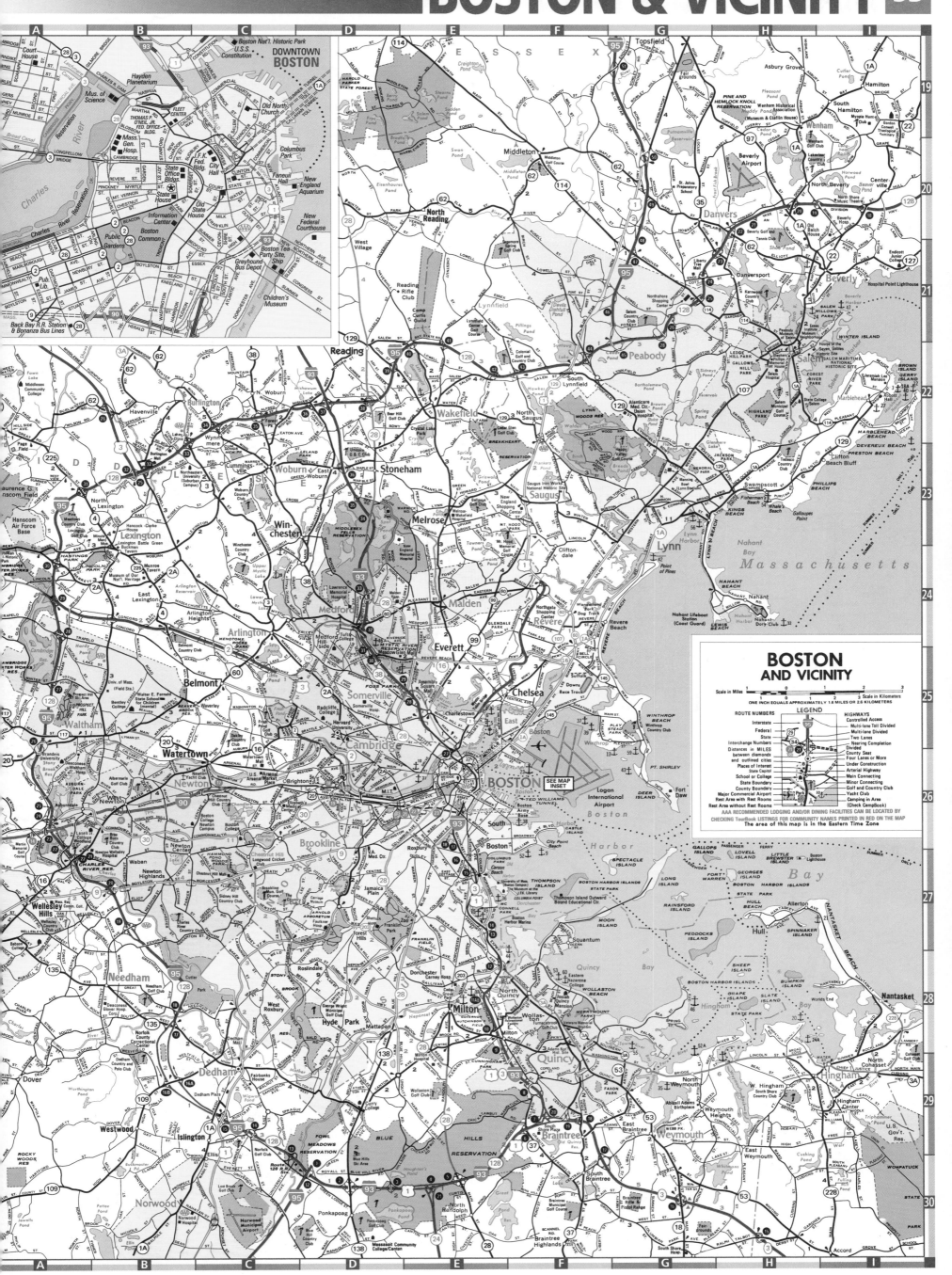

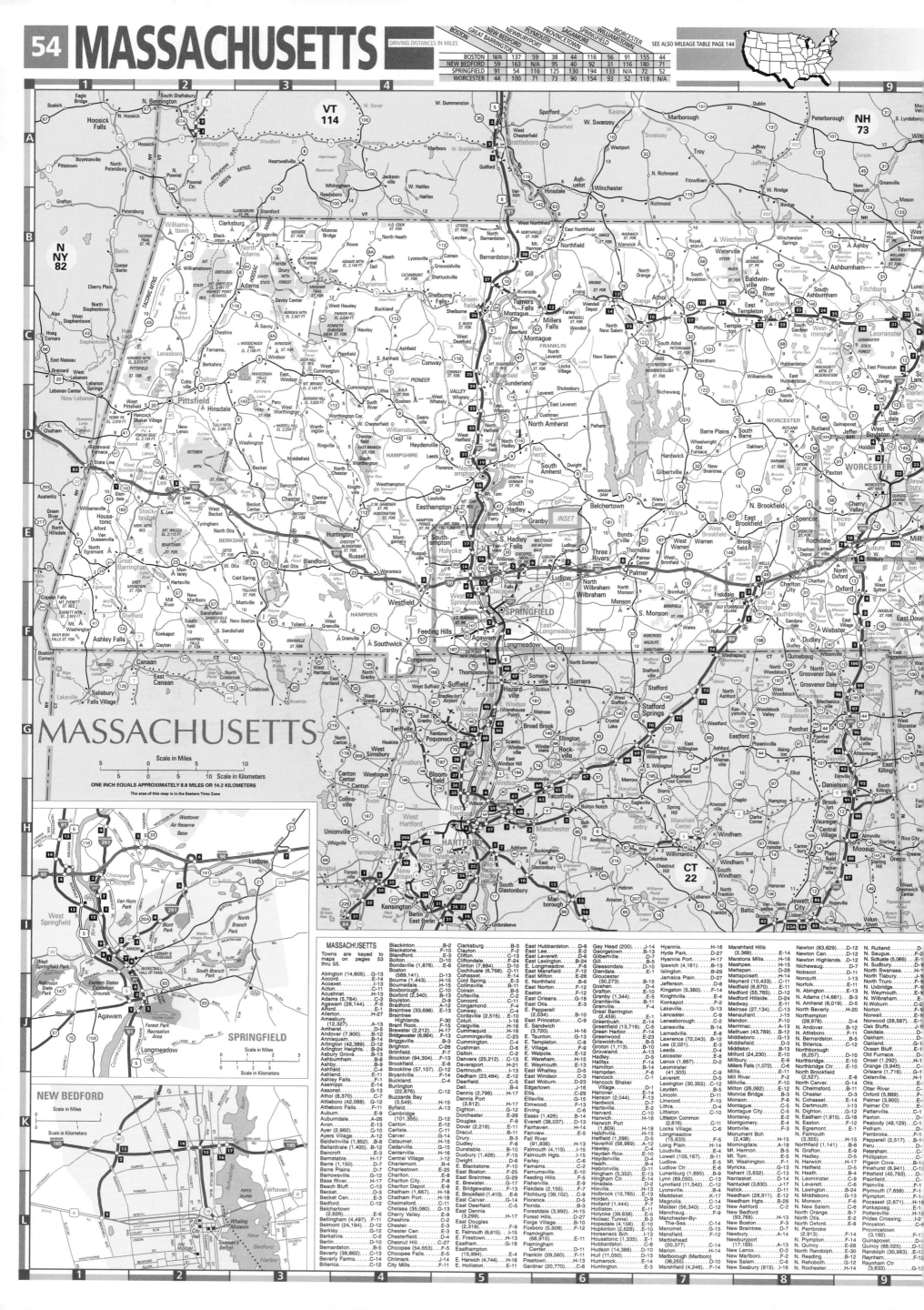

	BOSTON	GREAT BARRINGTON	NEW BEDFORD	NEWBURYPORT	PLYMOUTH	PROVINCETOWN	SAGAMORE	SPRINGFIELD	WILLIAMSTOWN	WORCESTER
BOSTON	N/A	137	59	38	44	116	56	91	155	44
NEW BEDFORD	59	163	N/A	95	40	92	31	116	180	71
SPRINGFIELD	91	54	116	125	130	194	133	N/A	72	52
WORCESTER	44	100	71	73	90	154	93	52	118	N/A

MASSACHUSETTS

Towns are keyed to maps on pages 53 thru 55.

MASSACHUSETTS

Scale in Miles

ONE INCH EQUALS APPROXIMATELY 8.8 MILES OR 14.2 KILOMETERS

The area of this map is in the Eastern Time Zone

SPRINGFIELD

Scale in Miles

NEW BEDFORD

Scale in Miles

CT 22

WORCESTER

DRIVING DISTANCES IN MILES

SEE ALSO MILEAGE TABLE PAGE 144

	BATTLE CREEK	BAY CITY	DETROIT	ESCANABA	FLINT	GRAND RAPIDS	IRONWOOD	LANSING	MARQUETTE	MUSKEGON	PORT HURON	SAULT STE. MARIE
DETROIT	122	115	N/A	435	68	151	691	90	454	195	63	343
FLINT	110	50	68	370	N/A	113	680	55	389	152	67	280
GRAND RAPIDS	80	158	151	394	113	N/A	578	68	413	40	179	296
LANSING	57	100	90	375	55	68	627	N/A	394	107	122	286
MUSKEGON	120	194	195	428	152	40	601	107	447	N/A	219	338

MICHIGAN

Towns with asterisk (*) are keyed to maps on pages 58-59. Towns on the Upper Peninsula are indexed with the map on pages 58-59.

FOR ADJOINING AREA SEE PAGES 58-59

ONE INCH EQUALS APPROXIMATELY 16.3 MILES OR 26.2 KILOMETERS

Scale in Miles
Scale in Kilometers

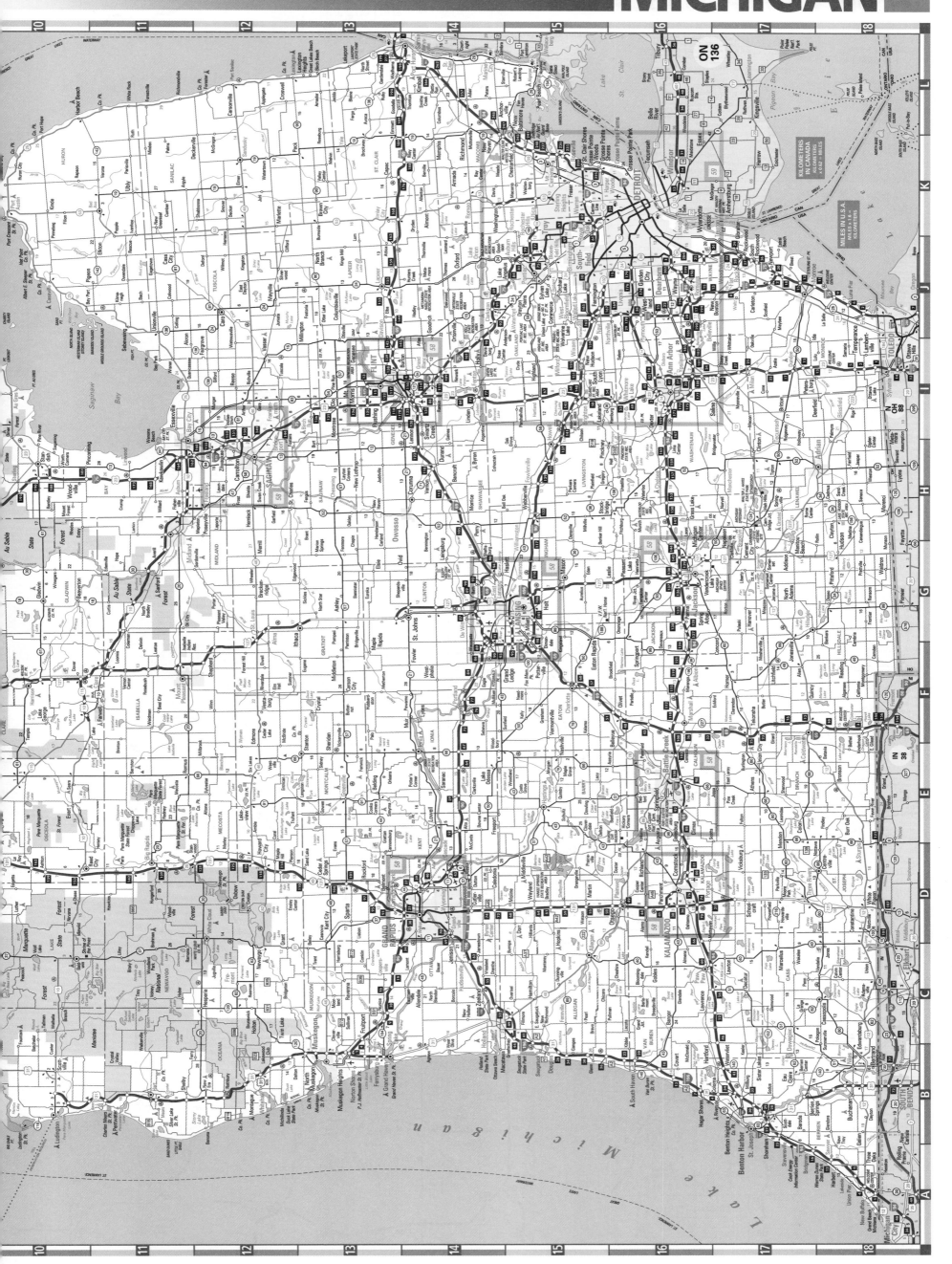

SEE ALSO MILEAGE TABLE PAGE 144

DRIVING DISTANCES IN MILES

	BATTLE CREEK	BAY CITY	DETROIT	ESCANABA	FLINT	GRAND RAPIDS	IRONWOOD	LANSING	MARQUETTE	MUSKEGON	PORT HURON	SAULT STE. MARIE
DETROIT	122	115		N/A	435	68	151	691	90	454	195	63	343
FLINT	110	50	68	370	N/A	113	680	55	389	152	67	280
GRAND RAPIDS	80	158	151	394	113	N/A	578	68	413	40	179	296
LANSING	57	100	90	375	55	68	627	N/A	394	107	122	286
MUSKEGON	120	194	195	428	152	40	601	107	447	N/A	219	338

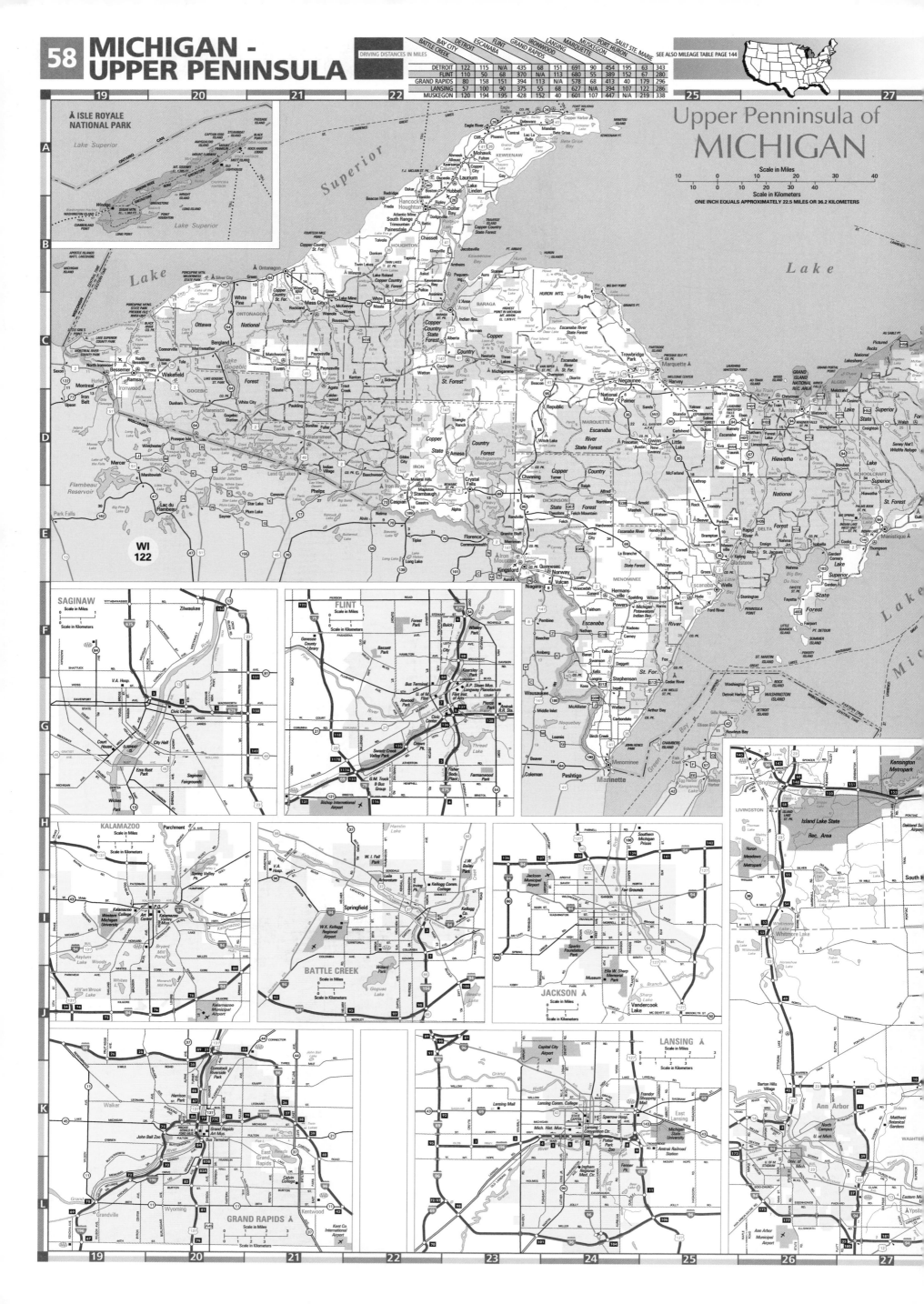

Upper Penninsula of MICHIGAN

Scale in Miles
10 0 10 20 30 40

Scale in Kilometers

ONE INCH EQUALS APPROXIMATELY 22.5 MILES OR 36.2 KILOMETERS

Isle Royale National Park

SAGINAW

FLINT

KALAMAZOO

BATTLE CREEK

JACKSON

LANSING

GRAND RAPIDS

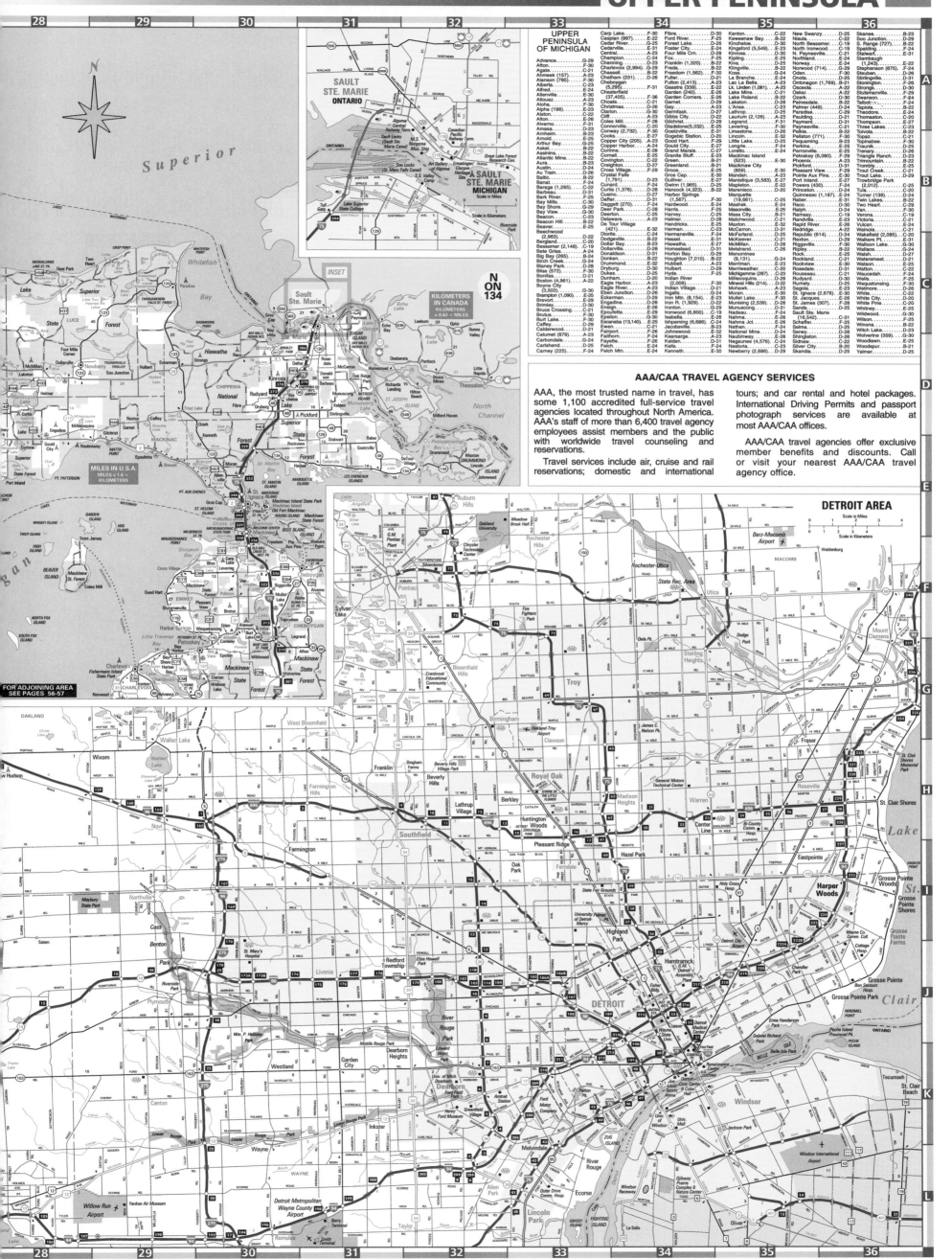

UPPER PENINSULA OF MICHIGAN

Advance...G-29	Carp Lake...F-30	Fibre...D-30	Kenton...C-22	New Swanzy...D-25	Skanee...B-23
Afton...F-30	Caspian (997)...E-22	Ford River...F-25	Keweenaw Bay...B-22	Nisula...D-22	Soo Junction...B-29
Agate...G-21	Cedar River...G-25	Forest Lake...C-24	Kinchiloe...D-30	North Bessemer...D-19	S. Range (727)...B-22
Ahmeek (157)...A-22	Cedarville...E-31	Foster City...F-24	Kingsford (5,549)...E-23	North Ironwood...D-19	Spalding...F-24
Alanson (785)...F-30	Centerville...C-31	Four Mile Crn...E-25	Kinross...D-30	N. Paynesville...D-24	Stalwart...E-31
Alberta...E-22	Champion...C-24	Fox...F-27	Kipling...E-25	Northland...C-24	Stambaugh...E-22
Alfred...E-24	Channing...D-23	Franklin (1,320)...B-22	Kiva...C-25	Norway...E-24	Stannard...C-21
Allenville...E-30	Charlevoix (2,994)...D-29	Freda...C-22	Klingville...B-24	Norwood (714)...D-29	Stephenson (875)...F-24
Allouez...A-22	Chassell...D-22	Freedom (1,562)...F-30	Koss...F-24	Oden...F-30	Steuben...D-26
Aloha...F-30	Chatham (231)...D-26	Fuller...D-25	La Branche...E-24	Okemos...D-25	Stirlingville...D-31
Alpha (198)...E-23	Cheboygan (5,295)...F-31	Gaastra (339)...E-22	La Salle...B-22	Ontonagon (1,769)...B-20	Stonington...E-25
Alston...C-22	Chesterfield...D-26	Garden (240)...E-25	Lk. Linden (1,081)...A-23	Osceola...A-22	Strongs...D-30
Alston...C-21	Choate...C-21	Garden Corners...E-25	Lake Mine...B-22	Oskar...B-22	Stutsmanville...E-29
Alverno...F-31	Christmas...D-26	Garnet...D-29	Lake Roland...C-22	Ozark...D-30	Swanson...F-24
Amasa...E-22	Clarion...D-30	Gay...A-23	Laketon...B-23	Painesdale...B-22	Tapiola...B-22
Arnheim...B-23	Coles Mill...F-28	Germfask...D-27	L'Anse...C-22	Palmer (449)...C-24	Theodore...E-24
Arnold...E-25	Connorville...C-20	Gibbs City...D-22	Lathrop...E-22	Paradise...C-29	Thomaston...C-21
Arthur Bay...B-23	Conway (2,732)...F-30	Gilchrist...D-28	Laurium (2,126)...A-23	Paulding...C-21	Thompson...E-26
Askel...B-22	Cooks...E-25	Gladstone(5,032)...E-25	Legrand...F-31	Payment...D-31	Three Lakes...C-23
Assinins...B-22	Copper City (205)...A-22	Goetzville...E-31	Limestone...C-24	Payne...B-22	Toivola...B-22
Atlantic Mine...B-22	Copper Harbor...A-22	Gogebic Station...D-20	Lincoln...E-22	Pelkie...C-22	Topaz...C-21
Aura...B-23	Cornell...E-25	Good Hart...E-29	Little Lake...E-25	Pelston (771)...F-30	Topinabee...F-30
Austin...D-27	Covington...C-22	Gould City...F-28	Longrie...F-24	Pequaming...B-23	Traunik...D-26
Au Train...D-26	Creighton...D-27	Grand Marais...C-28	Loretto...E-24	Perkins...E-25	Trenary...D-26
Baltic...B-22	Crystal Falls (1,791)...D-23	Granite Bluff...C-27	Mackinac Island...E-30	Perronville...E-25	Triangle Ranch...F-27
Banat...F-24	Curtis (1,378)...D-28	Greenland...B-21	Mackinaw City...E-30	Petoskey (6,080)...E-29	Trimountain...B-22
Baraga (1,285)...C-22	Cunard...E-25	Groos...E-23	Mandan...A-22	Phoenix...A-22	Trombly...D-25
Barbeau...E-31	Dafter...B-30	Gros Cap...E-30	Manistique (3,583)...E-27	Pickford...C-31	Trout Creek...C-21
Bark River...F-24	Daggett (270)...F-24	Gulliver...E-27	Mapleton...B-23	Pleasant View...F-29	Trout Lake...D-29
Bay Mills...C-30	Deer Park...C-28	Gwinn (1,965)...D-25	Marenisco...D-20	Pointe Aux Pins...E-30	Trowbridge Park (2,012)...C-24
Bay Shore...F-29	Deerton...D-26	Hancock (4,323)...B-22	Marquette (19,661)...C-25	Port Inland...E-27	Turner (139)...D-24
Bay View...E-29	Delaware...A-22	Harbor Springs (1,567)...E-29	Mass City...B-21	Powers (430)...F-24	Twin Lakes...B-22
Beacon...C-21	De Tour Village (421)...E-31	Hardwood...D-24	Mascoville...E-24	Pequaming...B-23	Two Heart...C-28
Beacon Hill...B-22	Diorite...C-24	Harvey...C-25	Matchwood...C-21	Quinnesec (1,187)...E-24	Van...C-23
Beaver...E-25	Dodgeville...B-22	Hendricks...E-27	Maxton...E-31	Raco...D-30	Verona...C-19
Beechwood (2,963)...C-21	Donken...B-22	Herman...C-23	McCarron...B-22	Ralph...E-24	Victoria...C-21
Bergland...C-21	Drummond...E-32	Hermansville...F-24	McFarland...C-25	Ramsay...E-19	Vulcan...E-24
Bessemer (2,148)...C-19	Dryburg...D-30	Hessel...E-31	McKeever...C-21	Randville...E-23	Wainola...C-21
Bete Grise...A-24	Dukes...D-25	Hiawatha...D-26	McMillan...D-28	Rapid River...E-26	Wakefield (2,085)...C-19
Big Bay (265)...B-24	Dunham...D-27	Homestead...D-21	Melstrand...C-26	Rexton...D-29	Walsh...D-27
Birch Creek...F-24	Eagle Harbor...A-23	Horton Bay...F-29	Menominee (9,131)...G-24	Republic (614)...D-24	Watersmeet...E-21
Blaney Park...D-28	Eagle River...A-22	Houghton (7,010)...B-22	Merriman...E-23	Ripley...B-22	Walkers Pt...E-25
Bliss (572)...E-29	Eben Junction...D-25	Hubbell...A-23	Merriweather...C-20	Rock...D-25	Walloon Lake...E-30
Bonifas...D-27	Eckerman...D-29	Hulbert...C-29	Michigamme (287)...C-23	Rockland...C-21	Wallace...F-24
Boyne City (3,503)...D-30	Engadine...D-28	Hyde...F-25	Milbrook...D-24	Rockview...D-30	Walton...F-30
Boyne Falls (294)...D-30	Ensign...E-26	Indian River...F-30	Millecoquins (9,131)...D-27	Rousseau...C-22	Watson...E-30
Brampton (1,090)...E-25	Epoufette...E-28	Indian Village...F-30	Mineral Hills (214)...D-22	Rudyard...D-30	Waucedah...E-24
Brevort...E-30	Epsilon...C-30	Ingalls...F-24	Mohawk...A-22	Rumely...D-25	Wells...E-25
Bruce Crossing...C-21	Escanaba (13,140)...E-25	Iron Mtn. (8,154)...E-23	Monico...E-25	Saginaw...F-25	Wequetonsing...F-29
Brutus...F-30	Ewen...C-21	Iron R. (1,929)...D-22	Montreal (9,539)...D-18	S. Ignace (2,678)...E-30	Wetmore...D-26
Burt Lake...F-30	Fairport...E-26	Ironton...D-29	Muskallonge...D-28	St. Jacques...E-26	White City...D-20
Caffey...F-27	Faithorn...F-24	Isabella...E-24	Munuscong...D-31	St. James (307)...D-29	White City...D-20
Caldorwood...D-21	Fayette...F-26	Ishpeming (6,886)...C-24		Sands...C-25	Whitney...E-26
Calumet (879)...A-23	Felch...E-24	Jacobsville...A-23	Nadeau...F-24	Saucier...E-31	Wilson...F-24
Carbondale...G-22	Felch Mtn....E-24	Johnswood...E-32	Nahma...E-26	Schaffer...C-25	Wolverine (359)...G-30
Carlshend...C-25		Kearsarge...A-23	Nahma Jct....E-25	Seney...D-27	Woodlawn...E-25
Carney (225)...F-24		Kelson...C-27	National Mine...C-24	Shingleton...D-26	Woodspur...D-20
		Kells...F-24	Nestoria...C-22	Sidnaw...C-22	Yalmer...D-25
		Kenneth...E-30	Newberry (2,686)...D-29	Silver City...B-20	
				Skandia...D-25	

FOR ADJOINING AREA SEE PAGES 56-57

AAA/CAA TRAVEL AGENCY SERVICES

AAA, the most trusted name in travel, has some 1,100 accredited full-service travel agencies located throughout North America. AAA's staff of more than 6,400 travel agency employees assist members and the public with worldwide travel counseling and reservations.

Travel services include air, cruise and rail reservations; domestic and international tours; and car rental and hotel packages. International Driving Permits and passport photograph services are available at most AAA/CAA offices.

AAA/CAA travel agencies offer exclusive member benefits and discounts. Call or visit your nearest AAA/CAA travel agency office.

DRIVING DISTANCES IN MILES

SEE ALSO MILEAGE TABLE PAGE 144

	ALBERT LEA	BEMIDJI	DULUTH	FARGO ND	INT'L FALLS	MINNEAPOLIS	ROCHESTER	ST. CLOUD	ST. PAUL	SIOUX FALLS SD
DULUTH	252	153	N/A	250	161	153	232	145	151	423
INT'L FALLS	390	114	161	278	N/A	293	371	283	289	560
MINNEAPOLIS	100	230	153	245	293	N/A	90	72	9	268
ROCHESTER	67	318	232	339	371	90	N/A	175	76	236

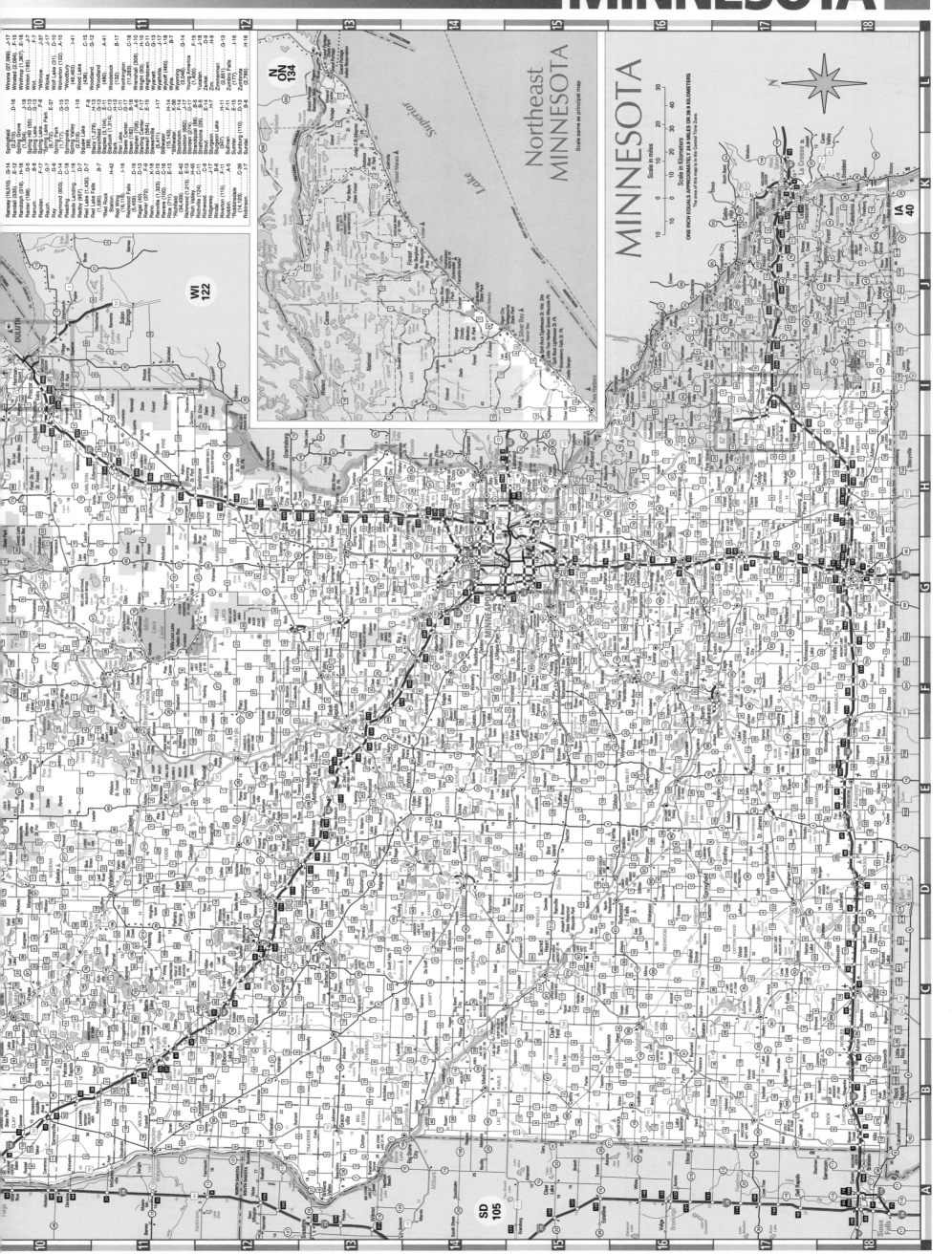

Northeast MINNESOTA

Scale same as principal map

MINNESOTA

Scale in miles

Scale in Kilometers

ONE INCH EQUALS APPROXIMATELY 24.9 MILES OR 38.9 KILOMETERS

The area of this map is in the Central Time Zone.

WI 122

IA 40

SD 105

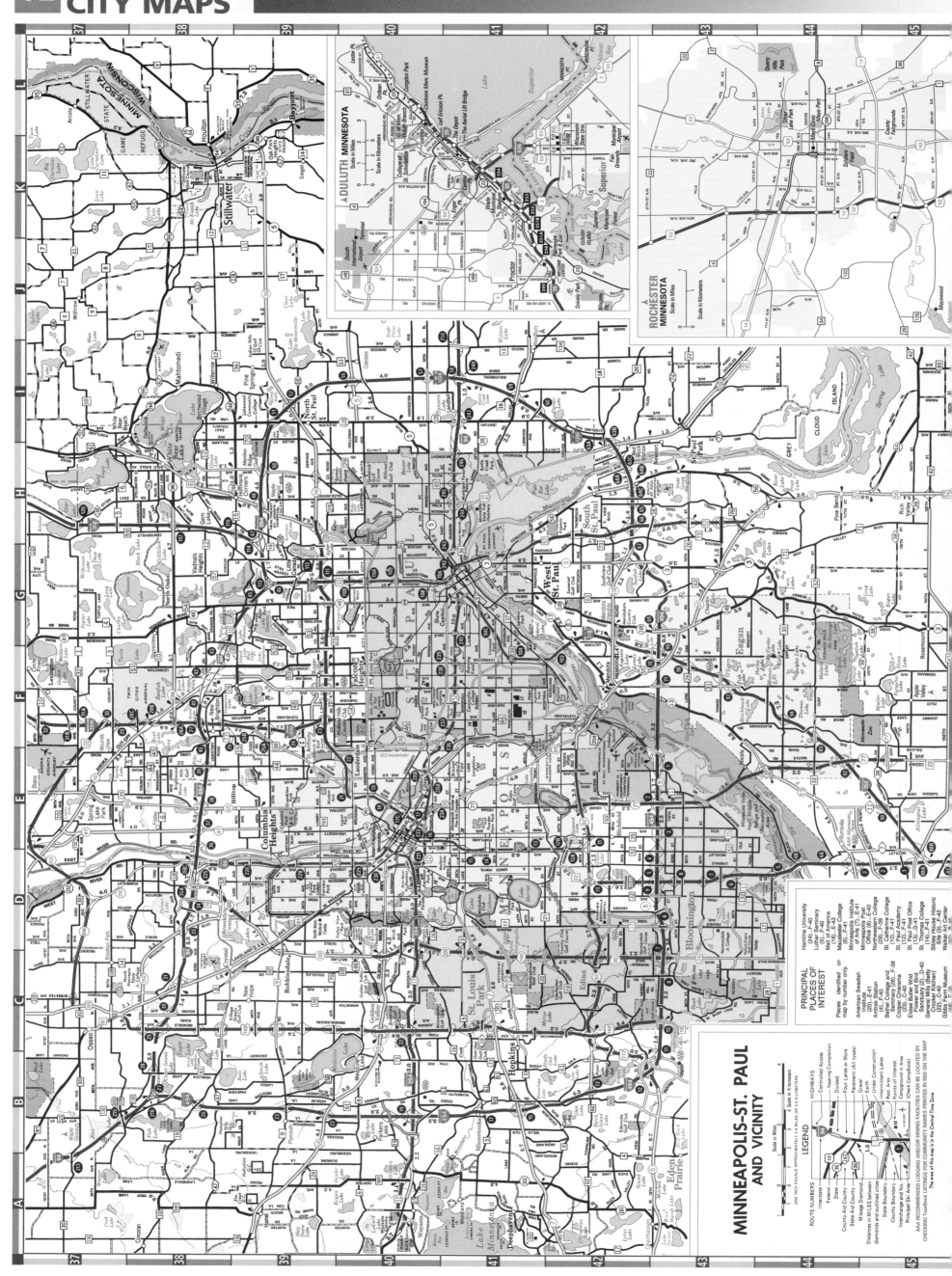

DULUTH MINNESOTA

ROCHESTER MINNESOTA

MINNEAPOLIS-ST. PAUL AND VICINITY

PRINCIPAL PLACES OF INTEREST

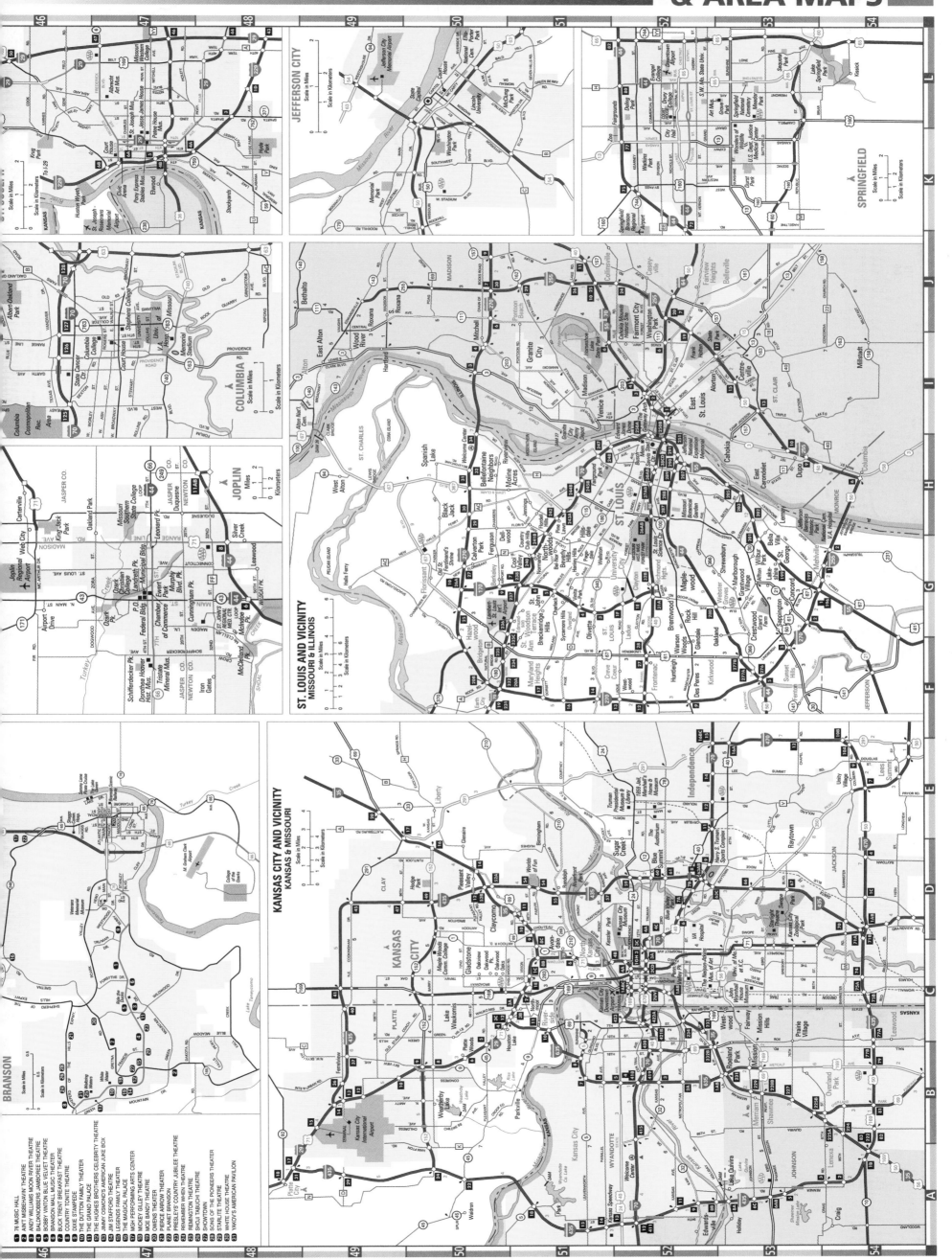

JEFFERSON CITY

SPRINGFIELD

COLUMBIA

JOPLIN

ST. LOUIS AND VICINITY
MISSOURI & ILLINOIS

BRANSON

KANSAS CITY AND VICINITY
KANSAS & MISSOURI

1. 76 MUSIC HALL
2. AIN'T MISBEHAVIN' THEATRE
3. ANDY WILLIAMS MOON RIVER THEATRE
4. BALDKNOBBERS JAMBOREE THEATRE
5. BOBBY VINTON BLUE VELVET THEATER
6. BRANSON MALL MUSIC THEATRE
7. BUCK TRENT BREAKFAST THEATRE
8. COUNTRY TONITE THEATRE
9. DIXIE STAMPEDE
10. THE DUTTON FAMILY THEATER
11. THE GRAND PALACE
12. THE HUGHES BROTHERS CELEBRITY THEATRE
13. JIM STAFFORD THEATRE
14. JIMMY OSMOND'S AMERICAN JUKE BOX
15. LEGENDS IN CONCERT
16. THE MAGICAL PALACE
17. MGH PERFORMING ARTS CENTER
18. MICKEY GILLEY THEATRE
19. MOE BANDY THEATER
20. OWENS THEATER
21. PIERCE ARROW THEATER
22. PRESLEYS' COUNTRY JUBILEE THEATRE
23. REMEMBER WHEN THEATRE
24. REMINGTON THEATRE
25. SHOJI TABUCHI THEATRE
26. SHOWTOWN
27. SONS OF THE PIONEERS THEATER
28. STARLITE THEATRE
29. TITANIC MUSEUM THEATRE
30. YAKOV'S AMERICAN PAVILION

DRIVING DISTANCES IN MILES

SEE ALSO MILEAGE TABLE PAGE 144

	BILOXI	CLARKSDALE	COLUMBUS	GULFPORT	HATTIESBURG	JACKSON	MERIDIAN	NATCHEZ	TUPELO	VICKSBURG
BILOXI	N/A	360	262	7	81	234	172	224	315	273
JACKSON	234	190	173	223	90	N/A	93	115	220	44
MERIDIAN	172	281	92	160	91	93	N/A	205	145	134
TUPELO	315	114	63	302	233	220	145	336	N/A	261

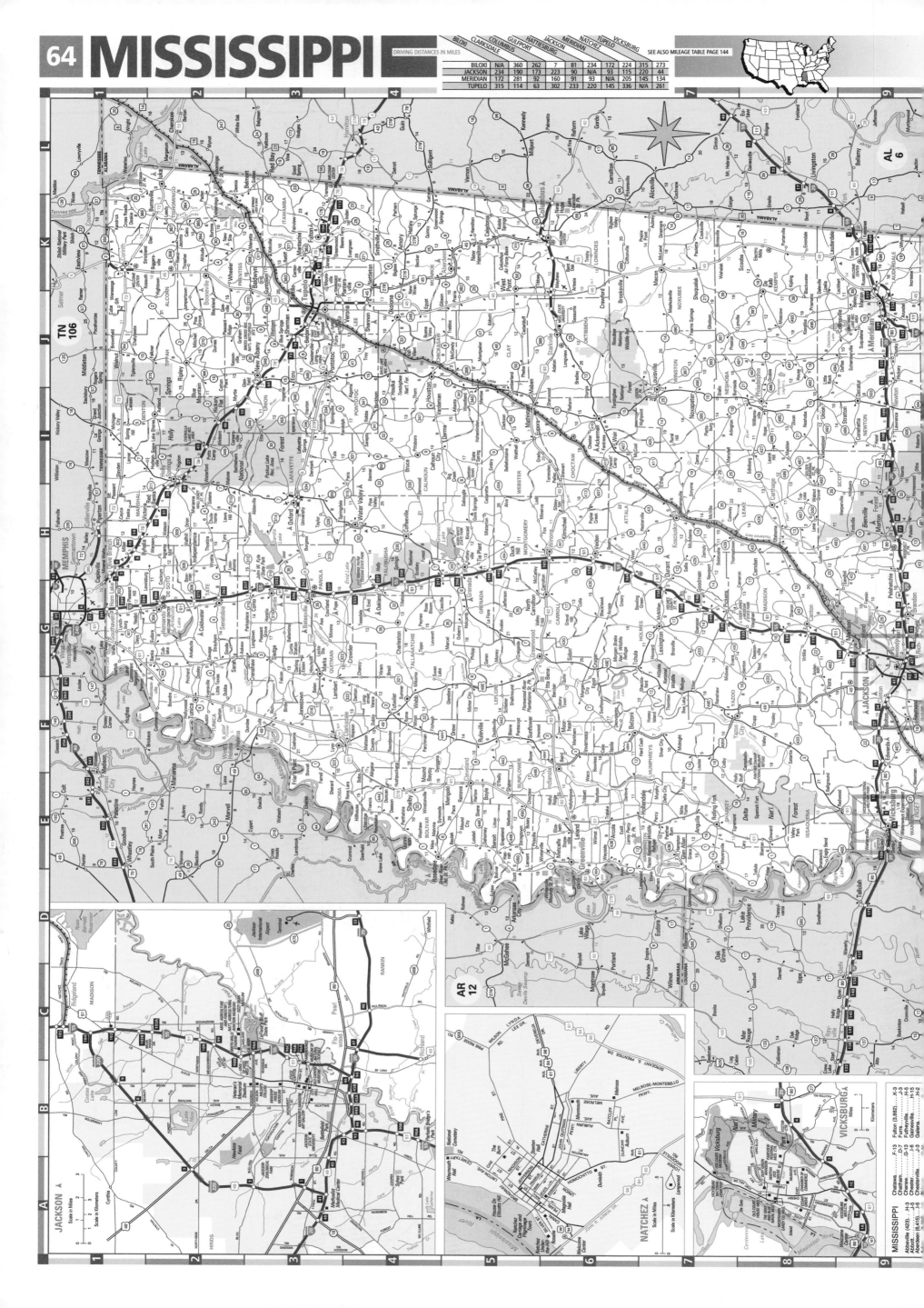

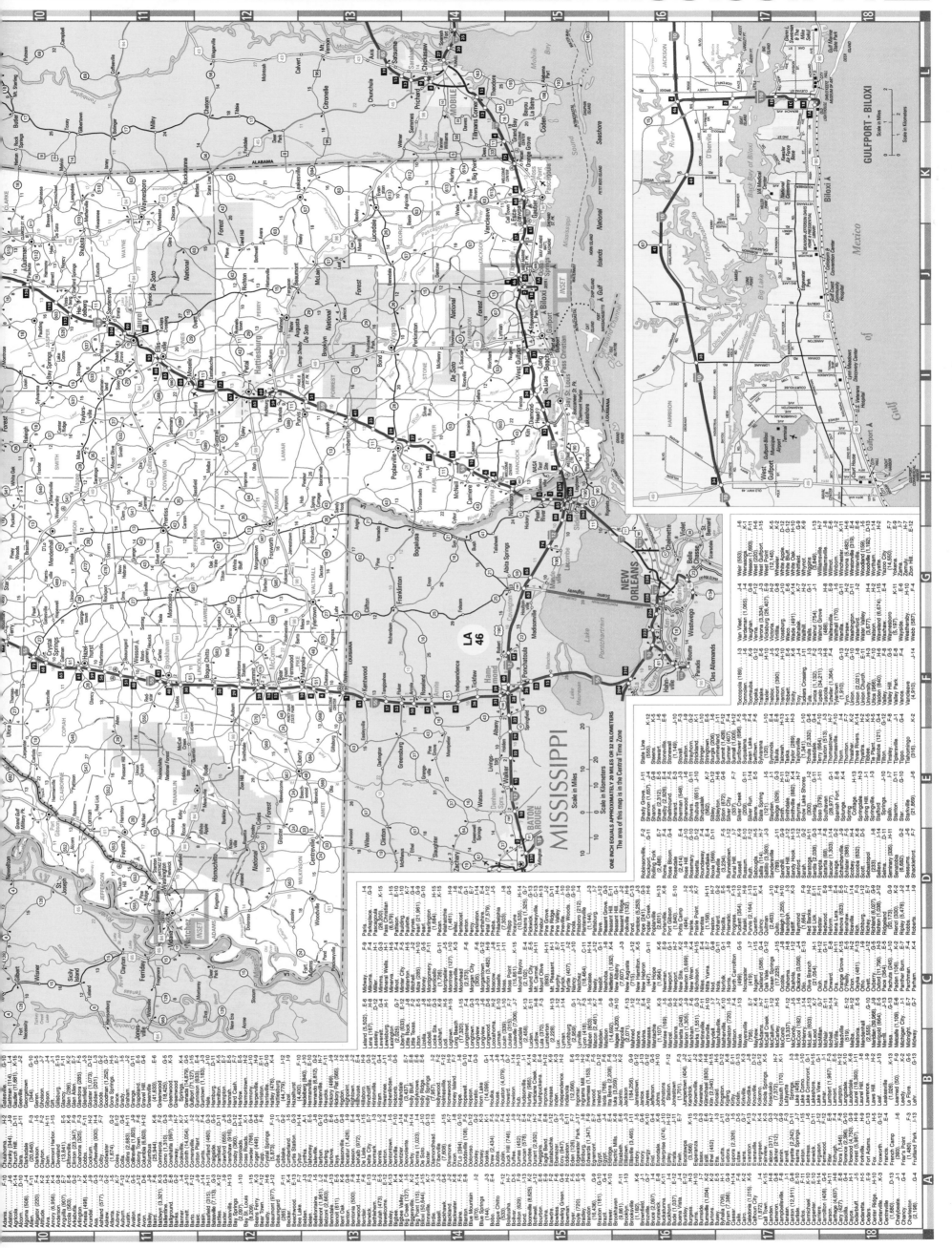

GULFPORT - BILOXI

MISSISSIPPI

Scale in Miles

Scale in Kilometers

ONE INCH EQUALS APPROXIMATELY 20 MILES OR 32 KILOMETERS

The area of this map is in the Central Time Zone

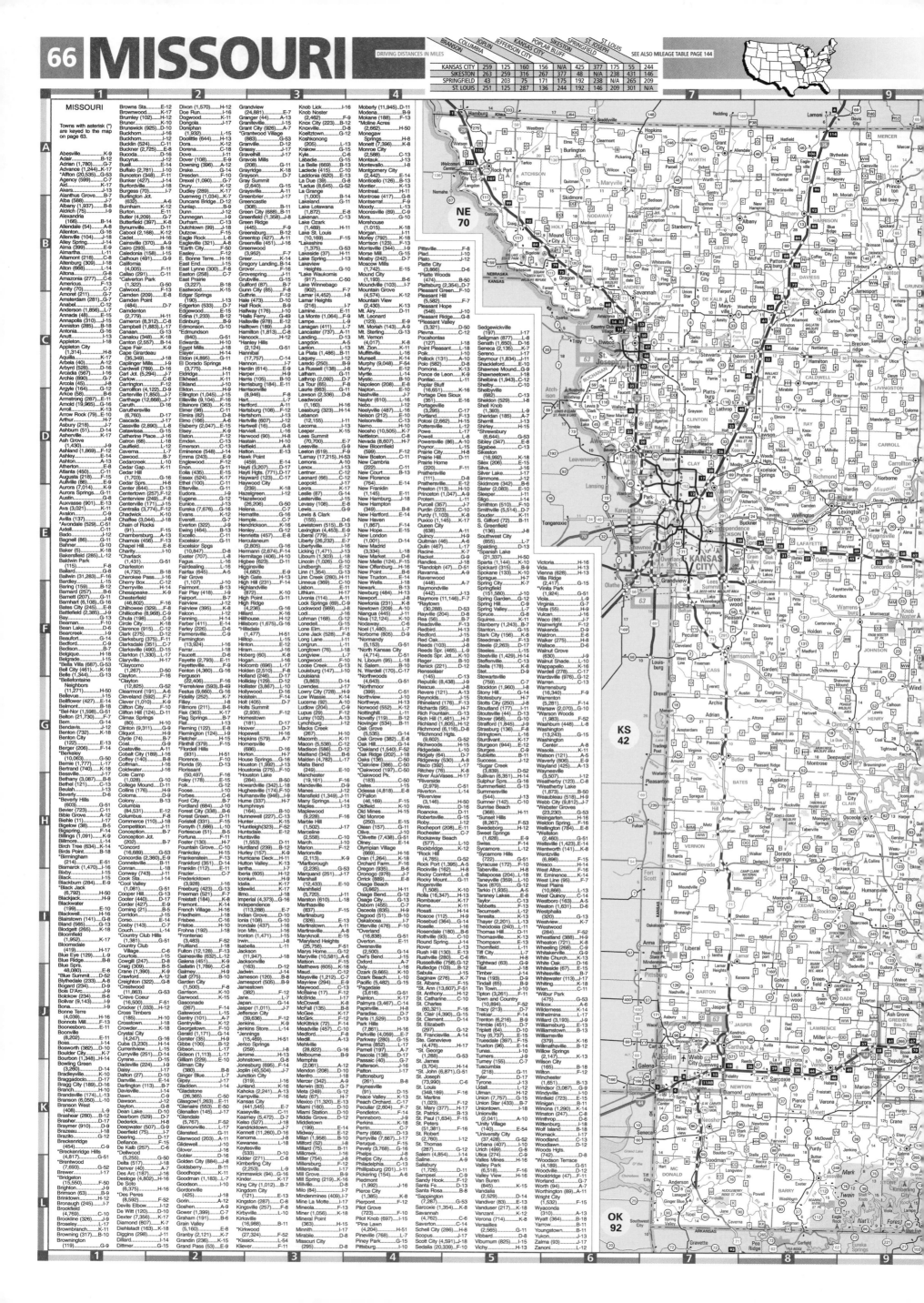

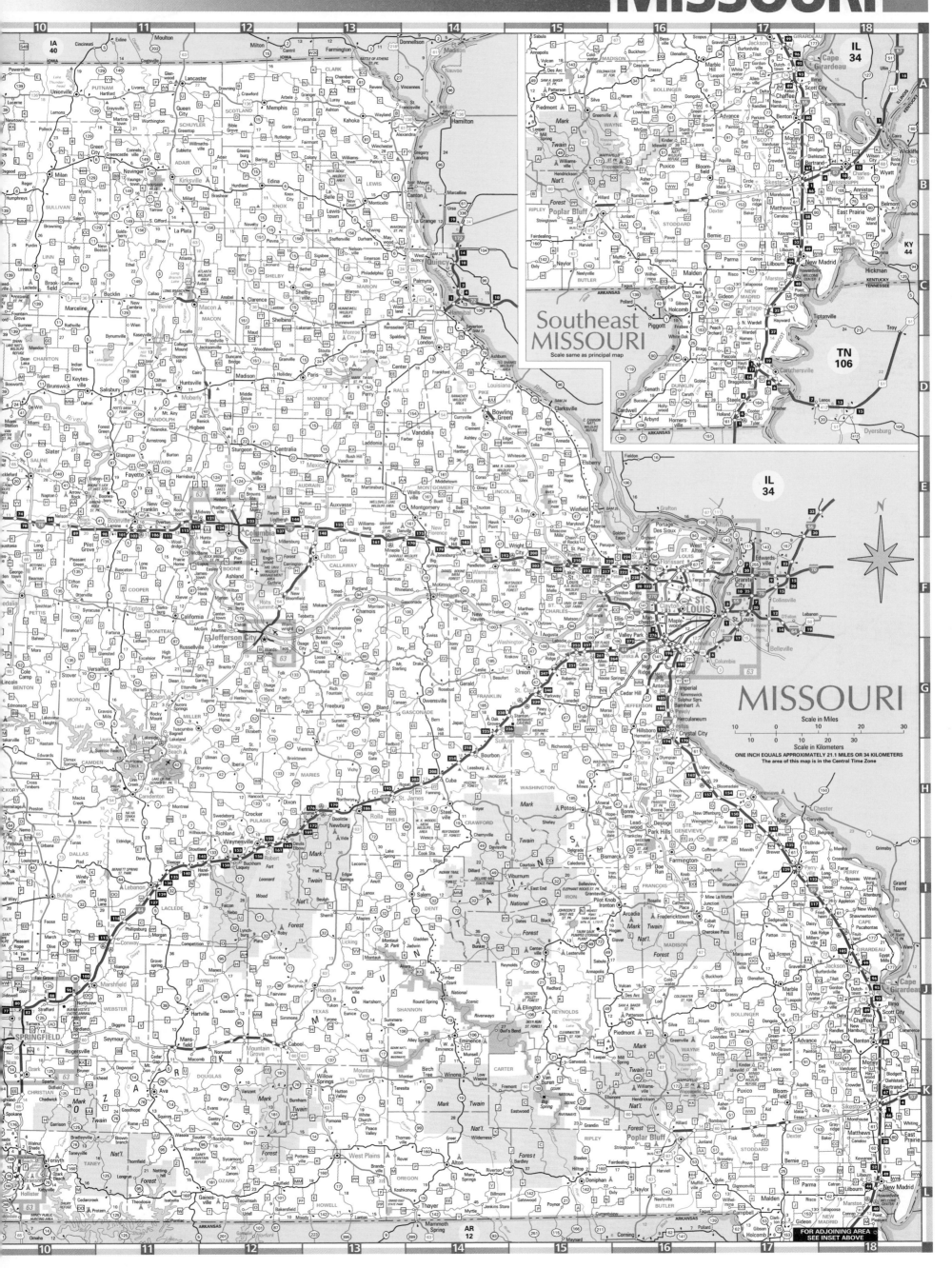

Southeast MISSOURI
Scale same as principal map

MISSOURI

Scale in Miles
Scale in Kilometers
ONE INCH EQUALS APPROXIMATELY 21.1 MILES OR 34 KILOMETERS
The area of this map is in the Central Time Zone

FOR ADJOINING AREA
SEE INSET ABOVE

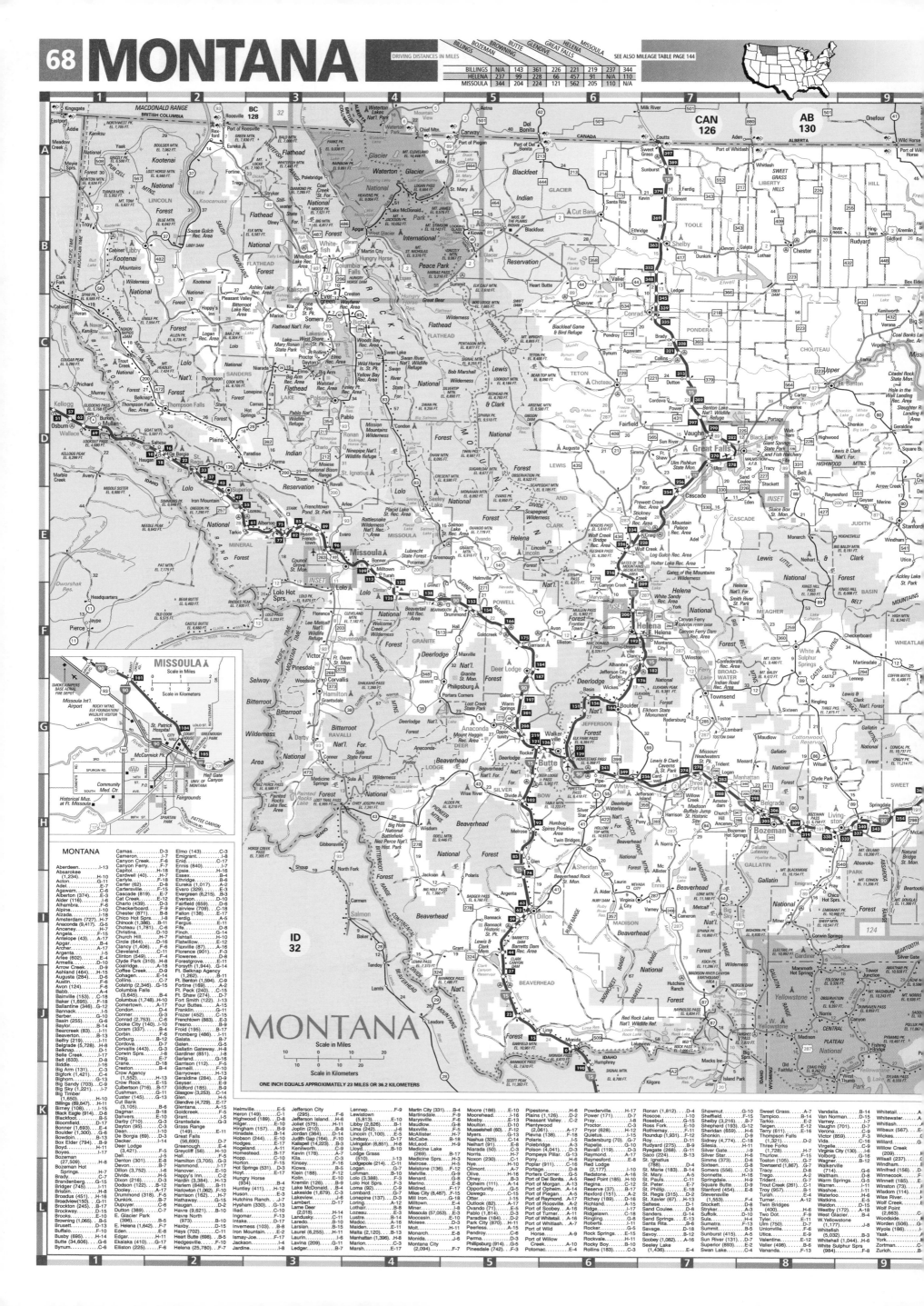

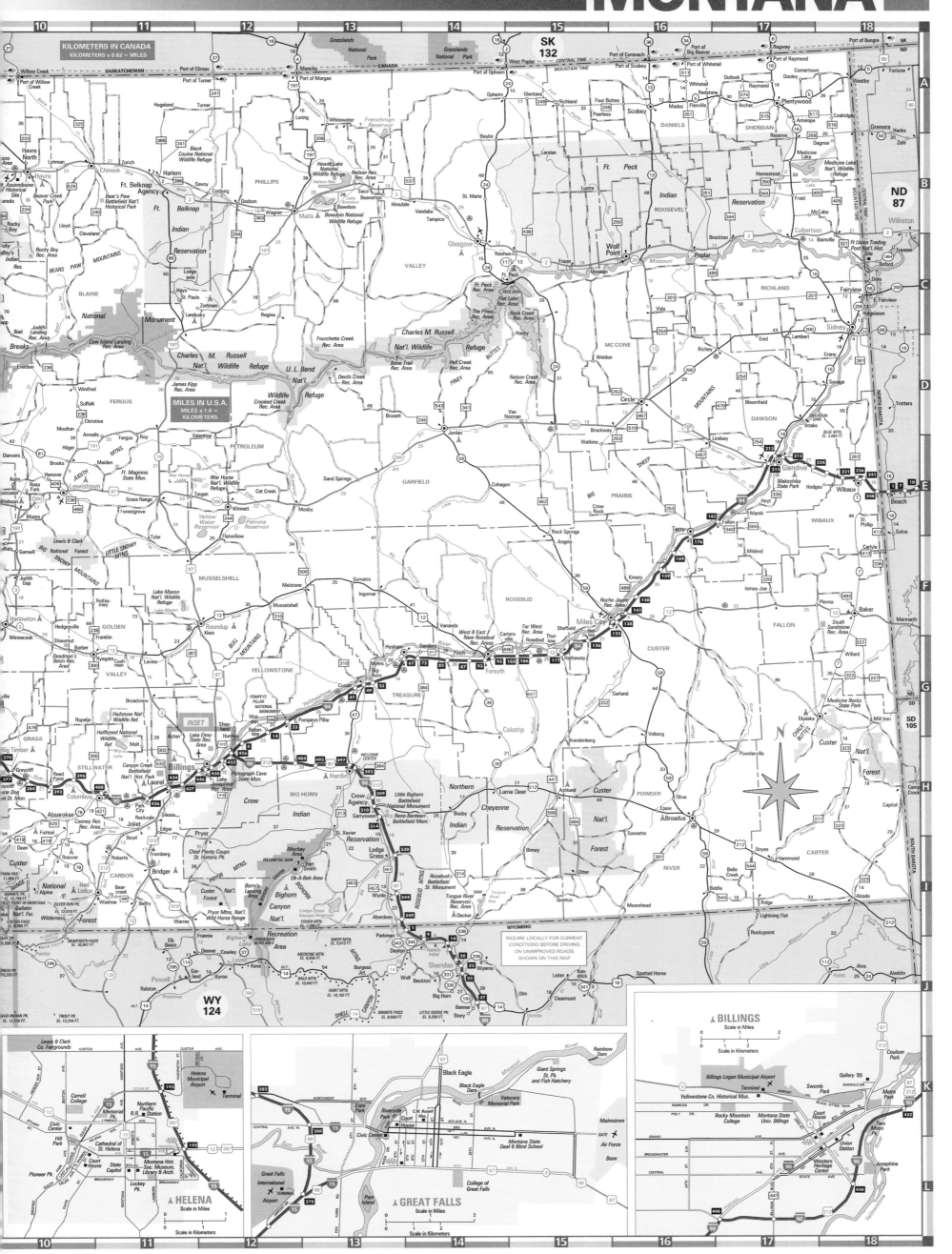

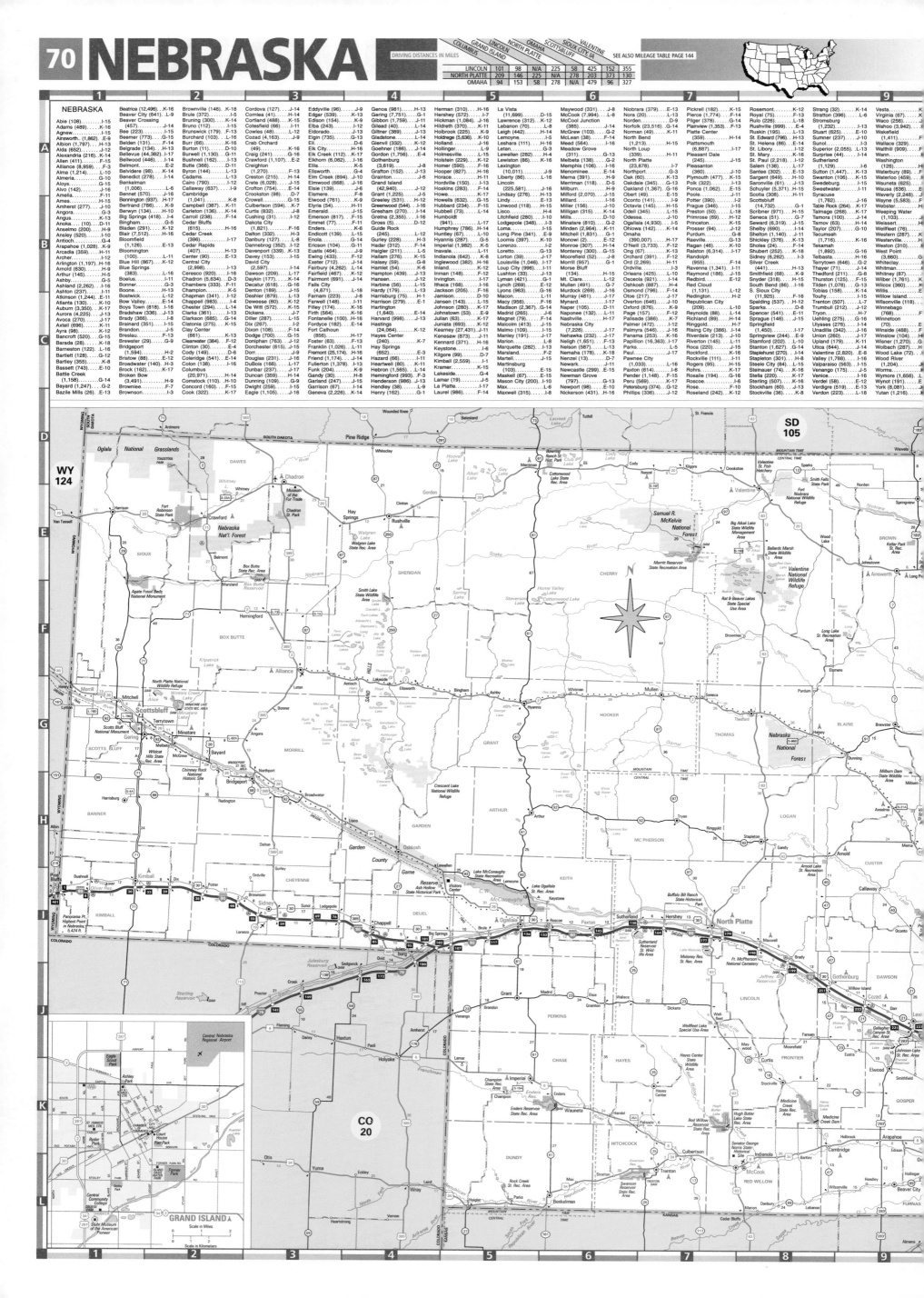

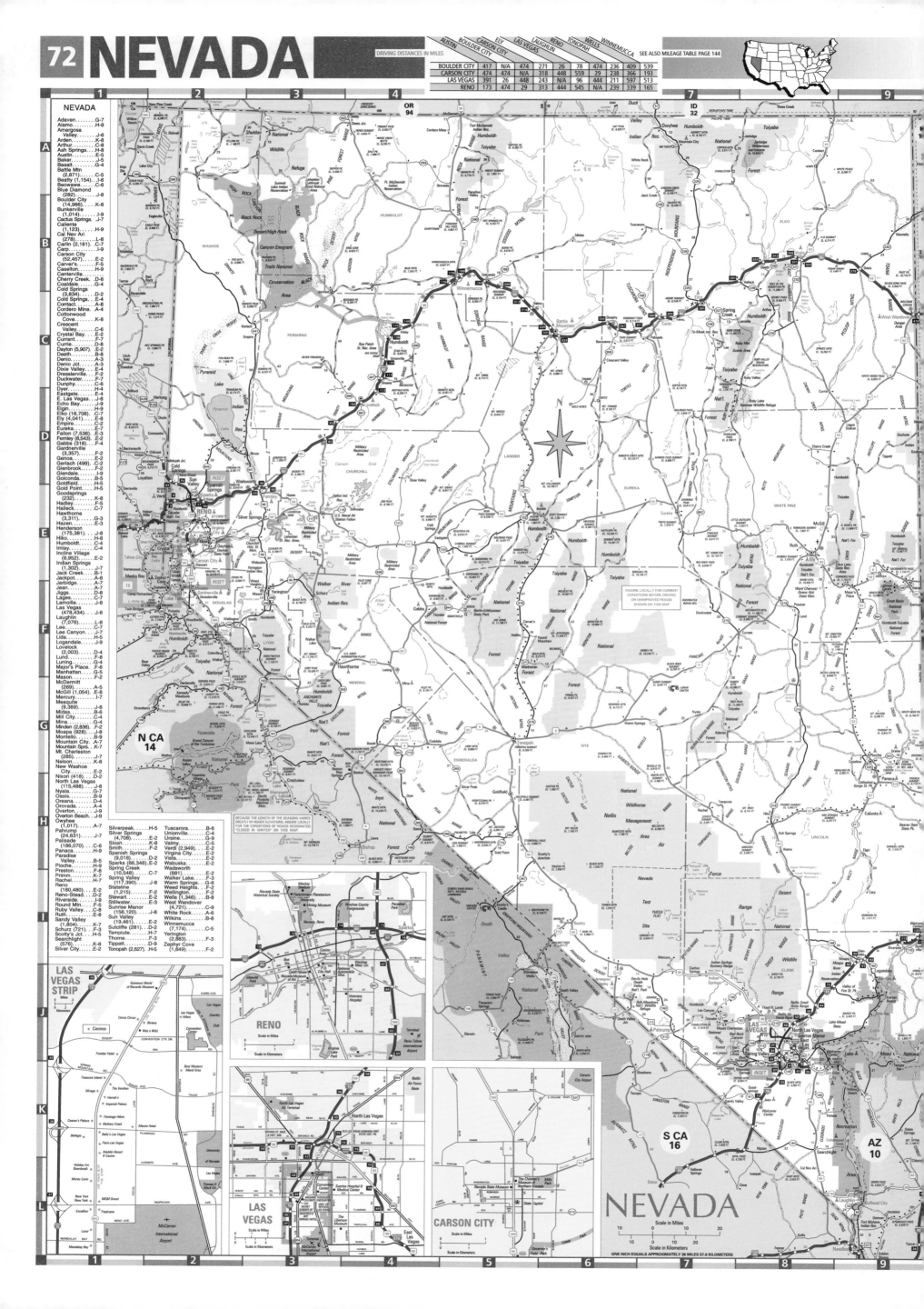

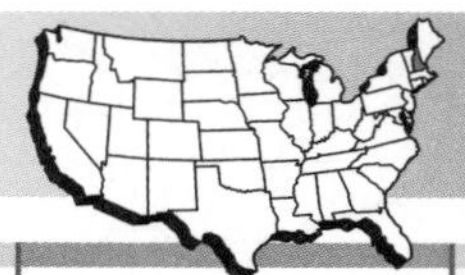

DRIVING DISTANCES IN MILES

	COLEBROOK	CONCORD	GORHAM	KEENE	LEBANON	MANCHESTER	NASHUA	PORTSMOUTH	PLYMOUTH	TWIN MOUNTAIN
CONCORD	165	N/A	149	54	59	17	35	58	44	84
MANCHESTER	181	17	166	56	71	N/A	18	43	69	101
NASHUA	199	35	184	49	88	18	N/A	61	78	118
PORTSMOUTH	172	58	140	99	111	43	61	N/A	101	141

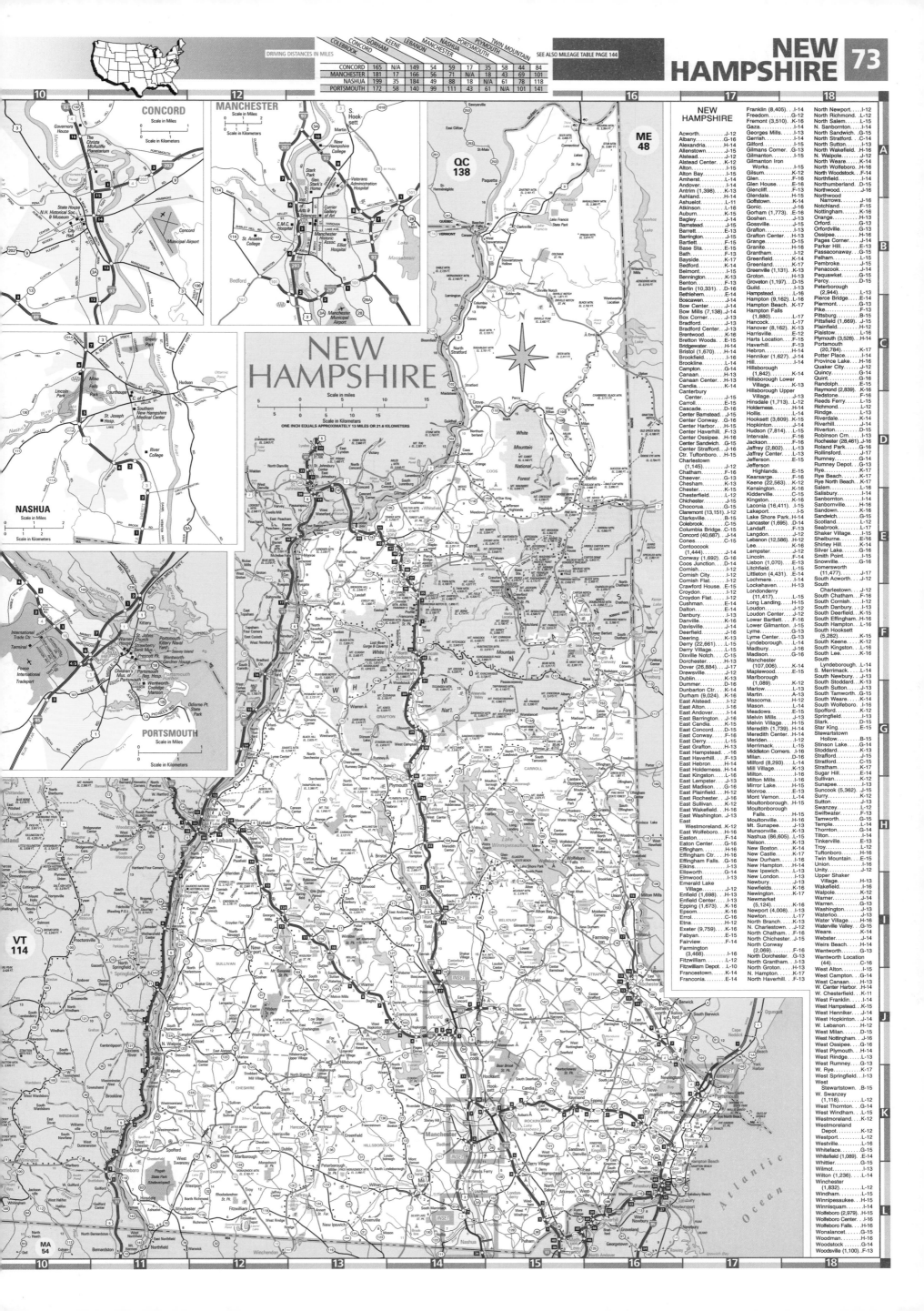

SEE ALSO MILEAGE TABLE PAGE 144

NEW HAMPSHIRE

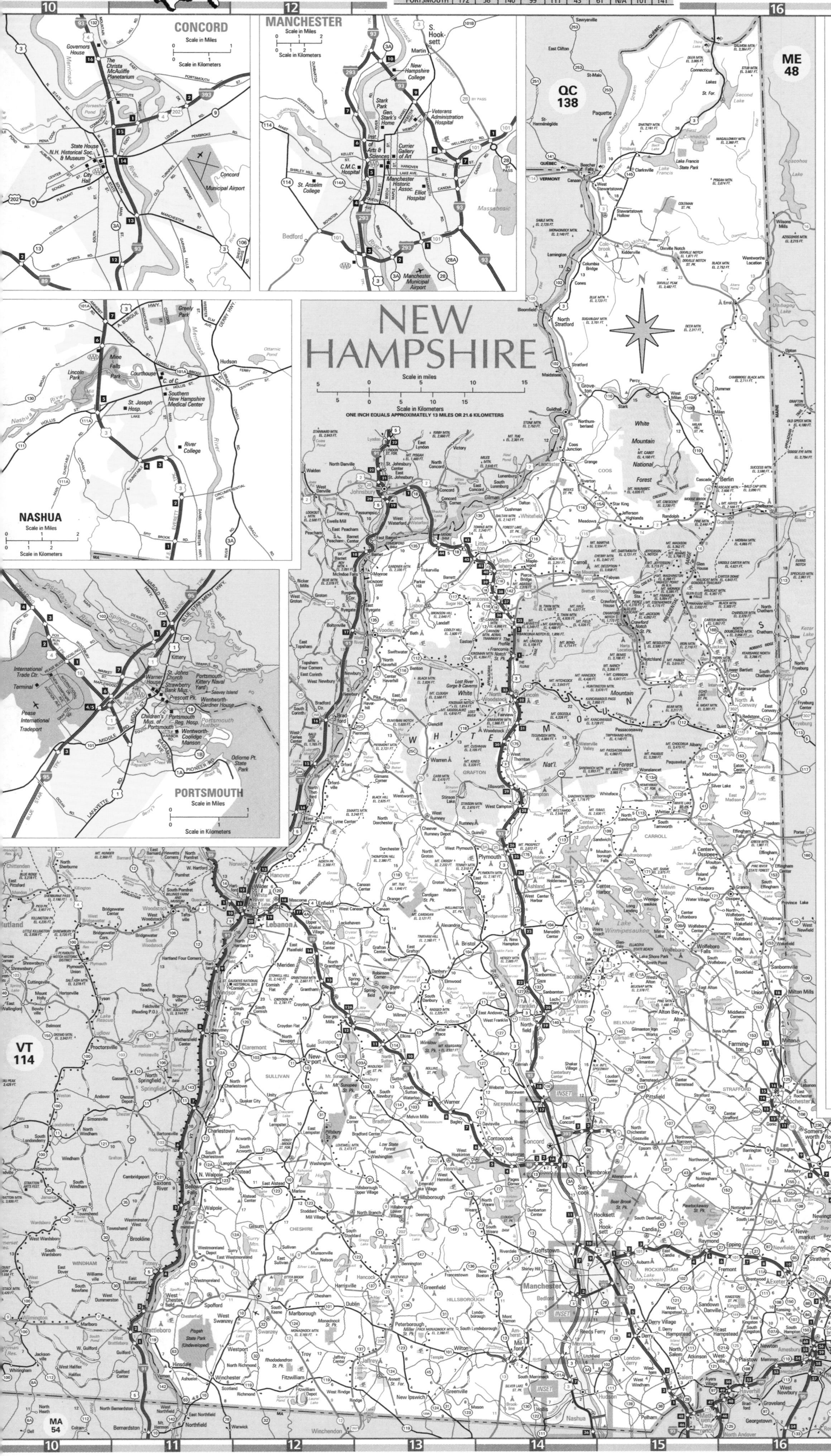

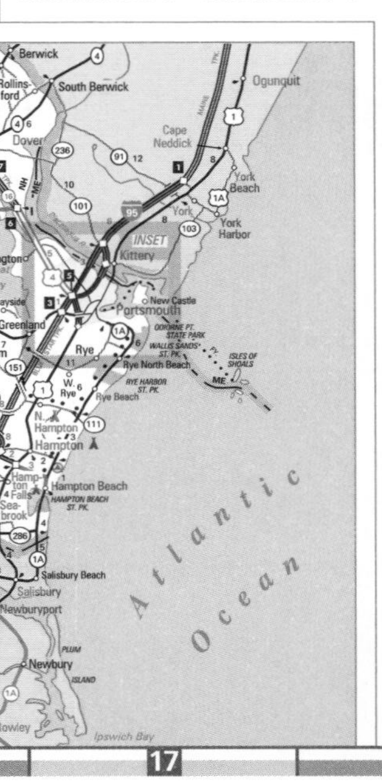

NEW HAMPSHIRE

Acworth....J-12
Albany....G-16
Alexandria....H-14
Allenstown....J-15
Alstead....J-12
Alstead Center....K-12
Alton....I-15
Alton Bay....I-15
Amherst....L-14
Andover....I-14
Antrim (1,398)....K-13
Ashland....H-14
Ashuelot....L-11
Atkinson....L-16
Auburn....K-15
Bagley....J-14
Barnstead....J-15
Barrett....E-13
Barrington....J-15
Bartlett....F-15
Base Sta....E-15
Bath....F-13
Bayside....K-17
Bedford....K-14
Belmont....I-15
Bennington....K-13
Benton....F-13
Berlin (10,331)....D-16
Bethlehem....E-14
Boscawen....J-14
Bow Center....J-14
Bow Mills (7,138)....J-14
Box Corner....J-13
Bradford....J-13
Bradford Center....J-13
Brentwood....K-16
Bretton Woods....E-15
Bridgewater....H-14
Bristol (1,670)....H-14
Brookfield....I-16
Brookline....L-14
Campton....G-14
Canaan....H-13
Canaan Center....H-13
Candia....K-14
Canterbury Center....J-15
Carroll....E-15
Cascade....D-16
Center Barnstead....J-15
Center Conway....G-16
Center Harbor....H-15
Center Haverhill....F-13
Center Ossipee....H-16
Center Sandwich....G-15
Center Strafford....J-16
Ctr. Tuftonboro....H-15
Charlestown (1,145)....J-12
Chatham....F-16
Cheever....G-13
Chesham....K-13
Chester....K-15
Chesterfield....L-12
Chichester....J-15
Chocorua....G-15
Claremont (13,151)....I-12
Clarksville....B-15
Colebrook....C-15
Columbia Bridge....C-15
Concord (40,687)....J-14
Cones....C-15
Contoocook (1,444)....J-14
Conway (1,692)....G-16
Coos Junction....D-14
Cornish....I-12
Cornish City....I-12
Cornish Flat....I-12
Crawford House....E-15
Croydon....I-12
Croydon Flat....I-12
Cushman....E-14
Dalton....E-14
Danbury....I-13
Danville....K-16
Davisville....J-14
Deerfield....J-16
Deering....K-13
Derry (22,661)....L-15
Derry Village....L-15
Dixville Notch....C-15
Dorchester....H-13
Dover (26,884)....J-17
Drewsville....J-12
Dublin....K-13
Dummer....D-16
Dunbarton Ctr....K-14
Durham (9,024)....K-16
East Alstead....I-12
East Alton....I-16
East Andover....I-14
East Barrington....J-16
East Candia....K-15
East Concord....D-15
East Conway....F-16
East Derry....L-15
East Grafton....H-13
East Hampstead....-16
East Haverhill....F-13
East Hebron....H-14
East Holderness....H-14
East Kingston....L-16
East Lempster....J-13
East Madison....G-16
East Plainfield....H-12
East Rochester....J-16
East Sullivan....K-12
East Wakefield....H-16
East Washington....J-13
East Westmoreland....K-12
East Wolfeboro....H-16
Easton....F-14
Eaton Center....G-16
Effingham....H-16
Effingham Ctr....H-16
Effingham Falls....G-16
Elkins....I-13
Ellsworth....G-14
Elmwood....I-13
Emerald Lake Village....J-12
Enfield (1,698)....H-13
Enfield Center....I-13
Epping (1,673)....K-16
Epsom....K-16
Errol....C-16
Etna....H-12
Exeter (9,759)....K-16
Fabyan....E-15
Fairview....F-14
Farmington (3,468)....I-16
Fitzwilliam....L-12
Fitzwilliam Depot....L-10
Francestown....K-14
Franconia....E-14
Franklin (8,405)....I-14
Freedom....G-12
Fremont (3,510)....K-16
Gaza....I-14
Georges Mills....I-13
Gerrish....I-14
Gilford....I-15
Gilmans Corner....G-13
Gilmanton....I-15
Gilmanton Iron Works....I-15
Gilsum....K-12
Glen....F-16
Glen House....E-16
Glencliff....F-13
Glendale....H-15
Goffstown....K-14
Gonic....J-16
Gorham (1,773)....E-16
Goshen....J-13
Gossville....J-15
Grafton....I-13
Grafton Center....H-13
Grange....D-15
Granite....H-16
Grantham....I-12
Greenfield....K-14
Greenland....K-17
Greenville (1,131)....K-13
Groton....H-13
Groveton (1,197)....D-15
Guild....I-13
Hampstead....L-16
Hampton (9,162)....L-16
Hampton Beach....K-17
Hampton Falls (1,880)....L-17
Hancock....L-17
Hanover (8,162)....K-13
Harrisville....E-12
Harts Location....F-15
Haverhill....F-13
Hebron....H-14
Henniker (1,627)....J-14
Hill....I-14
Hillsborough (1,842)....K-14
Hillsborough Lower Village....K-13
Hillsborough Upper Village....J-13
Hinsdale (1,713)....L-12
Holderness....H-14
Hollis....L-14
Hooksett (3,609)....K-15
Hopkinton....J-14
Hudson (7,814)....L-15
Intervale....F-16
Jackson....F-16
Jaffrey (2,802)....L-13
Jaffrey Center....L-13
Jefferson....E-15
Jefferson Highlands....E-15
Kearsarge....F-16
Keene (22,563)....K-12
Kensington....K-16
Kidderville....C-15
Kingston....K-16
Laconia (16,411)....I-15
Lakeport....I-5
Lake Shore Park....H-14
Lancaster (1,695)....D-14
Landaff....F-13
Langdon....J-12
Lebanon (12,586)....H-12
Lee....K-16
Lempster....J-12
Lincoln....F-14
Lisbon (1,070)....E-13
Litchfield....L-15
Littleton (4,431)....E-14
Lochmere....I-14
Lockehaven....H-13
Londonderry (11,417)....L-15
Long Landing....H-15
Loudon....J-12
Loudon Center....J-12
Lower Bartlett....F-16
Lower Gilmanton....I-15
Lyme....G-13
Lyme Center....G-13
Lyndeborough....L-14
Madbury....J-16
Madison....G-16
Manchester (107,006)....K-14
Maplewood....E-15
Marlborough (1,089)....K-12
Marlow....L-13
Martin....A-13
Mascoma....H-12
Mason....L-14
Meadows....E-15
Melvin Mills....J-13
Melvin Village....H-15
Meredith (1,739)....H-14
Meredith Center....H-14
Meriden....I-12
Merrimack....L-15
Middleton Corners....I-16
Milan....D-16
Milford (8,293)....L-14
Mill Village....K-13
Milton....I-16
Milton Mills....I-16
Mirror Lake....H-15
Monroe....E-13
Mont Vernon....L-14
Moultonborough....H-15
Moultonborough Falls....H-15
Moultonville....H-16
Mt. Sunapee....J-13
Munsonville....K-13
Nashua (86,605)....L-15
Nelson....K-13
New Boston....K-14
New Castle....K-17
New Durham....I-16
New Hampton....H-14
New Ipswich....L-13
New London....I-13
Newbury....J-13
Newfields....K-16
Newington....K-17
Newmarket (5,124)....K-16
Newport (4,008)....I-13
Newton....L-17
North Branch....K-13
N. Charlestown....J-12
North Chatham....F-16
North Chichester....J-15
North Conway (2,069)....F-16
North Dorchester....G-13
North Grantham....I-13
North Groton....H-13
N. Hampton....K-17
North Haverhill....F-13
North Newport....I-12
North Richmond....L-12
North Salem....L-15
N. Sanbornton....I-14
North Sandwich....G-15
North Stratford....C-14
North Sutton....I-13
North Wakefield....H-16
N. Walpole....J-12
North Weare....K-14
North Wolfeboro....H-16
North Woodstock....F-14
Northfield....I-14
Northumberland....D-15
Northwood....J-16
Northwood Narrows....J-16
Notchland....F-15
Nottingham....K-16
Orange....H-13
Orford....G-13
Orfordville....G-13
Ossipee....H-16
Pages Corner....J-14
Parker Hill....E-13
Passaconaway....G-15
Pelham....L-15
Pembroke....J-15
Penacook....J-14
Pequawket....G-15
Percy....D-15
Peterborough (2,944)....L-13
Pierce Bridge....E-14
Piermont....G-13
Pike....F-13
Pittsburg....B-15
Pittsfield (1,669)....J-15
Plainfield....H-12
Plaistow....L-16
Plymouth (3,528)....H-14
Portsmouth (20,784)....K-17
Potter Place....I-14
Province Lake....H-16
Quaker City....J-12
Quincy....G-14
Quint....G-16
Randolph....E-15
Raymond (2,839)....K-16
Redstone....F-16
Reeds Ferry....L-15
Richmond....L-12
Rindge....L-13
Riverdale....K-14
Riverhill....J-14
Riverton....D-15
Robinson Crn....I-13
Rochester (28,461)....J-16
Roland Park....G-16
Rollinsford....J-17
Rumney....G-14
Rumney Depot....G-13
Rye....K-17
Rye Beach....K-17
Rye North Beach....K-17
Salem....L-16
Salisbury....I-14
Sanbornton....I-14
Sanbornville....H-16
Sandown....K-16
Sandwich....G-15
Scotland....L-12
Seabrook....L-17
Shaker Village....I-15
Shelburne....E-16
Shirley Hill....K-14
Silver Lake....G-16
Smith Point....I-15
Snowville....G-16
Somersworth (11,477)....J-17
South Acworth....J-12
South Charlestown....J-12
South Chatham....F-16
South Cornish....I-12
South Danbury....I-13
South Deerfield....K-15
South Effingham....H-16
South Hampton....L-16
South Hooksett (5,282)....K-15
South Keene....K-12
South Kingston....L-16
South Lee....K-16
South Lyndeborough....L-14
S. Merrimack....L-14
South Newbury....J-13
South Stoddard....K-13
South Sutton....J-13
South Tamworth....G-15
South Weare....K-14
South Wolfeboro....I-16
Spofford....K-12
Springfield....I-13
Stark....D-15
Star King....E-15
Stewartstown Hollow....B-15
Stinson Lake....G-14
Stoddard....K-13
Strafford....J-15
Stratford....C-15
Stratham....K-17
Sugar Hill....E-14
Sullivan....K-12
Sunapee....I-13
Suncook (5,362)....J-15
Surry....K-12
Sutton....J-13
Swanzey....L-12
Swiftwater....F-13
Tamworth....G-15
Temple....L-14
Thornton....G-14
Tilton....I-14
Tinkerville....E-13
Troy....L-12
Tuftonboro....H-16
Twin Mountain....E-15
Union....I-16
Unity....J-12
Upper Shaker Village....H-13
Wakefield....I-16
Walpole....K-12
Warner....J-14
Warren....G-13
Washington....J-13
Waterloo....J-13
Water Village....H-16
Waterville Valley....G-15
Weare....K-14
Webster....J-14
Weirs Beach....H-14
Wentworth....G-13
Wentworth Location (44)....C-16
West Alton....I-15
West Campton....G-14
West Canaan....H-13
W. Center Harbor....H-14
W. Chesterfield....K-11
West Franklin....I-14
West Hampstead....K-15
West Henniker....J-14
West Hopkinton....J-14
W. Lebanon....H-12
West Milan....D-15
West Nottingham....J-16
West Ossipee....G-16
West Plymouth....H-14
West Rindge....L-13
West Rumney....G-13
W. Rye....K-17
West Springfield....I-13
West Stewartstown....B-15
W. Swanzey (1,118)....L-12
West Thornton....G-14
West Windham....L-15
Westmoreland....K-12
Westmoreland Depot....K-12
Westport....L-12
Westville....L-16
Whiteface....G-15
Whitefield (1,089)....E-14
Whittier....G-15
Wilmot....I-13
Wilton (1,236)....L-14
Winchester (1,832)....L-12
Windham....L-15
Winnipesaukee....H-15
Winnisquam....I-14
Wolfeboro (2,979)....H-15
Wolfeboro Center....I-16
Wolfeboro Falls....H-16
Wonalancet....G-15
Woodman....H-16
Woodstock....G-14
Woodsville (1,100)....F-13

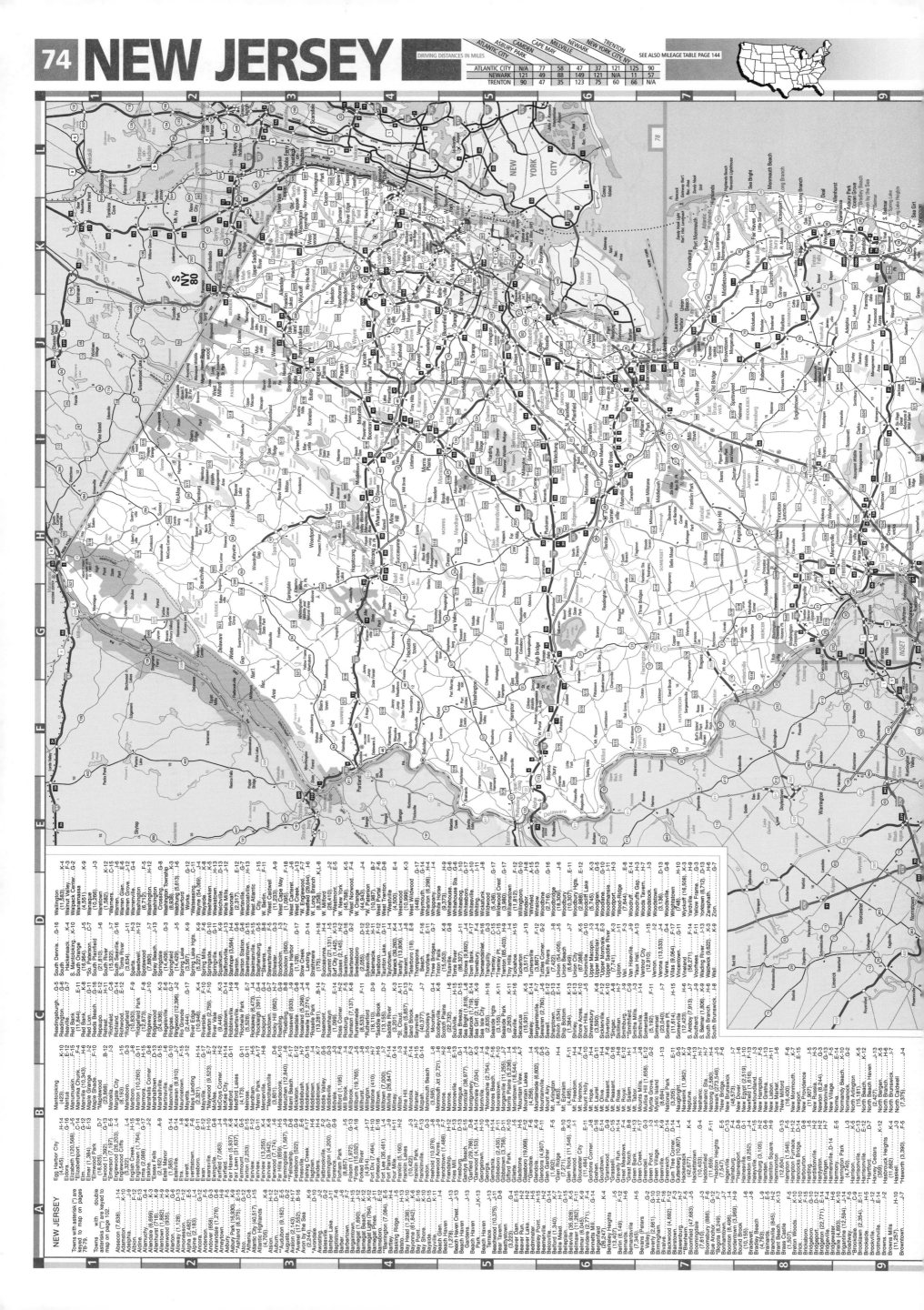

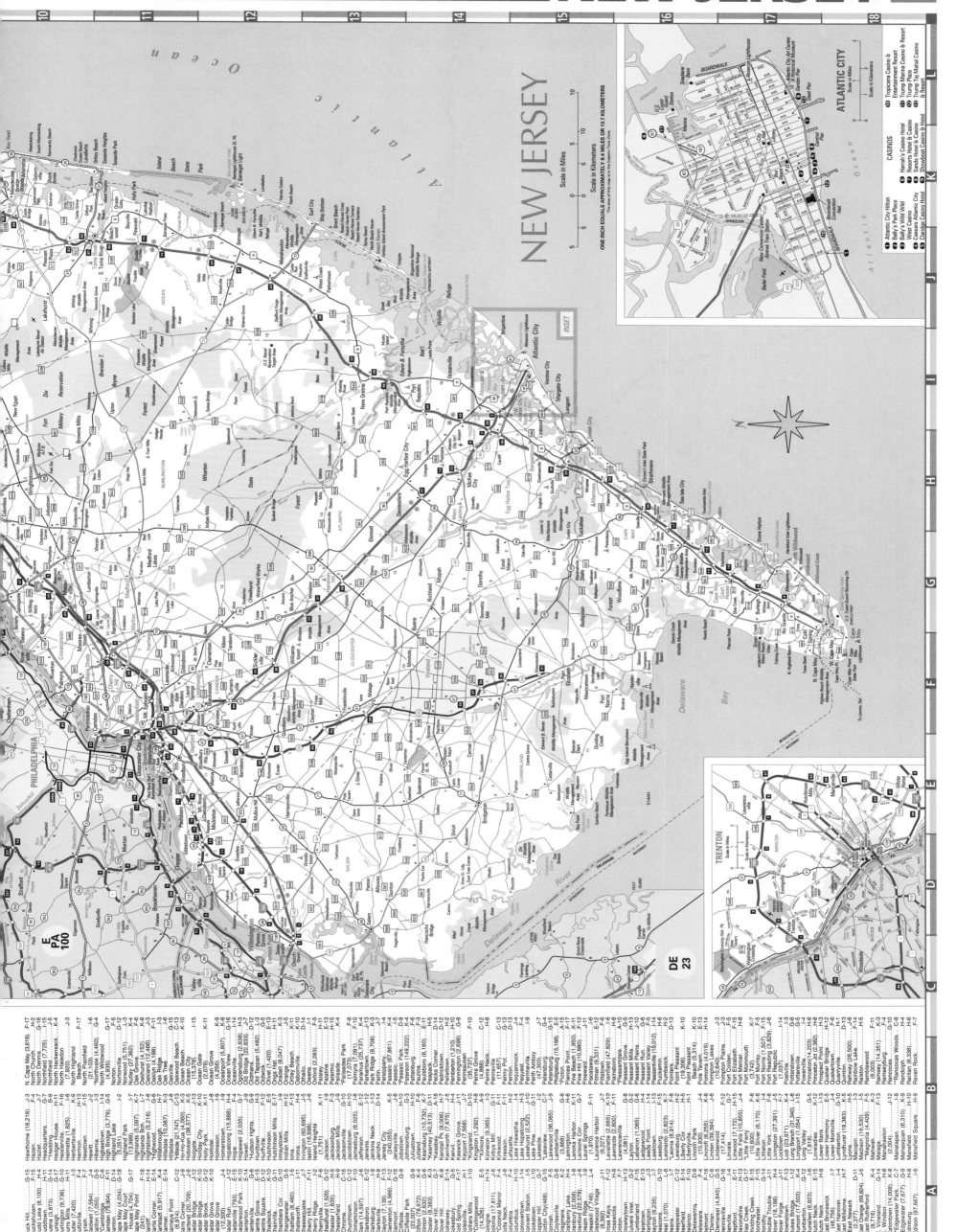

NEW JERSEY

Scale in Miles

Scale in Kilometers

ONE INCH EQUALS APPROXIMATELY 8.4 MILES OR 13.7 KILOMETERS
The area of this map is in the Eastern Time Zone.

ATLANTIC CITY

CASINOS
- Atlantic City Hilton
- Bally's Park Place
- Bally's Wild Wild West Casino
- Caesars Atlantic City
- Claridge Casino Hotel
- Harrah's Casino & Entertainment Resort
- Resorts Hotel & Casino
- Sands Hotel & Casino
- Showboat Casino & Hotel
- Tropicana Casino & Entertainment Resort
- Trump Marina Casino & Resort
- Trump Plaza
- Trump Taj Mahal Casino & Resort

TRENTON

Scale in Miles

PHILADELPHIA

DE 23

E PA 100

DRIVING DISTANCES IN MILES

SEE ALSO MILEAGE TABLE PAGE 144

	ALBUQUERQUE	EL PASO TX	FARMINGTON	GALLUP	LAS CRUCES	LORDSBURG	RATON	ROSWELL	SANTA FE	TUCUMCARI
ALBUQUERQUE	N/A	263	183	137	224	348	230	200	63	176
LAS CRUCES	224	45	405	362	N/A	119	452	185	285	399
ROSWELL	200	207	379	336	185	310	306	N/A	193	193
SANTA FE	63	327	209	198	285	409	176	193	N/A	170

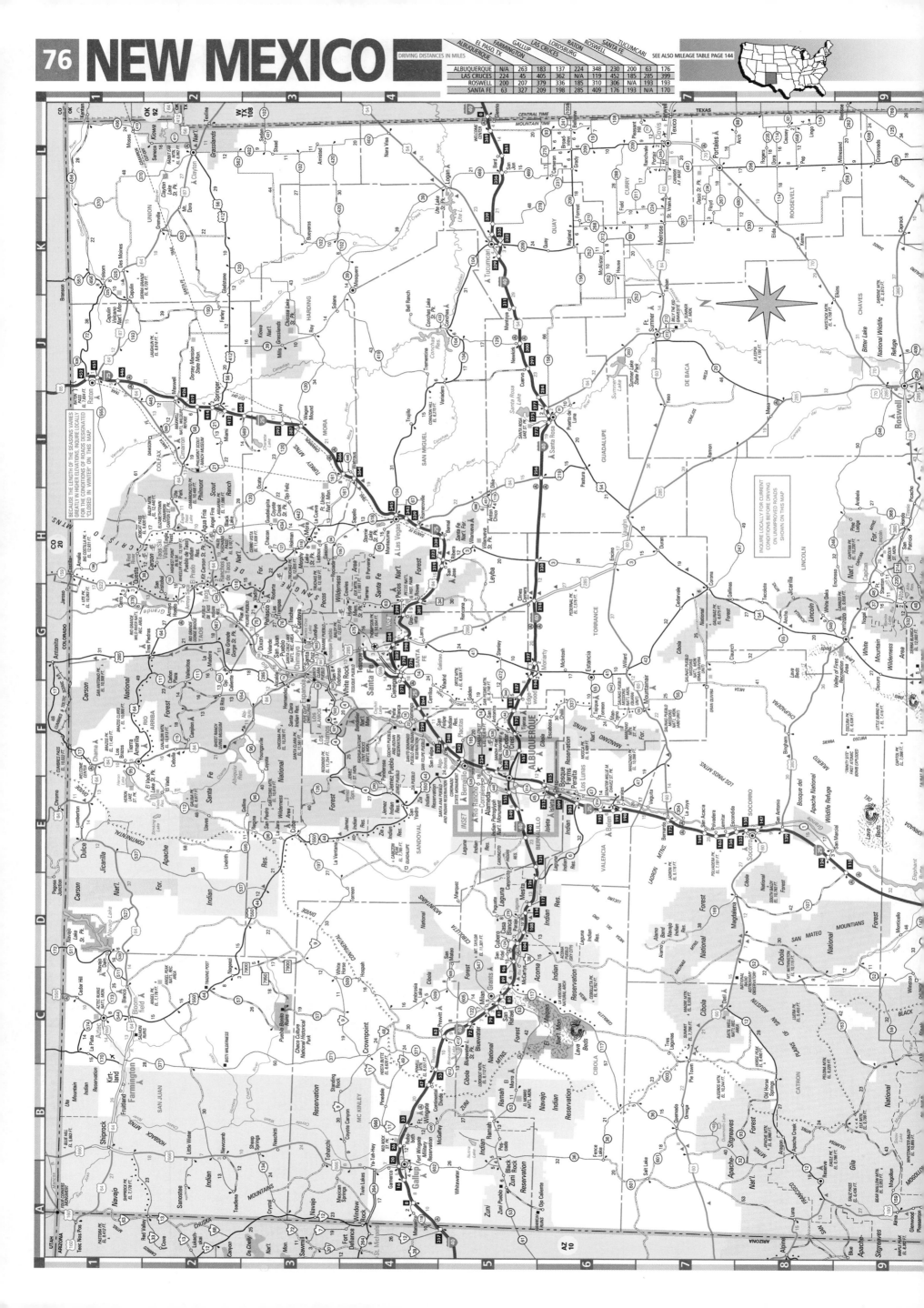

BECAUSE THE LENGTH OF THE SEASONS VARIES GREATLY IN HIGHER ELEVATIONS, INQUIRE LOCALLY FOR THE CONDITIONS OF ROADS DESIGNATED "CLOSED IN WINTER" ON THIS MAP.

INQUIRE LOCALLY FOR CURRENT CONDITIONS BEFORE DRIVING ON UNIMPROVED ROADS SHOWN ON THIS MAP.

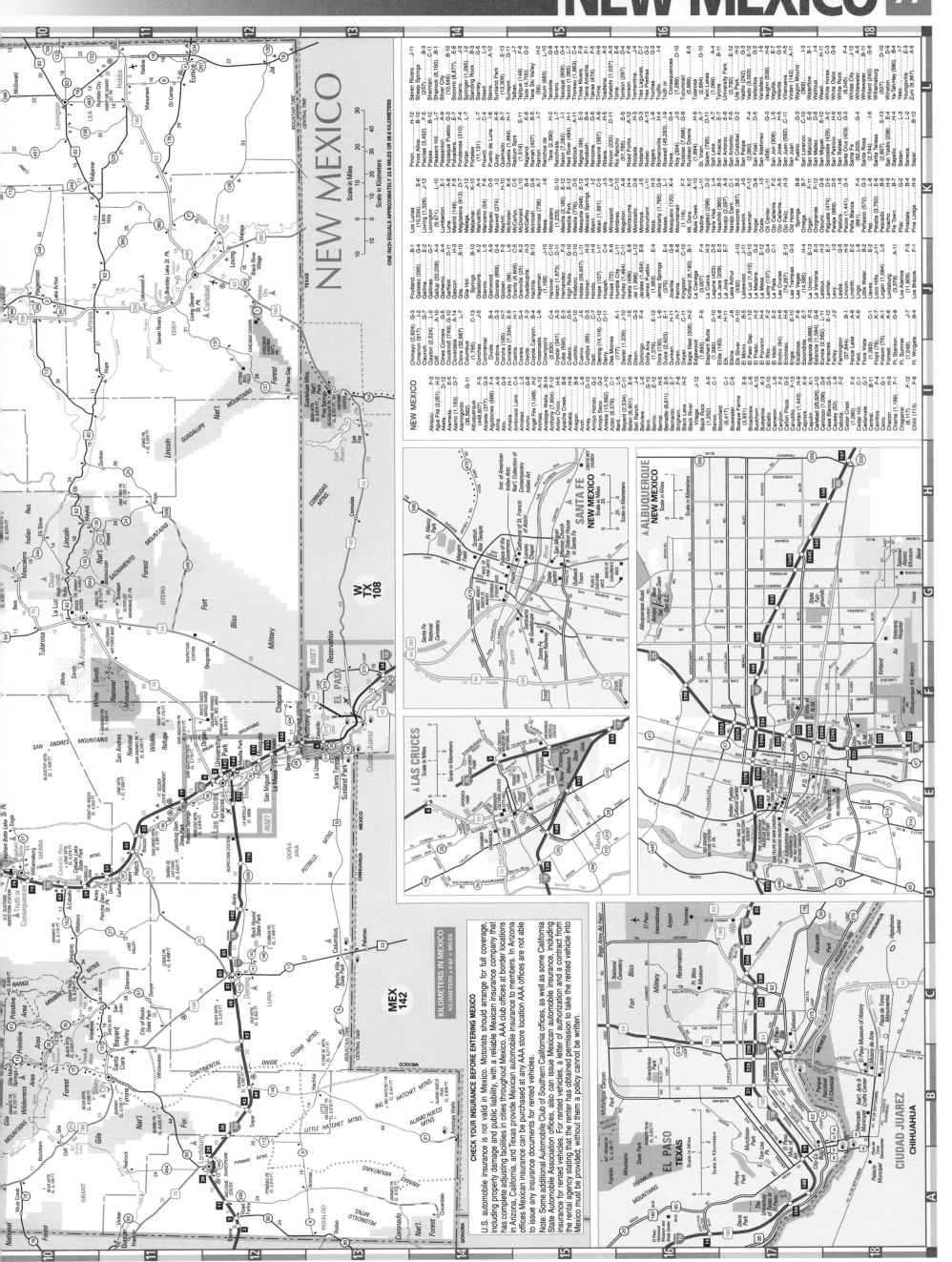

NEW MEXICO

SEE ALSO MILEAGE TABLE PAGE 144

DRIVING DISTANCES IN MILES

	ALBANY	BINGHAMTON	BUFFALO	CORNING	NEWBURGH	NIAGARA FALLS	NEW YORK CITY	PLATTSBURGH	ROCHESTER	SYRACUSE	UTICA	WATERTOWN
ALBANY	N/A	131	288	211	89	154	301	161	226	145	95	203
BUFFALO	288	223	N/A	158	360	394	21	437	73	149	198	212
NEW YORK CITY	154	186	394	247	75	N/A	406	314	331	245	246	314
ROCHESTER	226	160	73	104	297	331	86	374	N/A	87	135	150
SYRACUSE	145	73	149	98	211	245	162	293	87	N/A	55	69

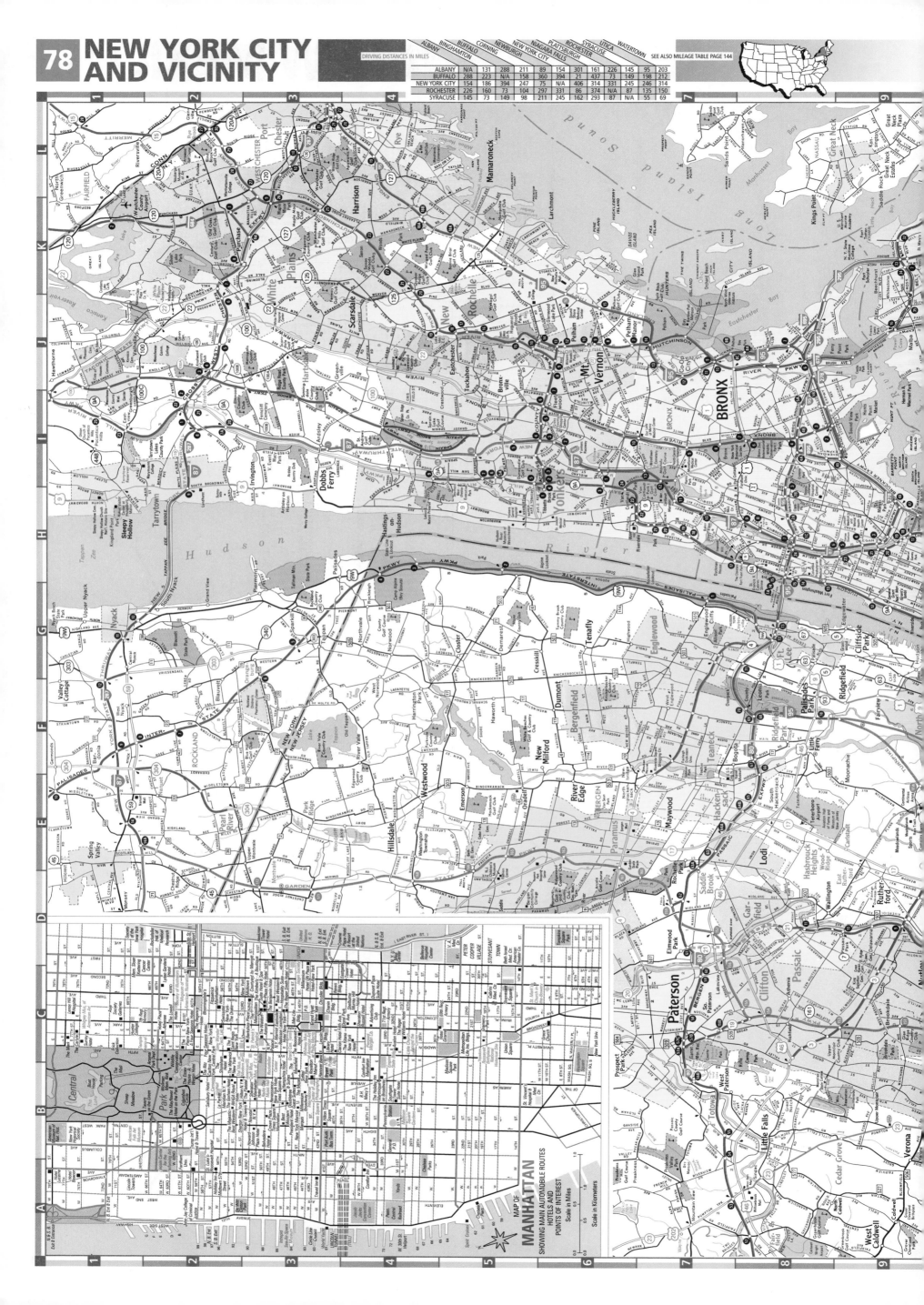

MANHATTAN

SHOWING MAIN AUTOMOBILE ROUTES
HOTELS AND
POINTS OF INTEREST

Scale in Miles

Scale in Kilometers

NEW YORK CITY AND VICINITY

LEGEND

HIGHWAYS

Controlled Access
Multi-lane, Divided
Toll Highways
Under Construction
Nearing Completion
Interchange Number
Four Lanes or More
Divided
Pavement (All Types)

ROUTE NUMBERS

Interstate
Federal
State
County

Distances in Miles between
intersections
County Boundary
State Boundary

Golf and Country Clubs
AAA Clubs
Principal Route
Place of Interest
Major Commercial Airport
Campground in Area (Check Campbook)

Rest Area With Rest Rooms
Rest Area Without Rest Rooms
Passenger Ferry
Automobile Ferry

Scale in Miles
Scale in Kilometers
ONE INCH EQUALS APPROXIMATELY 1.4 MILES OR 2.3 KILOMETERS

The area of this map is in the Eastern Time Zone.

MANHATTAN PRINCIPAL PLACES OF INTEREST

Advertising Club.......	C-4
American Craft Museum.....	B-3
American Museum of Natural History.....	B-1
Arsenal Park.....	C-2
Asia Society Galleries.....	C-1
Bellevue Hospital.....	D-4
Beth Israel Medical Center.....	D-5
Bloomingdale's.....	C-2
Bryant Park.....	B-3
Cabrini Med. Ctr......	D-5
Carnegie Hall.....	B-2
Central Park.....	C-3
Chanin Bldg......	C-3
Chelsea Piers.....	A-5
Chrysler Bldg......	C-3
Circle Line Tours.....	A-3
De Witt Clinton.....	
Museum.....	A-4
Cornell Medical.....	
University.....	D-3
Empire State Bldg......	C-4
Fordham.....	
University.....	B-2
Frick Collection.....	C-2
General P.O......	B-4
Gracie Mansion.....	D-1
Gramercy Park.....	C-5
Grand Central Terminal.....	C-3
Hunter College.....	C-1
International Center of Photography.....	B-3
Intrepid Sea-Air-Space Mus......	A-3
Jacob Javits Conv. Ctr......	A-4
Japan Society.....	D-3
John Jay College of Justice.....	A-2
Lenox Hill Hosp......	C-1
Lincoln Ctr. for the Performing Arts.....	A-2
Little Church around the Corner.....	C-4
Madison Square Garden.....	B-4
Madison Sq. Pk......	C-5
Mem. Sloan Kettering Cancer Ctr.......	C-1
Metropolitan Life Ins. Bldg......	C-5
Mus. of Modern Art.....	B-2
Mus. of TV & Radio.....	C-2
News Bldg......	C-3
New York City Police Mus......	C-5
New York Historical Society.....	B-1
New York Public Lib......	C-3
New York Univ......	C-6
N.Y.U. Medical Center.....	D-4
Peter Cooper Village.....	D-5
Pennsylvania Sta......	B-4
Pierpont Morgan Lib......	C-2
Port Auth. Bus Terminal.....	B-3
Radio City Music Hall.....	B-3
R.H. Macys.....	B-4
Rockefeller Ctr......	C-3
Rockefeller Inst......	D-2
St. Luke's Hosp......	B-1
St. Mark's Church in-the-Bowery.....	C-5
St. Patrick's Cathedral.....	C-3
St. Vincent's Hospital & Med. Ctr......	B-5
60th St. Heliport.....	D-2
Society of Illustrators.....	B-4
Mus. of American Illustration.....	C-2
Society of the New York Hosp......	D-1
The Sony IMAX Theatre.....	B-1
Sony Wonder Technology Lab......	C-2
Spirit Cruises.....	A-5
Stuyvesant Sq......	C-5
Tavern on the Green.....	B-2
Temple Emanu-el.....	C-2
Theatre Row.....	A-3
Tishman Nat'l Hist. Site.....	C-5
Times Square.....	B-3
Tompkins Sq. Park.....	D-6
Unicef House.....	D-3
Union Square.....	C-5
U.S.U.N. Headquarters.....	D-3
V.A. Med. Ctr......	D-5
Washington Sq......	B-6
W. 30th St. Heliport.....	A-4
Whitney Museum of American Art.....	C-1
Wildlife Cons......	C-3
Wollman Rink.....	B-2
World Yacht.....	A-3

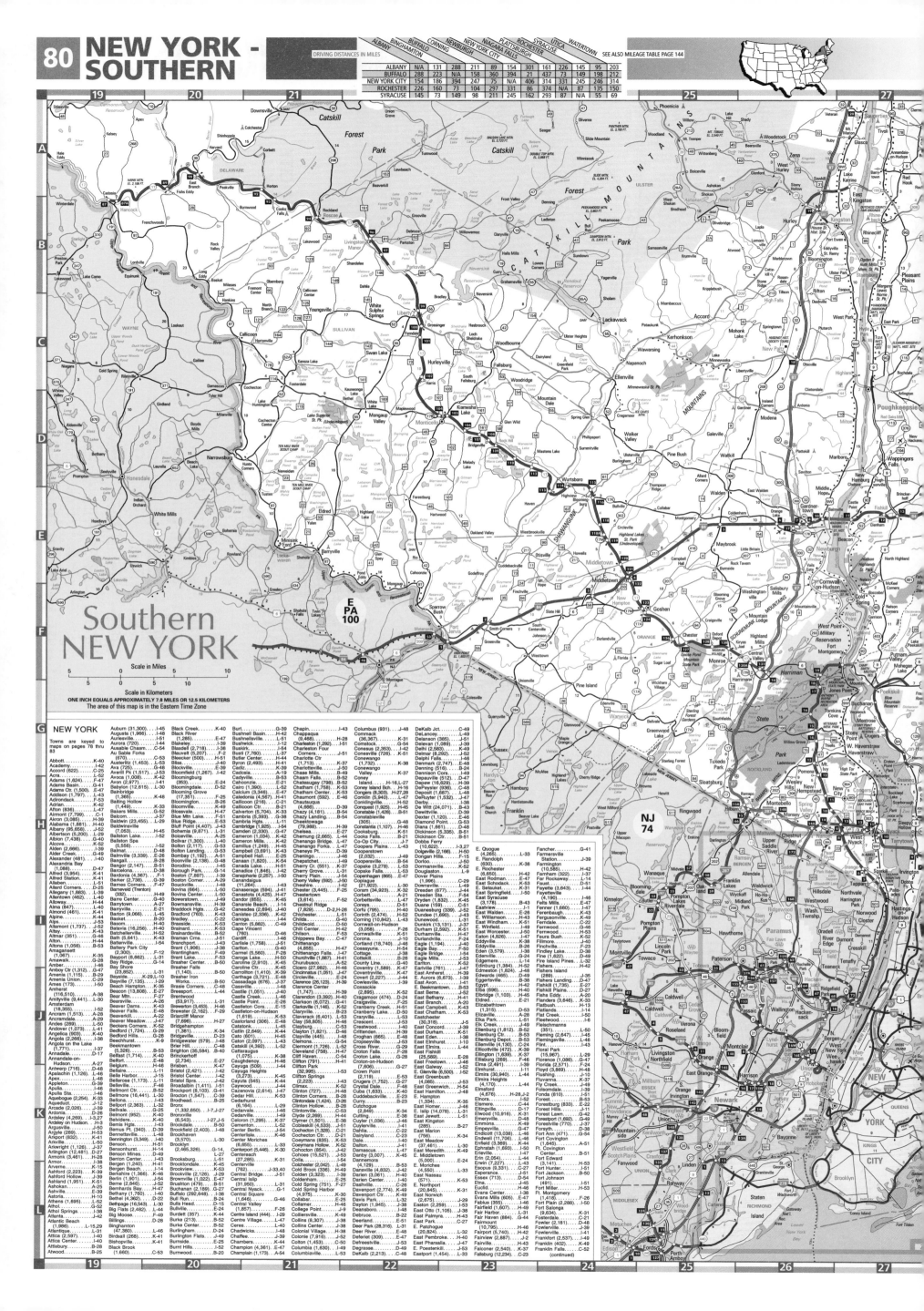

LONG ISLAND

DRIVING DISTANCES IN MILES

SEE ALSO MILEAGE TABLE PAGE 144

	ALBANY	BINGHAMTON	BUFFALO	CORNING	NEWBURGH	NEW YORK CITY	NIAGARA FALLS	PLATTSBURGH	ROCHESTER	SYRACUSE	UTICA	WATERTOWN
ALBANY	N/A	131	288	211	89	154	301	161	226	145	95	203
BUFFALO	288	223	N/A	158	360	394	21	437	73	149	198	212
NEW YORK CITY	154	186	394	247	75	N/A	406	314	331	245	246	314
ROCHESTER	226	160	73	104	297	331	86	374	N/A	87	135	150
SYRACUSE	145	73	149	98	211	245	162	293	87	N/A	55	69

BUFFALO

ROCHESTER

SYRACUSE

ALBANY

Western NEW YORK
Scale same as principal map

NIAGARA FALLS AREA

UTICA

Lake Erie

Lake Ontario

ON 136

ERIE

Lake Erie

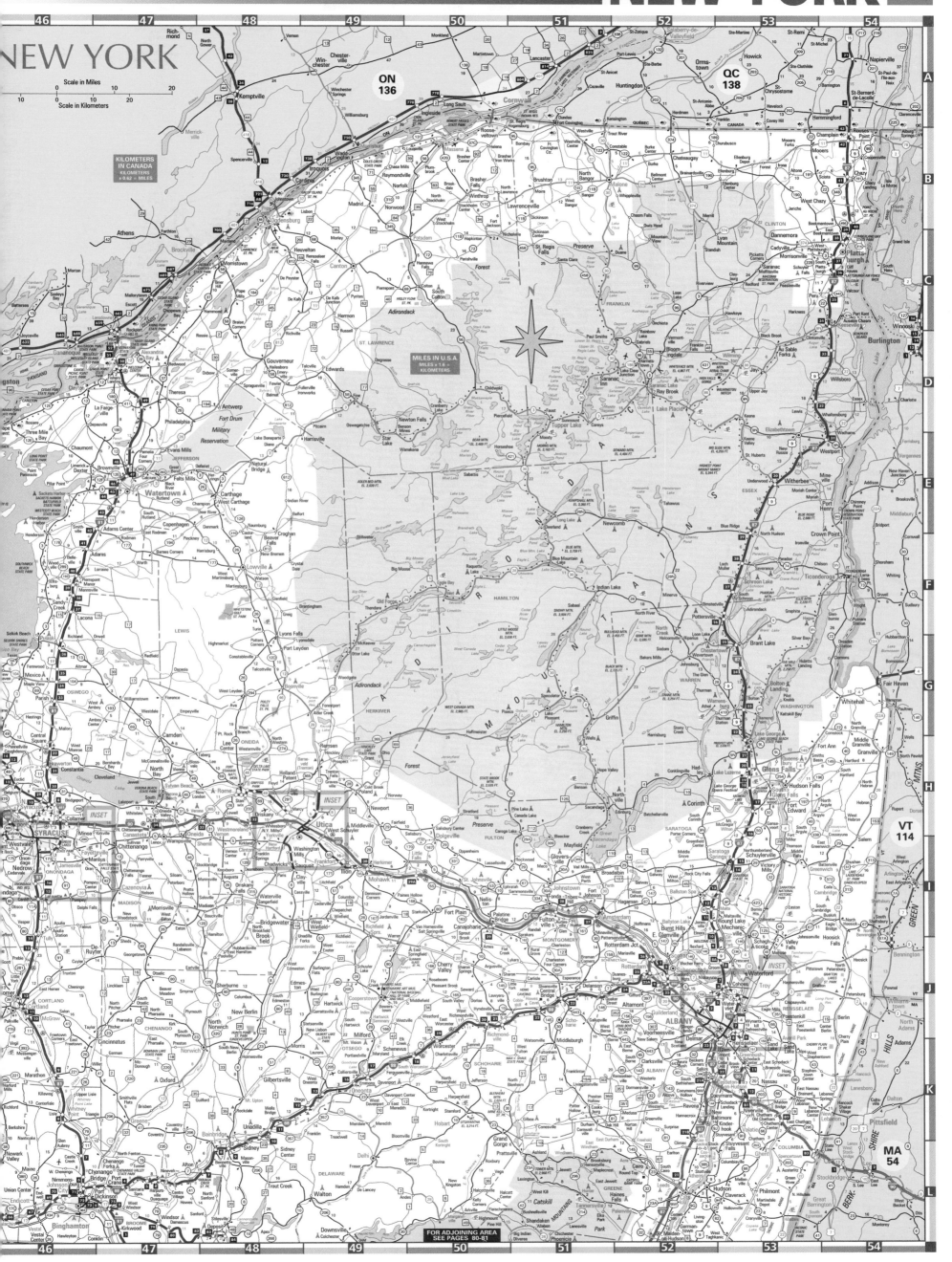

NEW YORK

FOR ADJOINING AREA
SEE PAGES 80-81

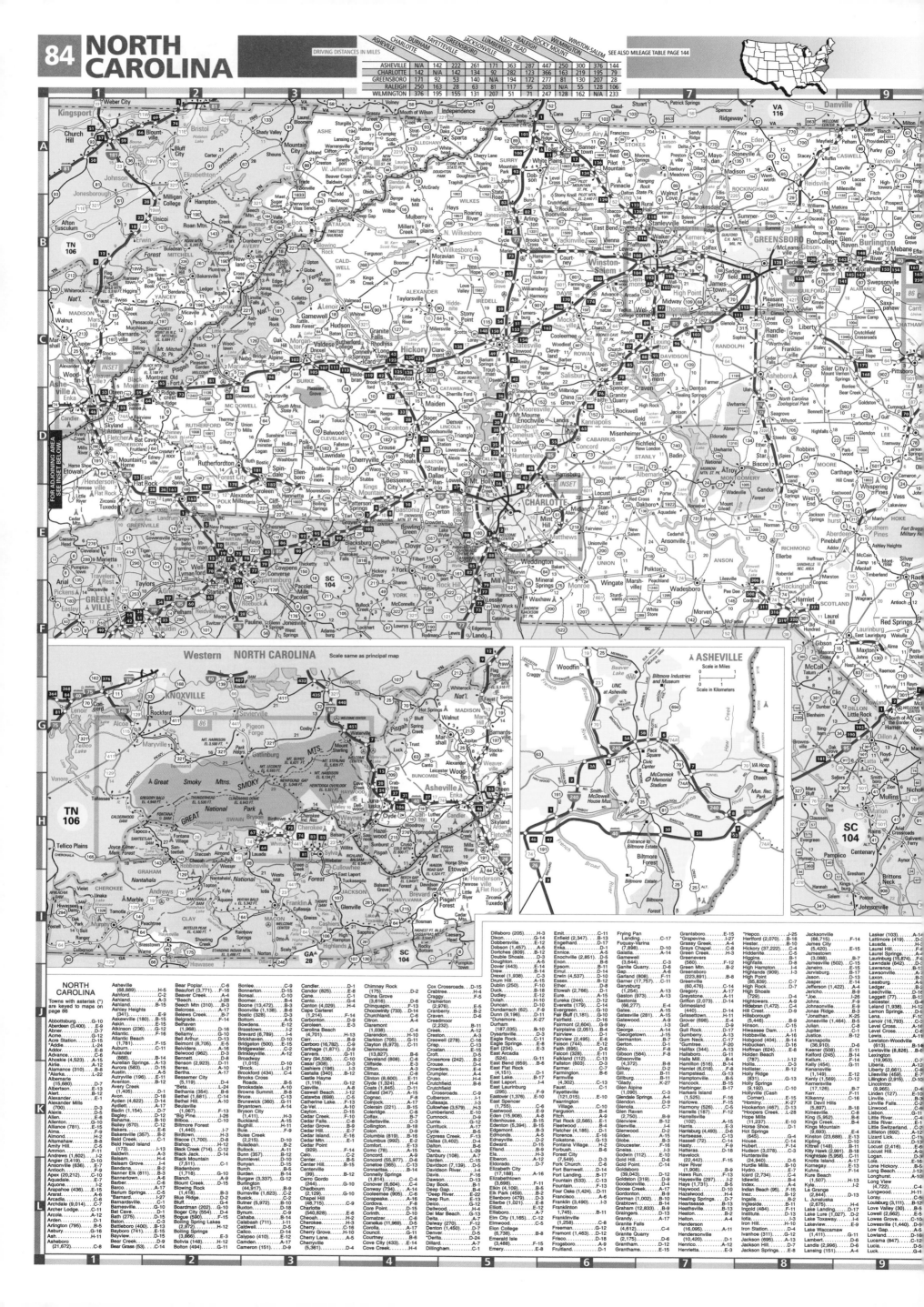

DRIVING DISTANCES IN MILES

SEE ALSO MILEAGE TABLE PAGE 144

	ASHEVILLE	CHARLOTTE	DURHAM	FAYETTEVILLE	GREENSBORO	JACKSONVILLE	LUMBERTON	NAGS HEAD	RALEIGH	ROCKY MOUNT	WILMINGTON	WINSTON-SALEM
ASHEVILLE	N/A	142	222	261	171	363	287	447	250	300	376	144
CHARLOTTE	142	N/A	142	134	92	283	123	366	163	215	195	79
GREENSBORO	171	92	53	140	N/A	194	172	277	81	130	207	28
RALEIGH	250	163	28	63	81	117	95	203	N/A	55	128	106
WILMINGTON	376	195	155	131	207	71	71	247	128	162	N/A	233

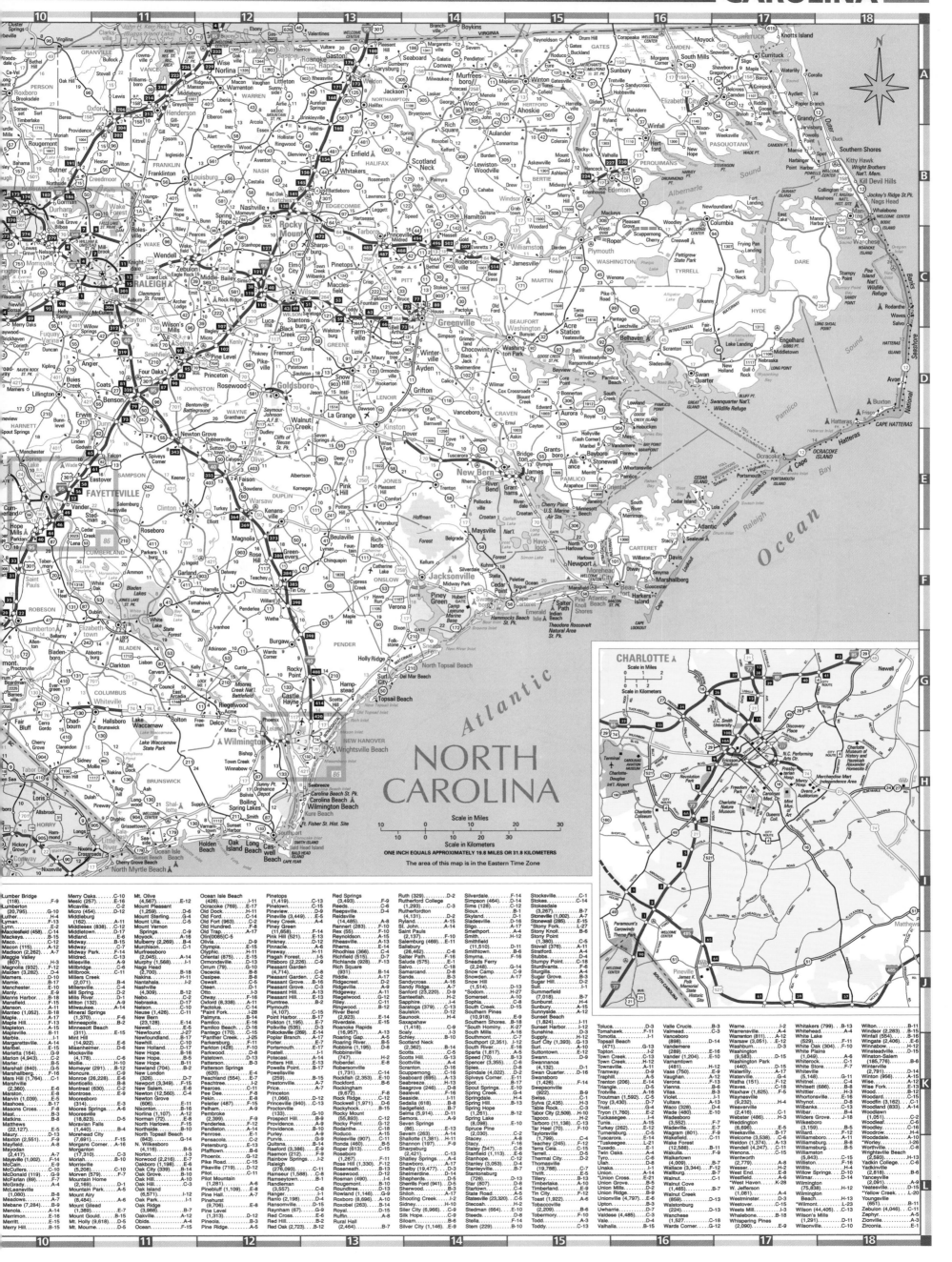

NORTH CAROLINA

Scale in Miles
10   0   10   20   30

Scale in Kilometers
10   0   10   20   30

ONE INCH EQUALS APPROXIMATELY 19.8 MILES OR 31.8 KILOMETERS

The area of this map is in the Eastern Time Zone

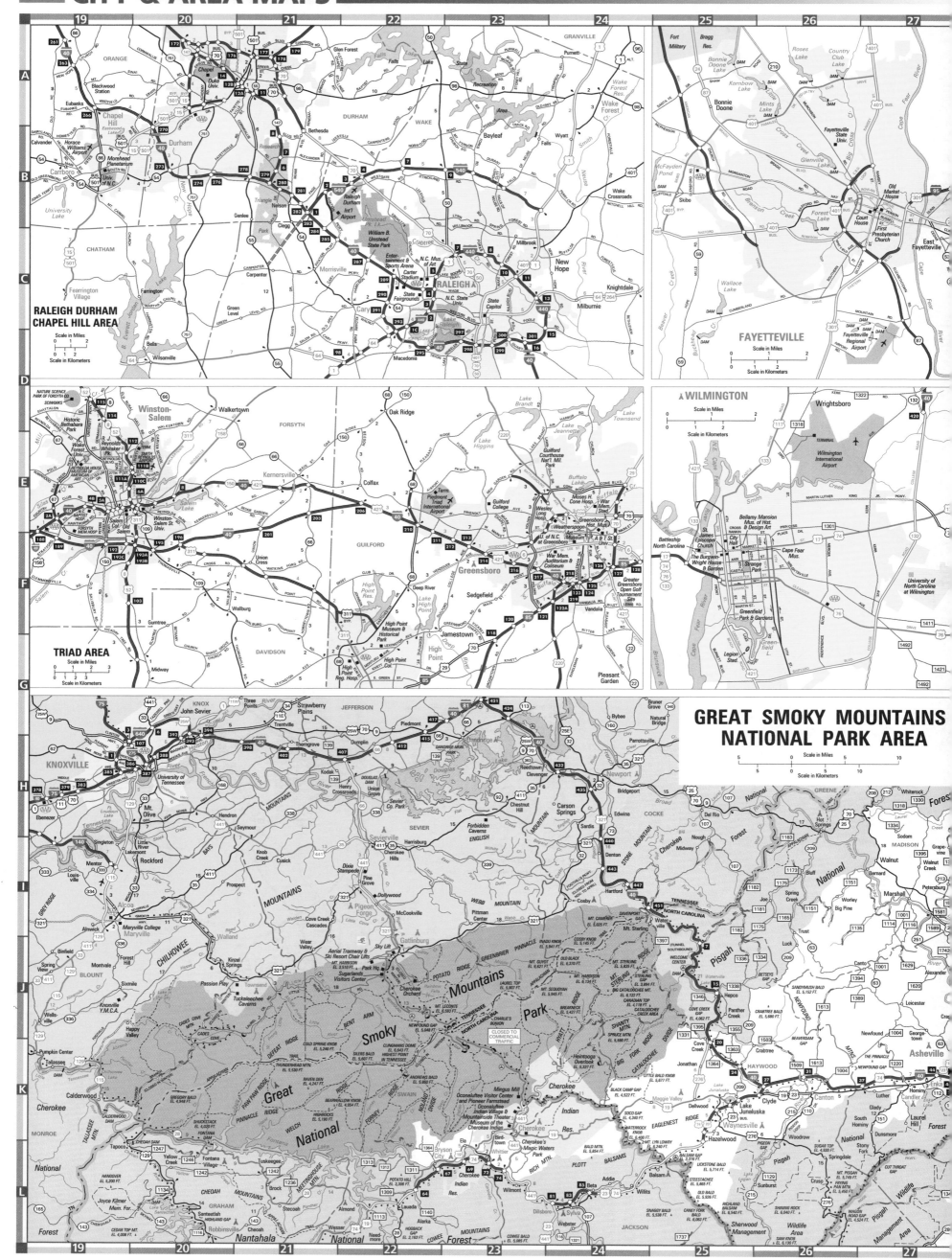

RALEIGH DURHAM CHAPEL HILL AREA
Scale in Miles
Scale in Kilometers

FAYETTEVILLE
Scale in Miles
Scale in Kilometers

TRIAD AREA
Scale in Miles
Scale in Kilometers

WILMINGTON
Scale in Kilometers

GREAT SMOKY MOUNTAINS NATIONAL PARK AREA
Scale in Miles
Scale in Kilometers

DRIVING DISTANCES IN MILES

SEE ALSO MILEAGE TABLE PAGE 144

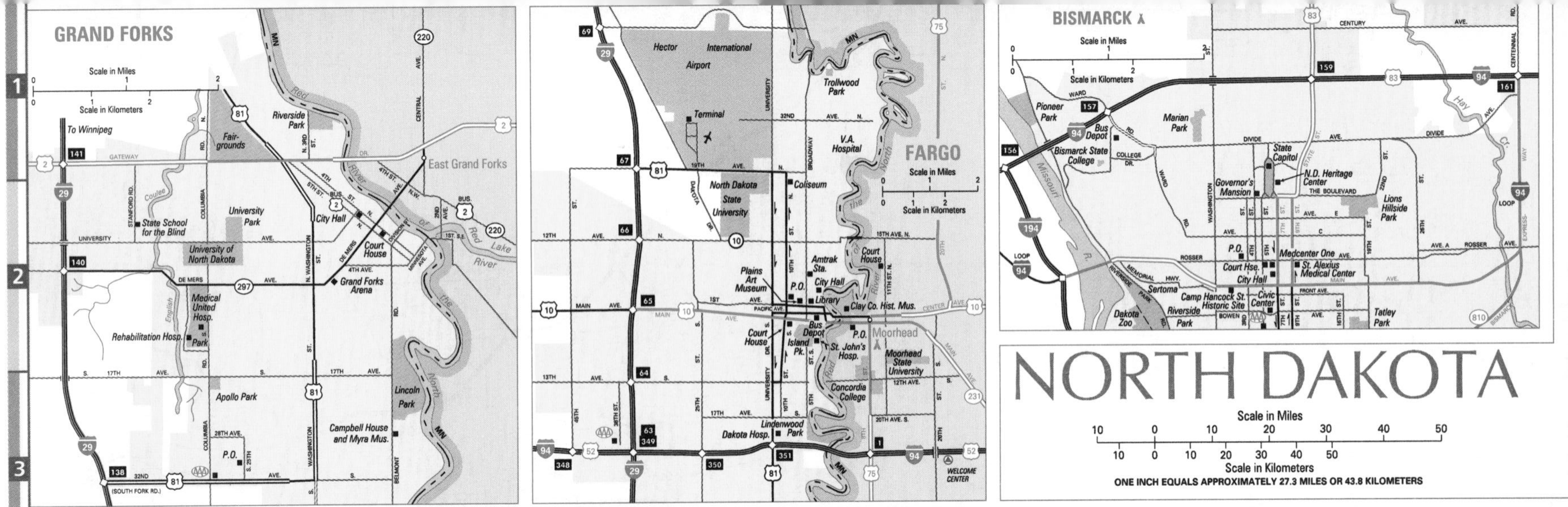

	BISMARCK	CHURCHS FERRY	DICKINSON	FARGO	GRAND FORKS	JAMESTOWN	MINOT	WILLISTON
BISMARCK	N/A	219	99	188	271	102	110	229
FARGO	188	189	294	N/A	75	97	262	424
GRAND FORKS	271	108	368	75	N/A	171	206	336

NORTH DAKOTA

BISMARCK

FARGO

GRAND FORKS

Scale in Miles

Scale in Kilometers

ONE INCH EQUALS APPROXIMATELY 27.3 MILES OR 43.8 KILOMETERS

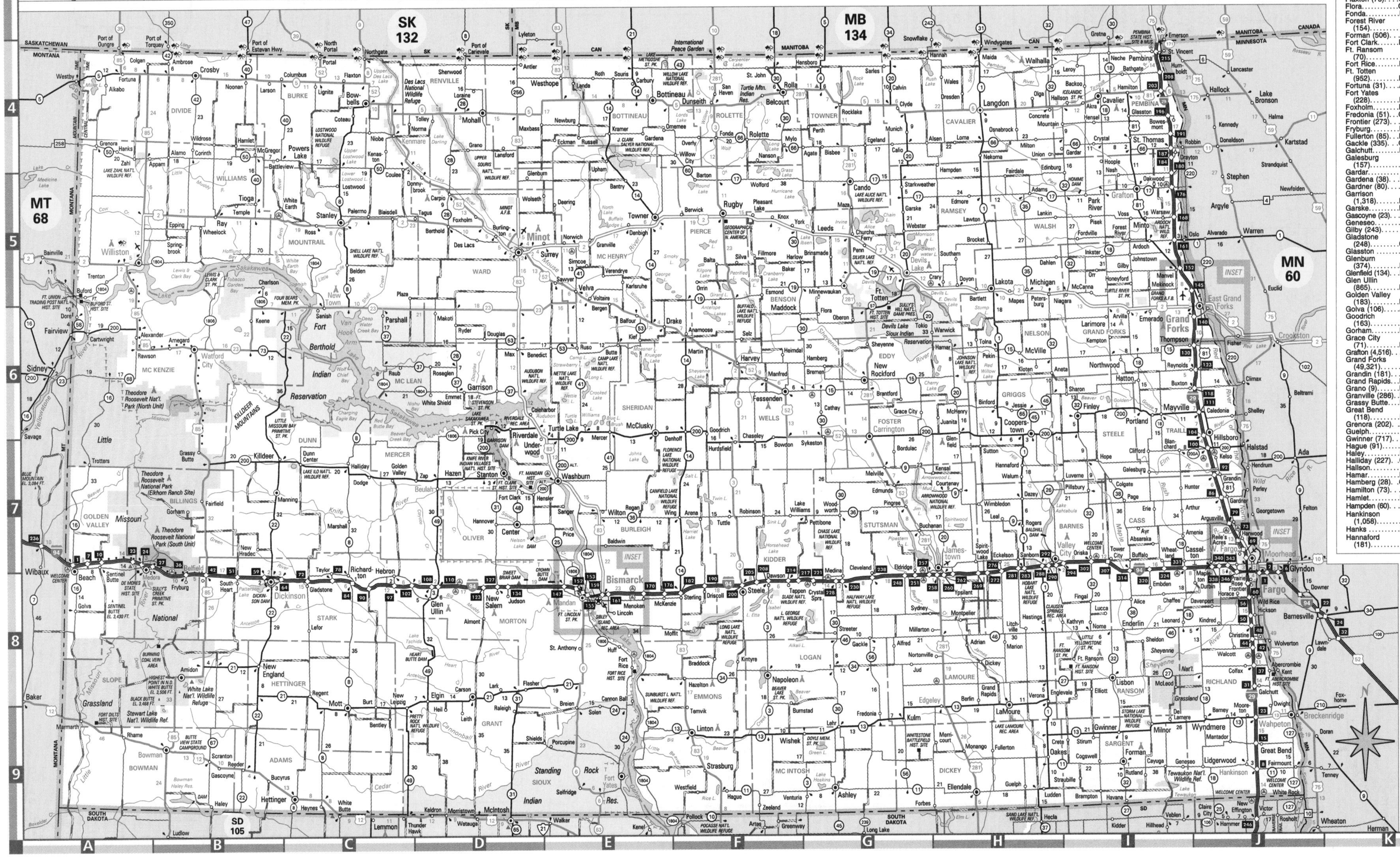

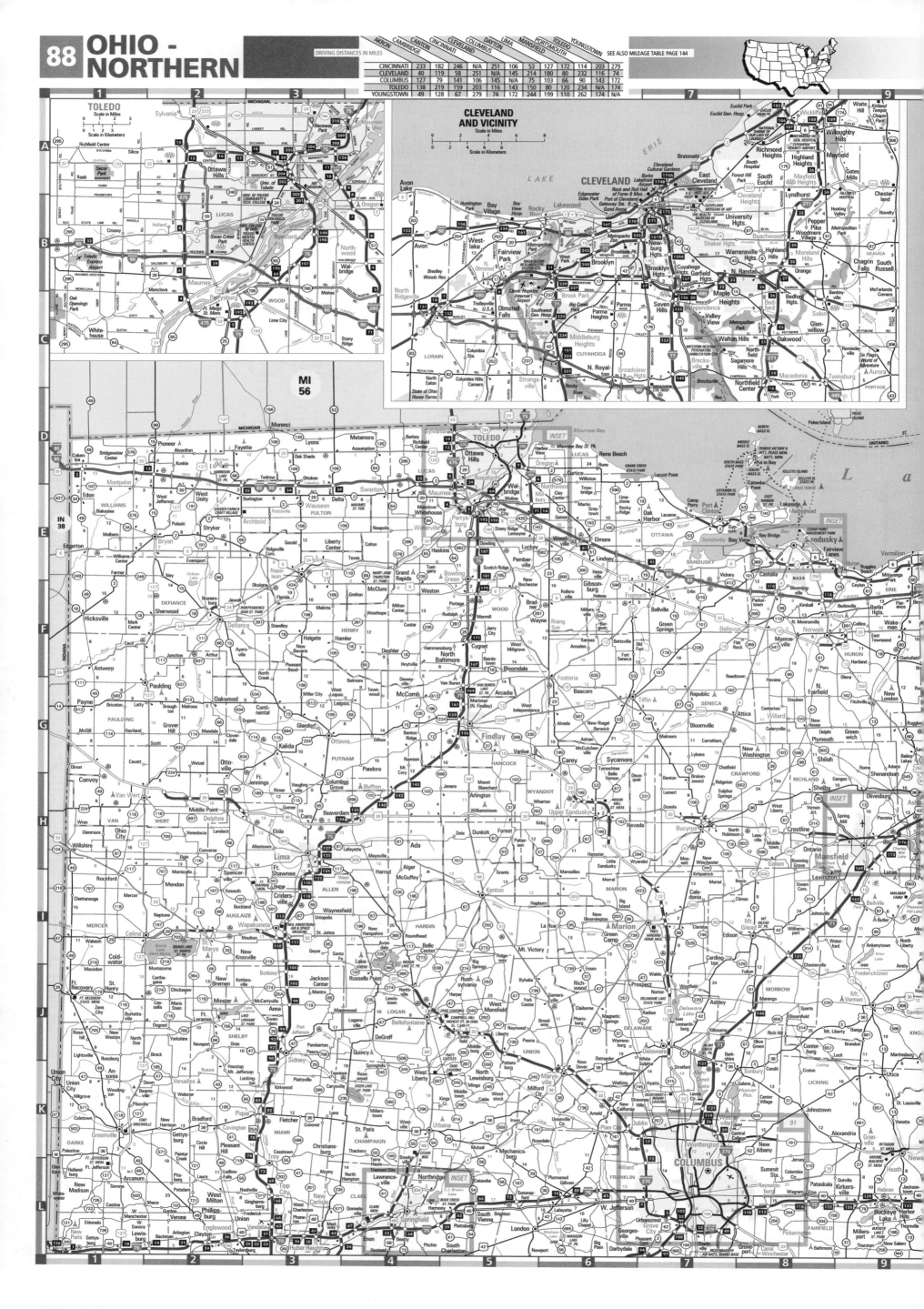

SEE ALSO MILEAGE TABLE PAGE 144

DRIVING DISTANCES IN MILES

	AKRON	CAMBRIDGE	CANTON	CINCINNATI	CLEVELAND	COLUMBUS	DAYTON	LIMA	MANSFIELD	PORTSMOUTH	TOLEDO	YOUNGSTOWN
CINCINNATI	233	182	246	N/A	251	106	53	127	172	114	203	279
CLEVELAND	40	119	58	251	N/A	145	214	180	80	232	116	74
COLUMBUS	127	79	141	106	145	N/A	75	103	66	90	143	172
TOLEDO	138	219	159	203	116	143	150	80	120	234	N/A	174
YOUNGSTOWN	49	128	62	279	74	172	244	199	110	262	174	N/A

TOLEDO

CLEVELAND AND VICINITY

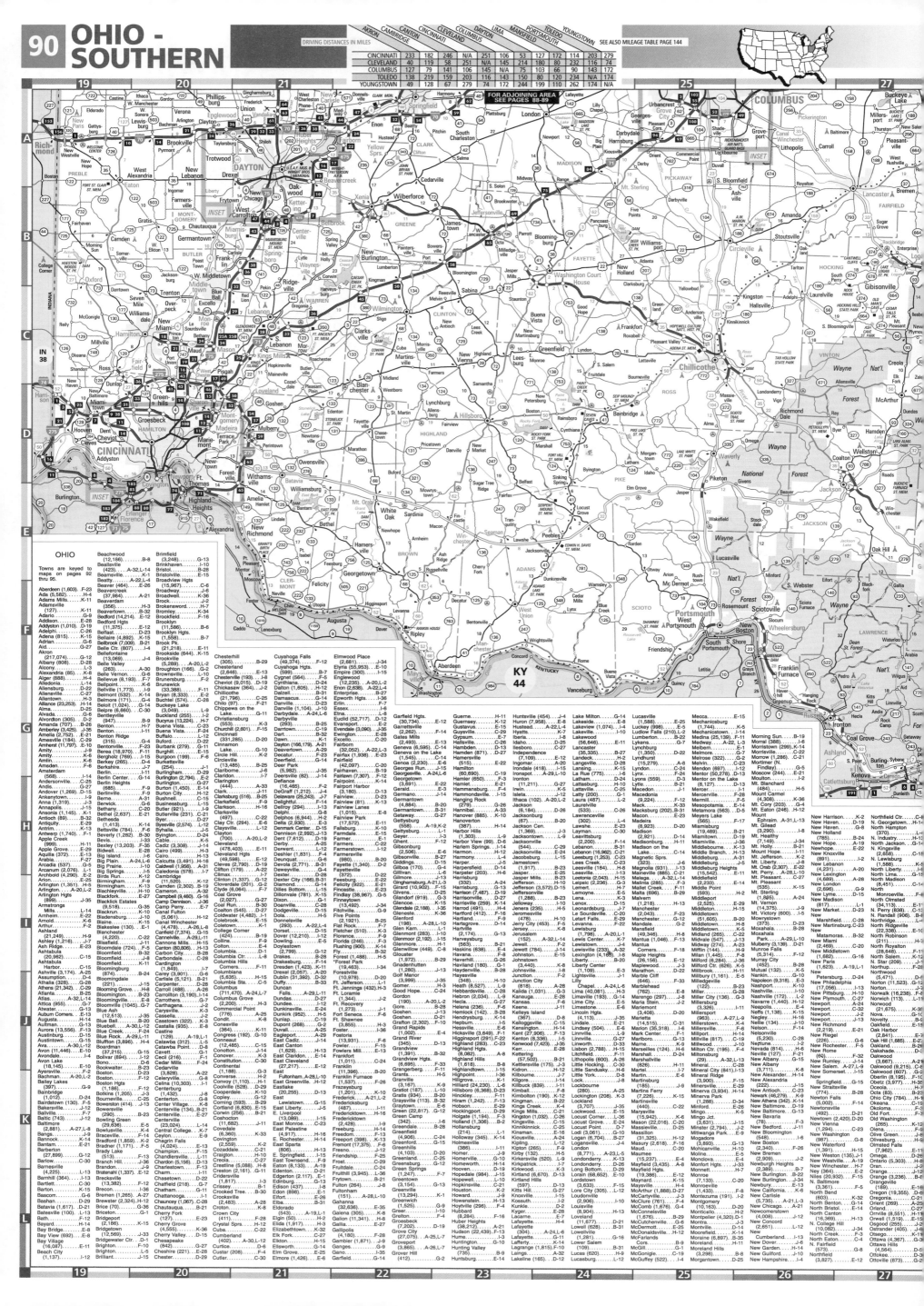

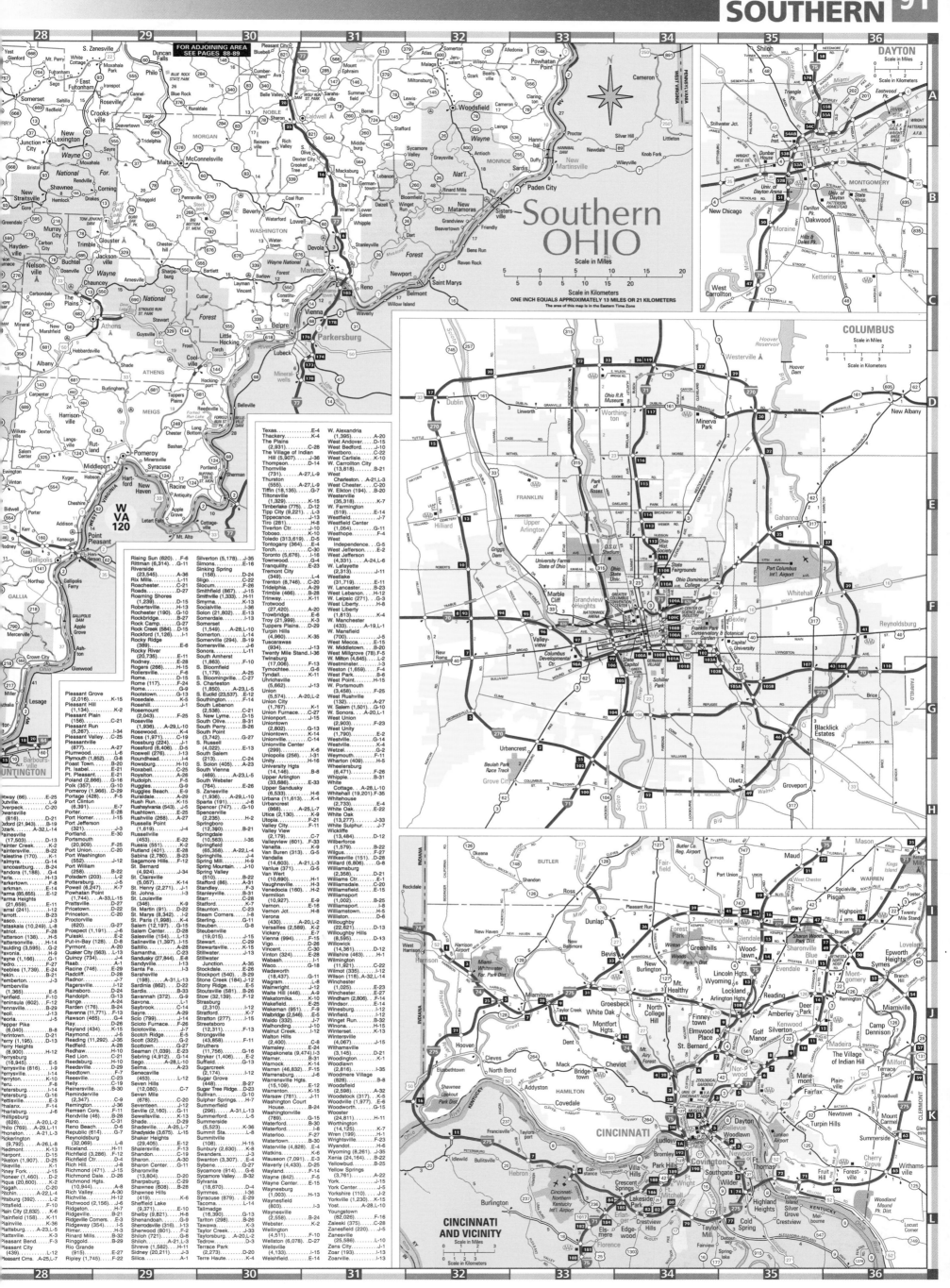

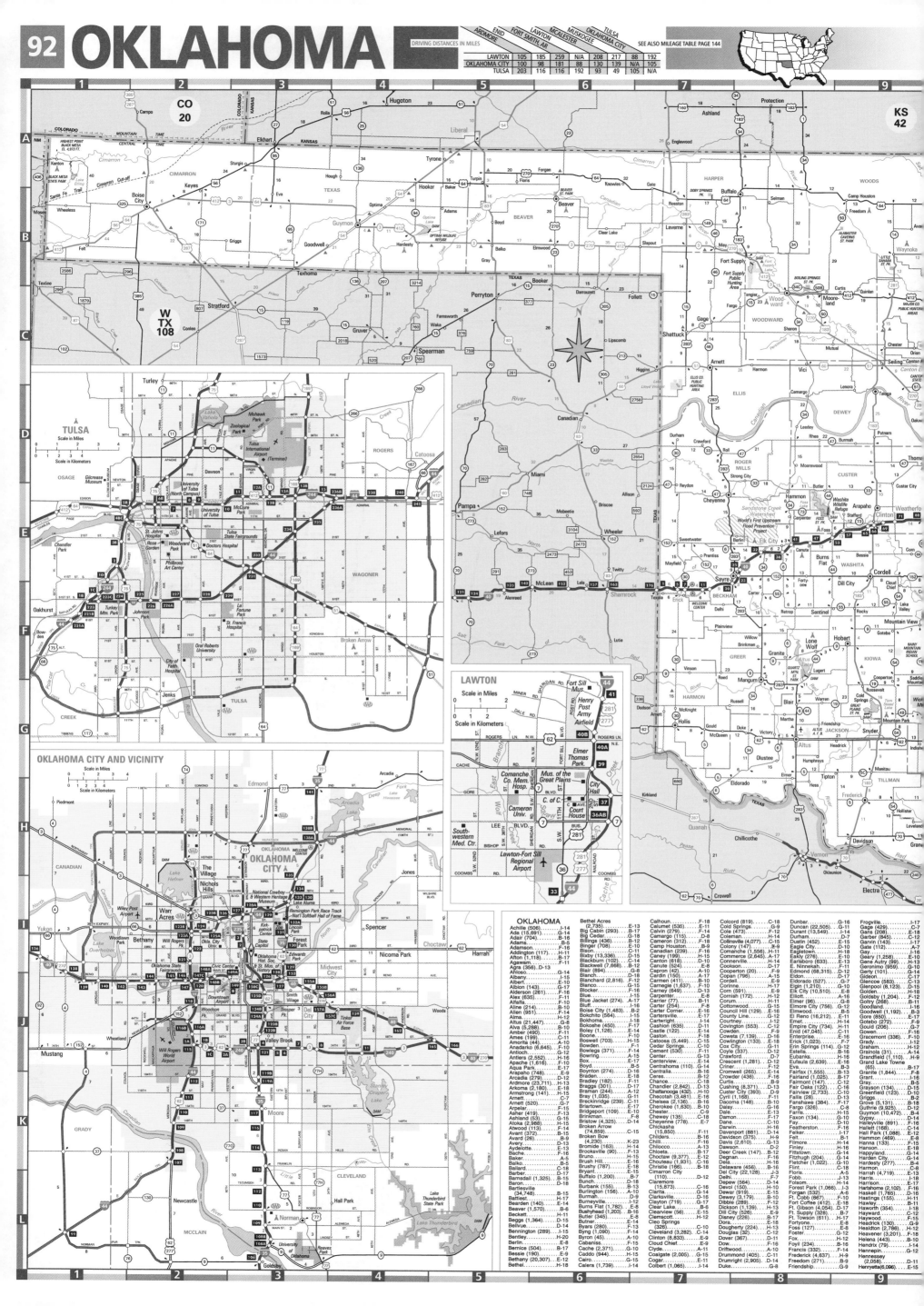

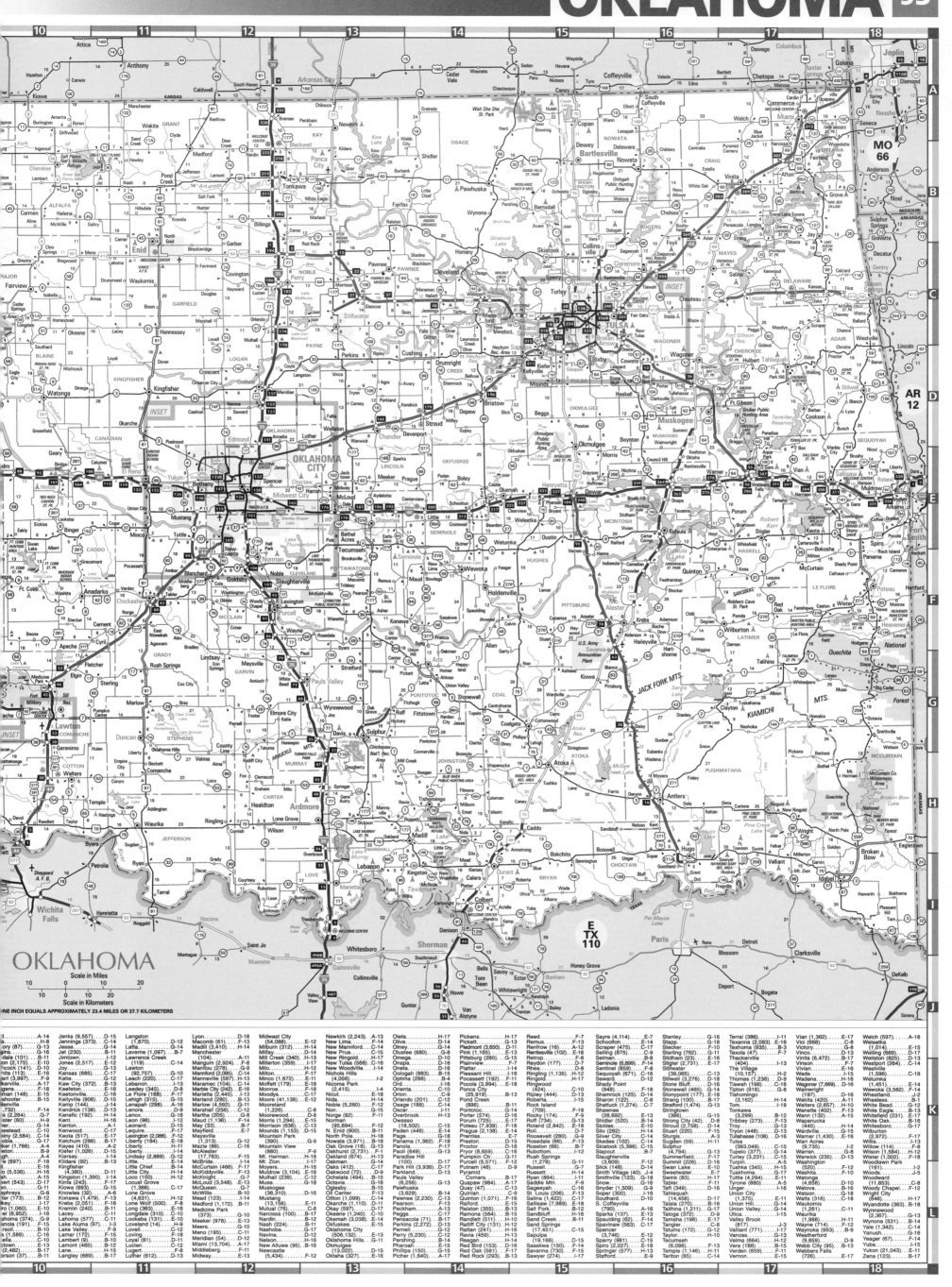

OKLAHOMA

Scale in Miles
10   10   20

Scale in Kilometers
10   10   20

ONE INCH EQUALS APPROXIMATELY 23.4 MILES OR 37.7 KILOMETERS

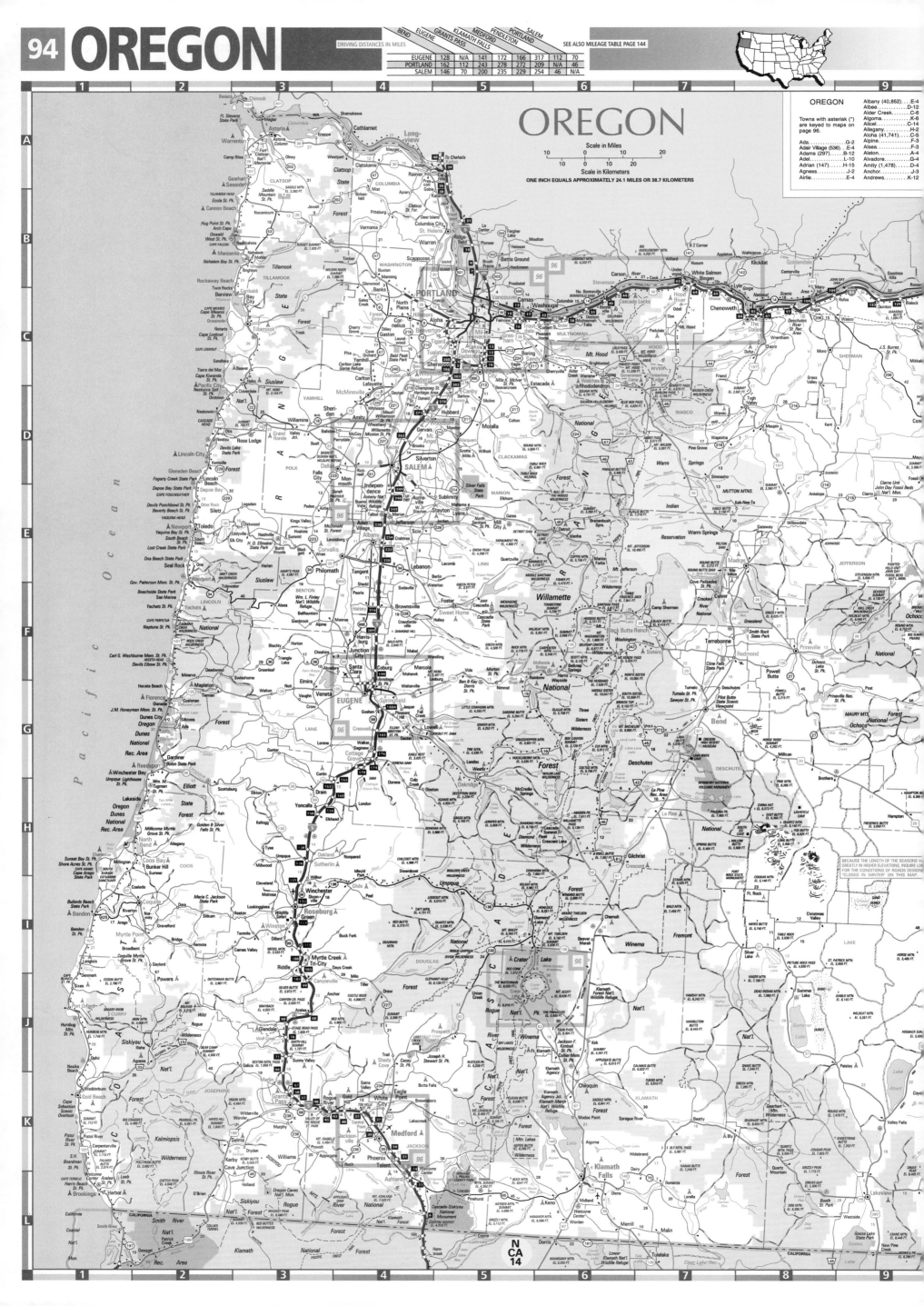

DRIVING DISTANCES IN MILES

SEE ALSO MILEAGE TABLE PAGE 144

	BEND	EUGENE	GRANTS PASS	KLAMATH FALLS	MEDFORD	PENDLETON	PORTLAND	SALEM
EUGENE	128	N/A	141	172	166	317	112	70
PORTLAND	162	112	243	278	272	209	N/A	46
SALEM	146	70	200	235	229	254	46	N/A

OREGON

Scale in Miles

Scale in Kilometers

ONE INCH EQUALS APPROXIMATELY 24.1 MILES OR 38.7 KILOMETERS

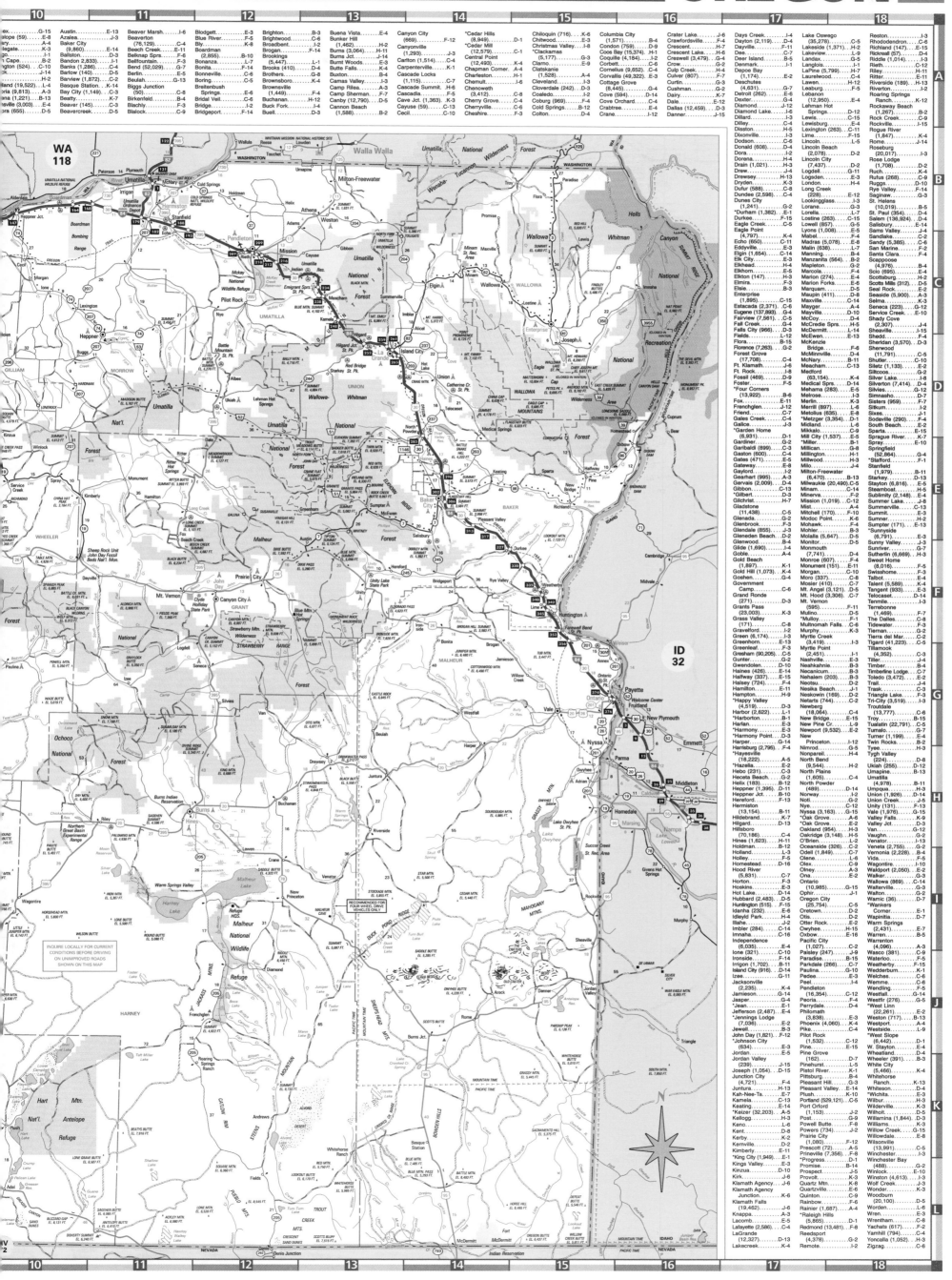

OREGON 95

10 11 12 13 14 15 16 17 18

ex............G-15
elope (59).......E-8
ary..............A-4
legate..........K-3
go...............I-1
Cape.........B-2
ngton (524). . .C-10
ck..............J-14
...............H-2
land (19,522). . .L-4
oria (9,813).....A-3
ena (1,221). . . .B-13
nsville (3,003). . . .E-4
ora (655).......D-5
Austin............E-13
Azalea.............J-3
Baker City (9,860).........E-14
Ballston............D-3
Bandon 2,833).......I-1
Banks (1,286).......C-4
Barlow (140).......D-5
Barview (1,872). . . .C-2
Basque Station. . .K-14
Bay City (1,149). . .C-3
Beatty..............K-7
Beaver (145).......C-3
Beavercreek.......D-5
Beaver Marsh.......I-6
Beaverton (76,129).........C-4
Beech Creek......E-11
Belknap Sprs.......F-6
Bellfountain........F-3
Bend (52,029).....G-7
Berlin..............E-5
Beulah...........G-13
Biggs Junction (50).............C-8
Birkenfeld..........B-4
Blachly.............F-3
Blalock............C-9
Blodgett............E-3
Blue River..........F-5
Bly.................K-8
Boardman (2,855).........B-10
Bonanza...........L-7
Bonita.............F-14
Bonneville.........C-6
Boring..............C-5
Breitenbush Springs..........E-6
Bridal Veil..........C-6
Bridge...............I-2
Bridgeport........F-14
Brighton............B-3
Brightwood.........C-6
Broadbent..........I-2
Brogan............F-14
Brookings (5,447)...........L-1
Brooks (410).......D-4
Brothers...........G-8
Brownsboro........K-4
Brownsville (1,449)...........F-4
Buchanan........H-12
Buck Fork...........I-4
Buell...............D-3
Buena Vista........E-4
Bunker Hill (1,462)..........H-2
Burns (3,064).....H-11
Burns Jct.........J-14
Burnt Woods.......E-3
Butte Falls.........K-4
Buxton.............B-4
Camas Valley.......I-3
Camp Rilea........A-3
Camp Sherman. . . .F-7
Canby (12,790). . . .D-5
Cannon Beach (1,588)..........B-2
Canyon City (669)..........F-12
Canyonville (1,293)...........J-3
Carlton (1,514).....C-4
Carpenterville......K-1
Cascade Locks (1,115)..........C-7
Cascade Summit. .H-6
Cascadia...........F-5
Cave Jct. (1,363). .K-3
Cayuse (59)......C-13
Cecil.............C-10
*Cedar Hills (8,949)..........D-1
*Cedar Mill (12,579).........C-1
Central Point (12,493).........K-4
Chapman Corner. .A-4
Charleston.........H-1
Chemult.............I-6
Chenoweth (3,412)..........C-8
Cherry Grove......C-4
Cherryville.........C-6
Cheshire..........F-3
Chiloquin (716). . . .K-6
Chitwood...........E-3
Christmas Valley. . . .I-8
*Clackamas (5,177)..........G-3
Clarno.............E-9
Clatskanie (1,528)..........A-4
Cleveland...........I-3
Cloverdale (242). . .D-3
Coaledo.............I-2
Coburg (969).......F-4
Cold Springs......B-12
Colton.............D-4
Columbia City (1,571)..........B-4
Condon (759)......D-9
Coos Bay (15,374). .H-1
Coquille (4,184).....I-2
Corbett............C-6
Cornelius (9,652). .C-4
Corvallis (49,322). .E-3
Cottage Grove (8,445)..........G-4
Cove (594).......D-14
Cove Orchard......C-4
Crabtree...........E-4
Crane.............I-12
Crater Lake........J-6
Crawfordsville......F-4
Crescent...........H-7
Crescent Lake.....H-6
Creswell (3,479). . .G-4
Crow..............G-2
Culp Creek........H-4
Culver (807)........F-7
Curtin..............G-3
Cushman..........G-2
Dairy..............K-7
Dale..............E-12
Dallas (12,459). . . .D-3
Danner............J-15
Days Creek..........I-4
Dayton (2,119).....D-4
Dayville...........F-11
Dee...............C-7
Deer Island........B-5
Denmark............I-1
Depoe Bay (1,174)..........E-2
Deschutes (4,631)..........G-7
Detroit (262).......E-6
Dexter.............G-4
Diamond.........J-12
Diamond Lake.......I-6
Dillard...............I-3
Dilley..............C-4
Disston............H-5
Dixonville...........I-3
Dodson............C-6
Donald (608).......D-4
Dora................I-2
Dorena.............H-4
Drain (1,021)......H-3
Drew...............J-4
Drewsey..........H-13
Dryden.............K-3
Dufur (588)........C-8
Dundee (2,598). . . .C-4
Dunes City (1,241)..........G-2
*Durham (1,382). . .E-1
Durkee............F-15
Eagle Creek.......C-5
Eagle Point (4,797)..........K-4
Echo (650)........C-11
Eddyville...........E-3
Elgin (1,654)......C-14
Elk City............E-3
Elkhead...........H-4
Elkhorn............E-5
Elkton (147).......H-3
Elmira..............F-3
Elsie...............B-3
Enterprise (1,895)........C-15
Estacada (2,371). .C-6
Eugene (137,893). . .G-4
Fairview (7,561). . .C-5
Fall Creek.........G-4
Falls City (966). . . .D-3
Fields.............L-12
Flora..............B-15
Florence (7,263). . . .G-2
Forest Grove (17,708).........C-4
Ft. Klamath.........J-6
Ft. Rock.............I-8
Fossil (469)........D-9
Foster..............F-5
*Four Corners (13,922).........B-6
Fox...............E-11
Frenchglen........J-12
Friend.............C-7
Gales Creek.......C-4
Galice..............J-3
*Garden Home (6,931)..........D-1
Gardiner..........G-2
Garibaldi (899).....C-3
Gaston (600).......C-4
Gates (471)........E-5
Gateway...........E-8
Gaylord.............I-2
Gearhart (995).....A-3
Gervais (2,009). . . .D-4
Gibbon...........C-13
*Gilbert............D-3
Gilchrist...........H-7
Gladstone (11,438).........C-5
Glenada...........G-2
Glenbrook..........F-3
Glendale (855).....J-3
Gleneden Beach. . .D-2
Glenwood..........B-4
Glide (1,690)........I-4
Goble..............A-4
Gold Beach (1,897)..........K-1
Gold Hill (1,073). . .K-4
Goshen............G-4
Government Camp............C-6
Grand Ronde (271)............D-3
Grants Pass (23,003).........K-3
Grass Valley (171)............C-8
Gravelford..........I-2
Green (6,174).......I-3
Greenhorn........E-13
Greenleaf..........F-3
Gresham (90,205). . .C-5
Gunter.............G-2
Gwendolen.......D-10
Haines (426)......E-14
Halfway (337).....E-15
Halsey (724).......F-4
Hamilton..........E-11
Hampton...........H-9
*Happy Valley (4,519)..........D-3
Harbor (2,622).....L-1
*Harborton.........B-1
Harlan.............E-3
*Harmony..........E-3
*Harmony Point. . . .D-3
Harper............G-14
Harrisburg (2,795). . .F-4
*Hayesville (18,222).........A-5
*Hazelia...........E-2
Hebo (231)........C-3
Heceta Beach. G-2
Helix (183)........B-12
Heppner (1,395). .D-11
Heppner Jct......B-10
Hereford..........F-13
Hermiston (13,154)........B-11
Hildebrand.........K-7
Hilgard...........D-13
Hillsboro (70,186).........C-4
Hines (1,623).....H-11
Holdman..........B-12
Holland.............L-3
Holley..............F-5
Homestead.......D-16
Hood River (5,831)..........C-7
Horton.............F-3
Hoskins............E-3
Hot Lake.........D-14
Hubbard (2,483). . .D-5
Huntington (515). . .F-15
Idanha (232).......E-6
Idleyld Park........H-4
Illahe...............J-2
Imbler (284)......C-14
Imnaha...........C-16
Independence (6,035).........E-4
Ione (321)........C-10
Ironside...........F-14
Irrigon (1,702). . . .B-11
Island City (916). . .D-14
Izee..............G-11
Jacksonville (2,235)..........K-4
Jamieson.........G-14
Jasper............G-4
*Jean..............E-1
Jefferson (2,487). . .E-4
*Jennings Lodge (7,036)..........E-2
Jewell.............B-3
John Day (1,821). . .F-12
*Johnson City (634)............E-3
Jordan.............E-5
Jordan Valley (239)...........J-15
Joseph (1,054). . .D-15
Junction City (4,721)...........F-4
Juntura...........H-13
Kah-Nee-Ta........E-7
Kamela...........C-13
Keating...........E-14
*Keizer (32,203). . .A-5
Kellogg............H-3
Keno...............L-6
Kent...............D-8
Kerby..............K-2
Kernville...........D-2
Kimberly..........E-11
*King City (1,949). . . .E-1
Kings Valley........E-3
Kinzua............D-10
Kirk................J-6
Klamath Agency. . . .J-6
Klamath Agency Junction.........K-6
Klamath Falls (19,462).........J-6
Knappa............A-3
Lacomb.............E-5
Lafayette (2,586). . . .C-4
LaGrande (12,327)........D-13
Lakecreek..........K-4
Lake Oswego (35,278).........C-5
Lakeside (1,371). . .H-2
Lakeview...........L-9
Landax............G-5
Langlois............I-1
LaPine (5,799).....H-7
Laurelwood........C-4
Lawen............H-12
Leaburg............F-5
Lebanon (12,950).........E-4
Lehman Hot Springs.........D-12
Lewis.............C-15
Lewisburg..........E-4
Lexington (263). . .C-11
Lime..............F-15
Lincoln.............L-5
Lincoln Beach (2,078)..........D-2
Lincoln City (7,437)..........D-2
Logdell...........G-11
Logsden...........E-3
London............H-4
Long Creek (228)...........E-12
Lookingglass........I-3
Lorane............G-3
Lorella.............L-7
Lostine (263).....C-15
Lowell (857).......G-5
Lyons (1,008)......E-5
Mabel..............F-4
Madras (5,078). . . .E-8
Malin (638).........L-7
Manning...........B-4
Manzanita (564). . .B-2
Mapleton..........G-2
Marcola............F-4
Marion (274).......E-4
Marion Forks.......E-6
Marquam..........D-5
Maupin (411).......D-8
Maxville..........C-14
Mayger.............A-4
Mayville..........D-10
McCoy.............D-4
McCredie Sprs.....H-5
McDermitt.........L-14
McEwen..........E-13
McKenzie Bridge...........F-6
McMinnville........D-4
McNary...........B-11
Meacham.........C-13
Medford (63,154).........K-4
Medical Sprs.....D-14
Mehama (283).....E-5
Melrose.............I-3
Merlin..............K-3
Merrill (897)........L-6
Metolius (635).....E-8
*Metzger (3,354). . .D-1
Midland............L-6
Mikkalo............C-9
Mill City (1,537). . . .E-5
*Miller.............B-1
Millican............G-8
Millington..........H-1
Millwood...........H-3
Milo...............J-4
Milton-Freewater (6,470).........B-13
Milwaukie (20,490).C-5
Minam...........C-14
Minerva............F-2
Mission (1,019). . .C-12
Mist...............A-4
Mitchell (170).....F-10
Modoc Point.......K-6
Mohawk............F-4
Mohler.............B-3
Molalla (5,647).....D-5
Monitor............D-5
Monmouth (7,741)..........D-4
Monroe (607)......F-4
Monument (151). . . .E-11
Morgan...........C-10
Moro (337).........C-8
Mosier (410).......C-7
Mt. Angel (3,121). .D-5
Mt. Hood (3,306). .C-7
Mt. Vernon (595)...........F-11
Mulino.............D-5
*Mulloy.............F-1
Multnomah Falls. . .C-6
Murphy............K-3
Myrtle Creek (3,419)............I-3
Myrtle Point (2,451)............I-1
Nashville...........E-3
Neahkahnie........B-3
Necanicum.........B-3
Nehalem (203).....B-3
Neotsu.............D-2
Nesika Beach......J-1
Neskowin (169). . . .D-2
Netarts (744)......C-2
Newberg (18,064).........C-4
New Bridge.......E-15
New Pine Cr.......L-9
Newport (9,532). . . .E-2
New Princeton........I-12
Nimrod............G-5
Nonpareil..........H-4
North Bend (9,544)..........H-2
North Plains (1,605)..........C-4
North Powder (489)...........D-14
Norway.............I-2
Noti...............G-2
Nye...............C-12
Nyssa (3,163). . . .G-15
*Oak Grove........A-6
*Oak Grove........E-2
Oakland (954).....H-3
Oakridge (3,148). . .H-5
O'Brien.............L-2
Oceanside (326). . .C-2
Odell (1,849).......C-7
Olene..............L-6
Olex...............C-9
Olney..............A-3
Ona...............E-2
Ontario (10,985)........G-15
Ophir...............J-1
Oregon City (25,754).........C-5
Oretown...........D-2
Otis...............D-2
Otter Rock.........E-2
Owyhee..........H-15
Oxbow...........E-16
Pacific City (1,027)..........C-2
Paisley (247)......J-9
Paradise.........B-15
Parkdale (266).....C-7
Paulina..........G-10
Pedee.............E-3
Peel................I-4
Pendleton (16,354)........C-12
Peoria.............F-4
Perrydale..........D-4
Philomath (3,838)..........E-3
Phoenix (4,060). . . .K-4
Pike...............C-4
Pilot Rock (1,532)........C-12
Pine..............E-15
Pine Grove (162)............D-7
Pinehurst..........L-5
Pistol River........K-1
Pittsburg..........B-4
Pleasant Hill.......G-3
Pleasant Valley. . .E-14
Plush.............K-10
Portland (529,121). . .C-5
Port Orford (1,153)..........J-2
Post...............G-9
Powell Butte.......F-8
Powers (734)......J-2
Prairie City (1,080).........F-12
Prescott (72)......A-5
Prineville (7,356). . .F-8
*Progress.........D-1
Promise..........B-14
Prospect...........J-5
Provolt............K-3
Quartz Mtn........K-8
Quartzville.........E-6
Quinton............C-9
Rainbow...........F-6
Rainier (1,687).....A-4
*Raleigh Hills (5,865)..........D-1
Redmond (13,481). . .F-8
Reedsport (4,378)..........G-2
Remote.............I-2
Reston..............I-3
Rhododendron.....C-6
Richland (147). . . .E-15
Rickreall (57)........D-4
Riddle (1,014).......I-3
Rieth.............C-12
Riley.............H-11
Ritter.............E-11
Riverside (189). . .H-13
Riverton.............I-2
Roaring Springs Ranch.........K-12
Rockaway Beach (1,267)..........B-2
Rock Creek........C-9
Rockville...........I-15
Rogue River (1,847)..........K-4
Rome.............J-14
Roseburg (20,017)...........I-3
Rose Lodge (1,708)..........D-2
Ruch...............K-4
Rufus (268)........C-9
Ruggs............D-10
Rye Valley........F-14
Saginaw...........G-3
St. Helens (10,019).........B-5
St. Paul (354)......D-4
Salem (136,924). . .D-4
Salisbury.........E-14
Sams Valley........J-4
Sandlake...........C-2
Sandy (5,385).....C-6
San Marine........F-2
Santa Clara........F-4
Scappoose (4,976)..........B-4
Scio (695).........E-4
Scottsburg.........H-2
Scotts Mills (312). . . .D-5
Seal Rock..........E-2
Seaside (5,900). . . .A-3
Selma..............K-3
Seneca (223).....G-12
Service Creek. . . .E-10
Shady Cove (2,307)...........J-4
Sheaville...........I-15
Shedd..............F-4
Sheridan (3,570). . .D-3
Sherwood (11,791).........C-5
Shutler...........C-10
Siletz (1,133)......E-2
Siltcoos...........G-2
Silver Lake..........I-8
Silverton (7,414). . .D-4
Silvies............G-12
Simnasho..........D-7
Sisters (959).......F-7
Sitkum..............I-2
Sixes...............J-1
Sodaville (290).....F-4
South Beach.......E-2
Sparta............E-15
Sprague River.....K-7
Spray.............E-10
Springfield (52,864).........G-4
*Stafford...........F-1
Stanfield (1,979).........B-11
Starkey...........D-13
Stayton (6,816). . . .E-5
Steamboat.........H-5
Sublimity (2,148). . .E-4
Summer Lake......J-8
Summerville......C-13
Summit.............E-3
Sumner............H-2
Sumpter (171). . . .E-13
*Sunnyside (6,791)..........E-3
Sunny Valley.......J-3
Sunriver...........G-7
Sutherlin (6,669). . .H-3
Sweet Home (8,016)..........F-5
Swisshome.........F-3
Talbot.............E-4
Talent (5,589)......K-4
Tangent (933)......E-3
Telocaset.........D-14
Tenmile.............I-3
Terrebonne (1,469)..........F-7
The Dalles.........C-8
Tidewater..........F-3
Tiernan............G-2
Tierra del Mar......C-2
Tigard (41,223). . . .C-5
Tillamook (4,352)..........C-3
Tiller...............J-4
Timber.............B-4
Timberline Lodge. . . .C-7
Toledo (3,472).....E-2
Trail................J-4
Trask..............C-3
Triangle Lake......F-3
Tri-City (3,519)......I-3
Troutdale (13,777).........C-6
Troy..............B-15
Tualatin (22,791). . .C-5
Tumalo............G-7
Turner (1,199). E-4
Twin Rocks........B-2
Tyee...............H-3
Tygh Valley (224)............D-8
Ukiah (255).......D-12
Umapine..........B-13
Umatilla (4,978).........B-11
Umpqua...........H-3
Union (1,926).....D-14
Union Creek........J-5
Unity (131)........F-13
Vale (1,976)......G-15
Valley Falls........K-9
Valley Jct..........D-3
Van...............G-12
Vaughn............G-2
Venator............I-13
Veneta (2,755).....G-2
Vernonia (2,228). . .B-4
Vida...............F-5
Wagontire.........I-10
Waldport (2,050). . .E-2
Walker.............G-3
Wallowa (869). . . .C-14
Walterville.........G-3
Walton.............G-2
Wamic (36)........D-7
*Wankers Corner...........E-1
Wapinitia...........D-7
Warm Springs (2,431).........E-7
Warren.............B-5
Warrenton (4,096)..........A-3
Wasco (381).......C-9
Waterloo...........F-5
Weatherby........F-15
Wedderburn........K-1
Welches...........C-6
Wemme............C-6
Wendling...........F-5
Westfall..........G-14
Westfir (276).......G-5
*West Linn (22,261).........E-2
Weston (717).....B-13
Westport..........A-4
Westside...........L-9
*West Slope (6,442)..........D-1
W. Stayton.........E-4
Wheatland.........D-4
Wheeler (391).....B-3
White City (5,466)..........K-4
Whitehorse Ranch.........K-13
Whiteson..........D-4
*Wichita............E-3
Wilbur.............H-3
Wilderville.........K-3
Wilhoit.............D-5
Willamina (1,844). .D-3
Williams...........K-3
Willow Creek.....G-15
Willowdale.........E-8
Wilsonville (13,991).........C-5
Winchester..........I-3
Winchester Bay (488)............G-2
Winlock...........E-10
Winston (4,613).....I-3
Wolf Creek.........J-3
Wonder............K-3
Woodburn (20,100).........D-5
Worden.............L-6
Wren...............E-3
Wrentham.........C-8
Yachats (617)......F-2
Yamhill (794).......C-4
Yoncalla (1,052). . .H-3
Zigzag.............C-6

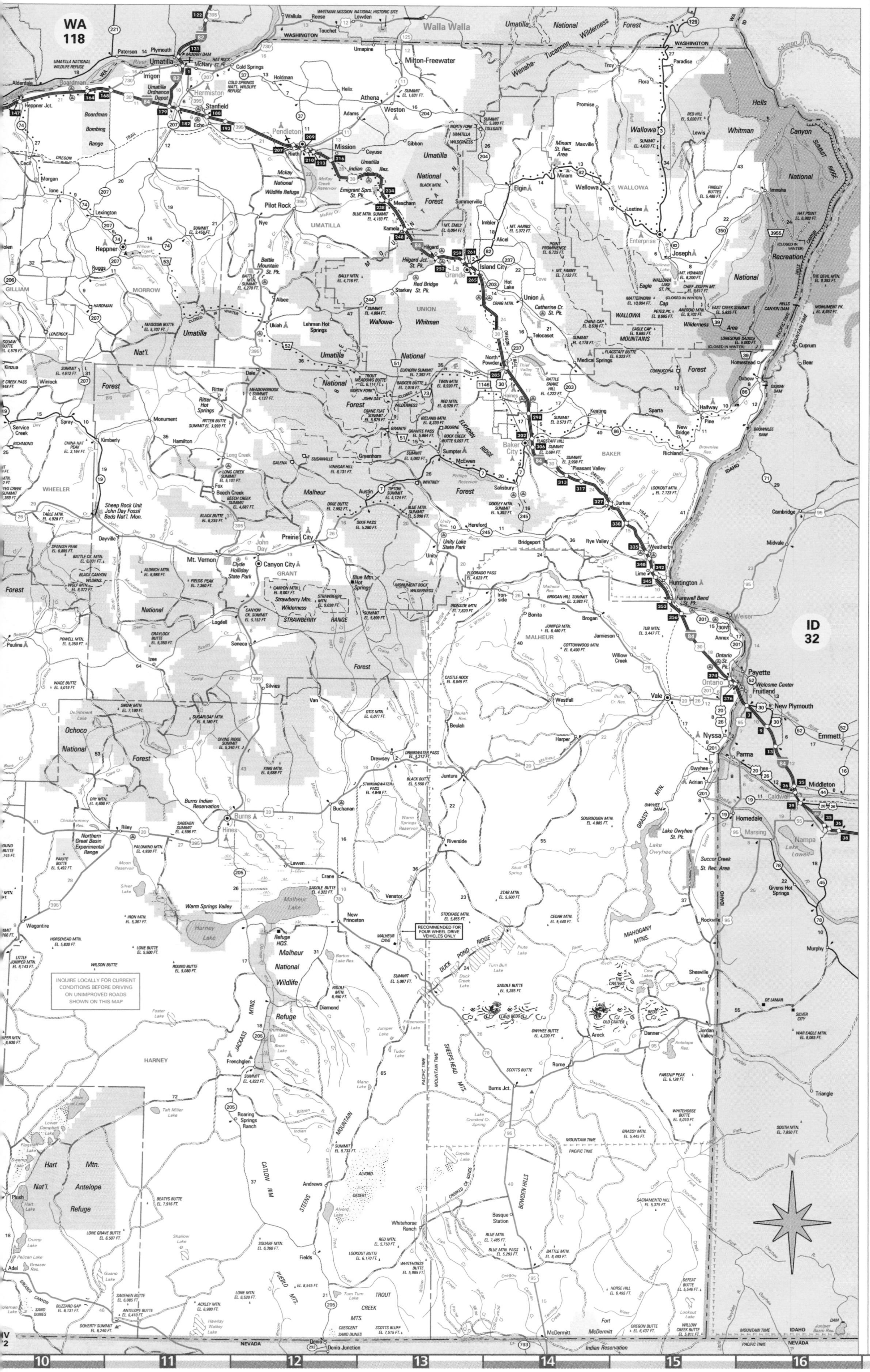

10 11 12 13 14 15 16 17 18

COLUMBIA RIVER SCENIC AREA

PORTLAND AND VICINITY

SALEM

CRATER LAKE NATIONAL PARK

EUGENE

MEDFORD

PENNSYLVANIA DUTCH COUNTRY-LANCASTER AREA

Legend (Lancaster Area):

1. Quality Inn & Suites
2. Sunset Valley Motel
3. Fairfield Inn by Marriott
4. Hilton Garden Inn Lancaster
5. Gardens of Eden Bed & Breakfast
6. Best Western Eden Resort Inn & Suites
7. Hampton Inn-Lancaster
8. Holiday Inn Visitors Center
9. Ramada Inn Brunswick Conference Center
10. The King's Cottage
11. O'Flaherty's Dingeldein House Bed & Breakfast
12. Country Living Inn
13. Hawthorn Inn & Suites
14. Country Inn of Lancaster
15. Travel Inn
16. Howard Johnson Inn
17. Econo Lodge North
18. Econo Lodge South
19. Days Inn
20. Continental Inn
21. Garden Spot Motel
22. Country Inn & Suites by Carlson, Lancaster
23. McIntosh Inn of Lancaster
24. Ramada Inn-Lancaster
25. Rodeway Inn Italian Villa East
26. Classic Inn
27. Lancaster Host Resort & Conference Center
28. Park Inn
29. Fulton Steamboat Inn
30. Willow Valley Family Resort & Conference Center
31. Country Squire Motor Inn
32. The Hollander Motel
33. Comfort Inn
34. Leaman's Country Lodging
35. Leola Village Inn & Suites
36. Kitchen Kettle Village Lodging
37. Travelers Rest Motel
38. Best Western Intercourse Village Inn
39. Intercourse Village Bed & Breakfast Suites
40. Harvest Drive Family Motel
41. Folk Craft Center Bed and Breakfast
42. Village Inn of Bird-In-Hand
43. Amish Country Motel
44. Bird-In-Hand Family Inn
45. Smoketown Motor Lodge
46. Mill Stream Country Inn
47. Quiet Haven Motel
48. Olde Amish Inn
49. Eastbrook Inn
50. Weathervane Motor Court
51. Cherry Lane Motor Inn
52. Candlelight Inn Bed & Breakfast
69. After Eight B&B
70. Best Western Revere Inn & Suites
71. Beiler's Bed & Breakfast Suites & Efficiencies
72. Best Western The Inn at Millersville
73. Dutch Treat Motel
74. Amish Lanterns Motel
75. Historic Strasburg Inn
76. Strasburg Village Inn
77. Carriage House Motor Inn
78. Australian Walkabout Inn B&B

Restaurants:
1. Isaac's Restaurant & Deli
2. The Olde Greenfield Inn
3. Isaac's Restaurant & Deli
4. Stockyard Inn
5. Horse Inn Restaurant
6. Tobias S Frogg
7. Isaac's Restaurant & Deli
8. D & S Brasserie
9. The Pressroom
10. People's Restaurant
11. Mazzi Designed Dining Pennsylvania Dutch
13. Haydn Zug's
21. The Kling House Restaurant
24. Das Cafe Haus
25. Stoltzfus Farm Restaurant
26. Amish Barn Restaurant & Gift Shop
27. Plain & Fancy Farm Dining Room
30. Dinner With Dee Dee
38. Good 'N Plenty Restaurant
12. Miller's Smorgasbord & Bakery
35. Hershey Farm Restaurant
37. Washington House Restaurant
39. Isaac's Restaurant & Deli

HERSHEY

YORK

WILKES-BARRE PENNSYLVANIA
Scale in Miles
Scale in Kilometers

Luzerne, Forty Fort, Plains, Hudson, Kingston, Larksville, Mercy Hosp., Georgetown, Laurel Run, Sugar Notch, Ashley, Newtown, Riverside

SCRANTON PENNSYLVANIA
Scale in Miles
Scale in Kilometers

Scranton Country Club, Dickson City, Throop, Worthington Scranton Campus Penn. State Univ., Mercy Hosp., Dunmore, Memorial Stadium, Pennsylvania Anthracite Heritage Museum, Lackawanna Station, Steamtown Nat'l Hist. Site, Scranton Iron Furnace, Taylor, Old Forge, Moosic, Lackawanna Co. Stadium, Nay Aug Park, Univ. of Scranton, LACKAWANNA

ALLENTOWN
ALLENTOWN-BETHLEHEM
Scale in Miles
Scale in Kilometers

Catasauqua, West Catasauqua, Mechanicsville, Hanoverville, Schoenersville, Lehigh Valley International Airport, Bethlehem, Farmersville, Whitehall, Fullerton, Muhlenberg Medical Center, Butztown, Orefield, Guthsville, Schnecksville, Greenawalds, Moravian College, Middletown, Wescosville, Muhlenberg College, Cetronia, Liberty Bell Shrine, Lehigh University, Fountain Hill, Freemansburg, Steel City, Dorneyville, Lehigh Valley Hospital-Cedar Crest, Farmington, Seidersville, Gauff Hill, Wydnor, Hellertown, Lower Saucon, NORTHAMPTON, LEHIGH

PITTSBURGH AND VICINITY
Scale in Miles
Scale in Kilometers

Mars, Downieville, BUTLER, Freedom, BEAVER, Conway, Bakerstown, Bairdford, Garvers Ferry, ARMSTRONG, Pleasant Hill Church, Warrendale, Wexford, Natrona Hts., Brackenridge, Tarentum, Lower Burrell, Shearersburg, Economy, Baden, Duff City, Bell Acres, North Park, Wildwood, Dorseyville, Creighton, New Kensington, ALLEGHENY, Aliquippa, Ambridge, Wireton, Glenwillard, Sewickley, Osborne, Perrysville, Hartwood Acres, Allison Park, Indianola, Springdale, Cheswick, Logans Ferry, Markle, Ben Avon, Avalon, Bellevue, West View, Glenshaw, Etna, Sharpsburg, Aspinwall, Fox Chapel, Oakmont, Verona, Plum, Penn Hills, New Texas, Sardis, Camp Jo-Ann, Carnot, Coraopolis, Moon Crest, Groveton, Emsworth, McKees Rocks, Pittock, Ingram, Millvale, Highland Park, Wilkinsburg, Boyce Regional Park, WEST-MORELAND, Pittsburgh International Airport, Imperial, Crafton, Mt. Oliver, PITTSBURGH, Churchill, Forest Hills, Monroeville, Murrysville, Oakdale, Rennerdale, Heidelberg, Carnegie, Dormont, Swissvale, Homestead, Braddock, East Pittsburgh, Turtle Creek, Trafford, North Huntingdon, Harrison City, Noblestown, Federal, Mt. Lebanon, Brentwood, Whitehall, West Mifflin, Duquesne, McKeesport, North Irwin, Irwin, McDonald, Morgan, Kirwan, Castle Shannon, Bethel Park, Drayosburg, Port Vue, White Oak, Boston, Treveskyn, Gladden, Bridgeville, Upper St. Clair, Pleasant Hills, Clairton, Versailles, Glassport, Venice, Bishop, Cecil, Muse, South Park, Fair Grounds, Jefferson Hills, WASHINGTON

HARRISBURG PENNSYLVANIA
Scale in Miles
Scale in Kilometers

PERRY, Summerdale, Colonial Park, West Enola, Enola, Harrisburg Area Comm. Col., Harrisburg State Hospital, Penbrook, Progress, West Fairview, Italian L. Park, Farm Show Bldg., Rutherford Heights, Wormleysburg, Reservoir Park, National Civil War Museum, Fire Museum of Greater Harrisburg, Riverfront, State Capitol Art Assoc. of Harrisburg, City Island Park, Oakleigh, Lawnton, Lemoyne, CUMBERLAND, Camp Hill, Steelton, Oberlin, DAUPHIN, Shiremanstown, Enhaut, Bressler, Shiremanstown, New Cumberland, Capital City Airport, Highspire, Green Lane Farms, Allendale, Defense Distribution Region East, Harrisburg International Airport, YORK

ERIE
Scale in Miles
Scale in Kilometers

Lake Erie, Presque Isle State Park, U.S. Coast Guard Station, Presque Isle Bay, Erie Maritime Museum, Homeport Brig. Niagara, Lawrence Park, Wesleyville, Erie Civic Center, Hamot Med. Center, McClelland Park, Penn State Erie, The Behrend College, Frontier Park, Waldameer Park and Water World, St. Vincent Health Ctr., Mercyhurst College, Belle Valley, William L. Scott Park, Erie International Airport, West Millcreek, Zuck Park, Glenwood Park, Kearsarge, Asbury Community Park

ALTOONA
Scale in Miles
Scale in Kilometers

Buckhorn, Mill Run Reservoir, Altoona Railroaders Mem. Mus., Fort Roberdeau, Altoona Hosp., Horseshoe Curve Nat'l Hist. Landmark, Kittanning Res., Bon Secours Holy Family Sys., James E. Van Zandt VA Mem. Med. Ctr., Baker Mansion Museum, Lake Altoona, Highland Park, Benzel's Pretzel Factory, Sugar Run, Lakemont, Lakemont Park, Frankstown, Hollidaysburg, Duncansville, State Game Lands 109

STATE COLLEGE
Miles
Kilometers

University Park Airport, Fox Hill Rd., Penn State Research Park, Agricultural Arena, Centre Community Hosp., Pennsylvania State University, Beaver Stadium, Spring Creek Park, Lemont, Walnut Springs Park, Palmer Museum of Art, Lederer Park, Haymarket Park, Orchard Park, Oak Hill, Shingletown

JOHNSTOWN
Scale in Miles
Scale in Kilometers

Hinckston Run Reservoir, Conemaugh, South Fork, Johnstown Flood Mus., Brownstown, Johnstown Inclined Plane, Stackhouse Park, Conemaugh Mem. Med. Center, Johnstown-Cambria County Airport, Grandview Cem., Ferndale, Geistown, Elton, CAMBRIA, SOMERSET

GETTYSBURG NATIONAL MILITARY PARK PENNSYLVANIA
Scale in Miles
Scale in Kilometers

Eternal Light Peace Memorial, Gettysburg Coll., Gettysburg, National Park Visitor Center, Gettysburg Nat'l Cem., Cyclorama Center, Culps Hill Observation Tower, Spangler's Spring, SEMINARY RIDGE, Gen. Meade's Hqs., Eisenhower Nat'l Hist. Site, The Peach Orchard, The Wheatfield, Devil's Den, Little Round Top, Confederate Memorial, Round Top

READING
Scale in Miles
Scale in Kilometers

Tuckerton, Temple, Laureldale, Blue Marsh, Leinbachs, Mid-Atlantic Air Mus., Reading Regional Airport, Berks Co. Heritage Center, Wernersville, Sinking Spring, Reading Hosp. & Med. Ctr., Hampden Park, Pennside, West Lawn, Reading Public Museum, St. Joseph Med. Ctr., Pagoda, Mt. Penn, Wyomissing, Stony Creek Mills, St. Lawrence, Alvernia Coll., Shillington, Gouglersville, Mohnton

DRIVING DISTANCES IN MILES

SEE ALSO MILEAGE TABLE PAGE 144

	ALLENTOWN	ALTOONA	ERIE	GETTYSBURG	HARRISBURG	JOHNSTOWN	LANCASTER	PHILADELPHIA	PITTSBURGH	READING	SCRANTON	YORK
ERIE	371	227	N/A	306	300	178	337	403	128	358	322	329
HARRISBURG	85	134	300	37		136	38	105	198	59	123	24
PHILADELPHIA	63	236	404	130	105	238	79		297	62	124	105
PITTSBURGH	283	96	128	184	198	99	237	297		N/A	235	220
SCRANTON	76	185	322	160	123	229	137	124	321	106		146

Western PENNSYLVANIA

WESTERN PENNSYLVANIA

Towns keyed to maps on pages 97 thru 99.

Towns with asterisk (*) appear on maps on page 97.

Scale in Miles

Scale in Kilometers

ONE INCH EQUALS APPROXIMATELY 12.5 MILES OR 20.2 KILOMETERS

The area of this map is in the Eastern Time Zone.

FOR ADJOINING AREA SEE PAGES 100-101

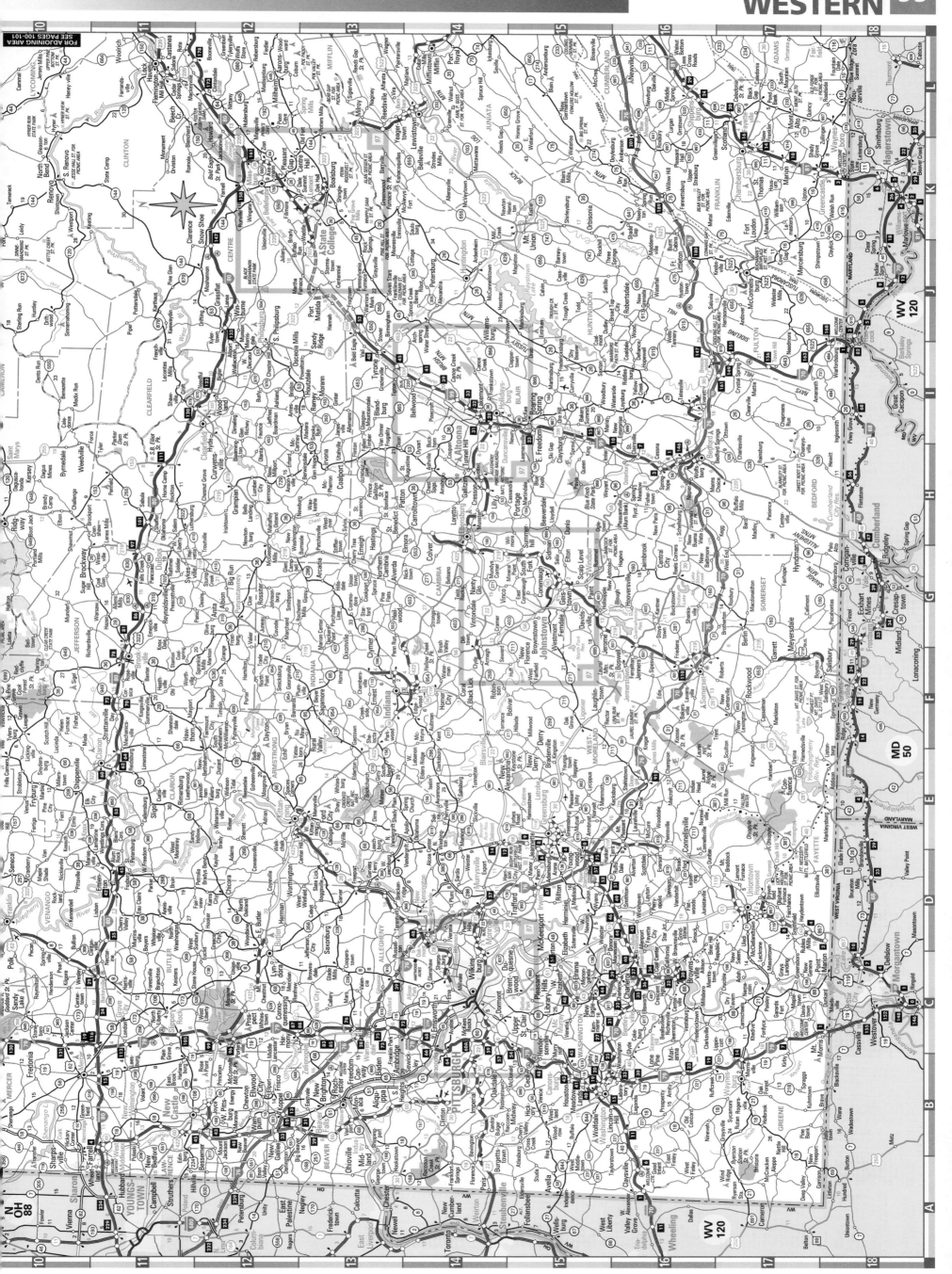

DRIVING DISTANCES IN MILES

SEE ALSO MILEAGE TABLE PAGE 144

	ALLENTOWN	ALTOONA	ERIE	GETTYSBURG	HARRISBURG	JOHNSTOWN	LANCASTER	PHILADELPHIA	PITTSBURGH	READING	SCRANTON	YORK
ERIE	371	227	N/A	306	300	178	337	403	128	358	322	329
HARRISBURG	85	134	300	37	—	105	38	105	198	59	123	24
PHILADELPHIA	63	236	404	130	105	238	79	N/A	297	62	124	105
PITTSBURGH	283	96	128	184	198	99	237	297	N/A	259	321	220
SCRANTON	76	185	322	160	123	223	137	124	321	106	N/A	146

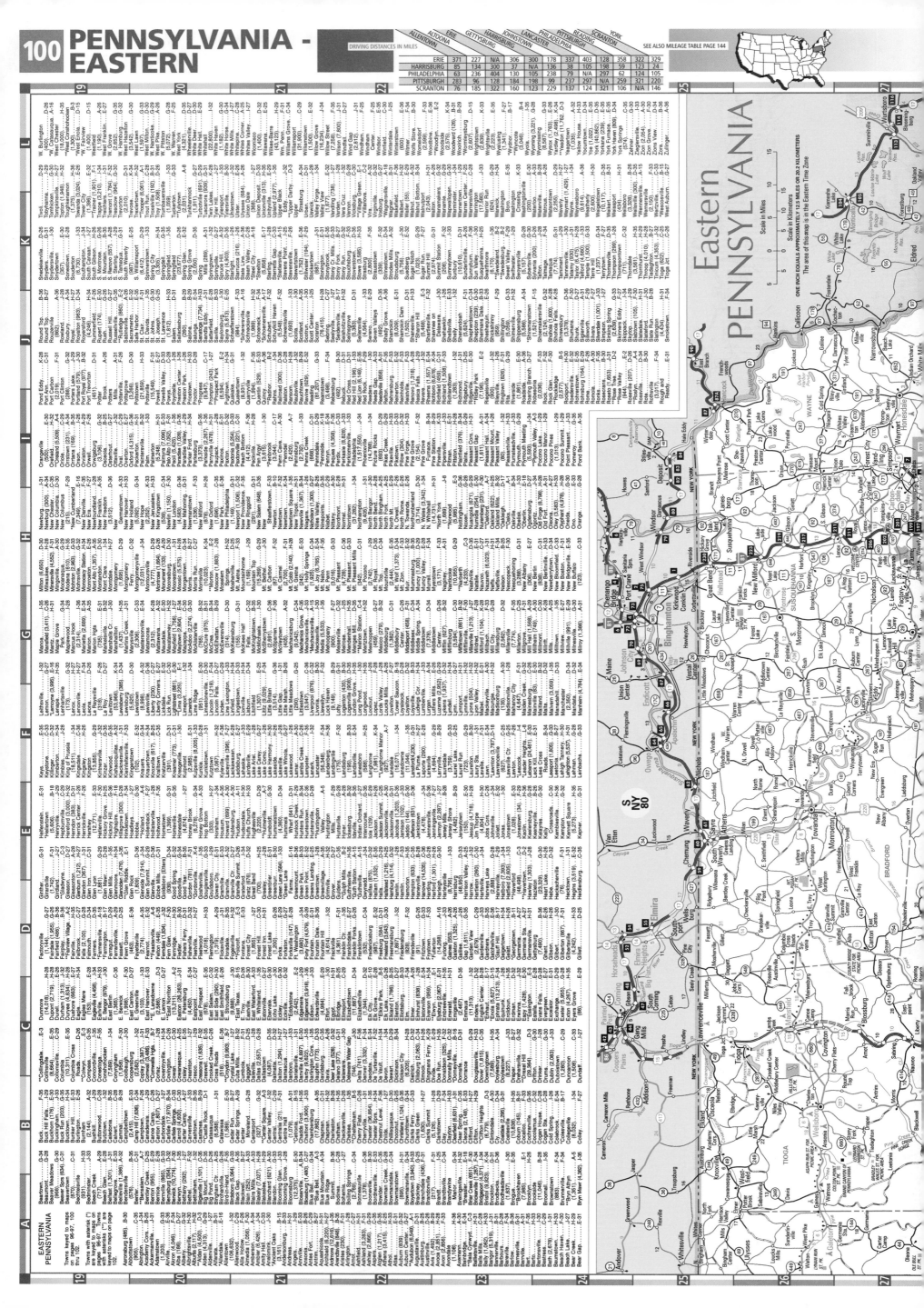

Eastern PENNSYLVANIA

Scale in Miles

ONE INCH EQUALS APPROXIMATELY 12.5 MILES OR 20.2 KILOMETERS
The area of this map is in the Eastern Time Zone

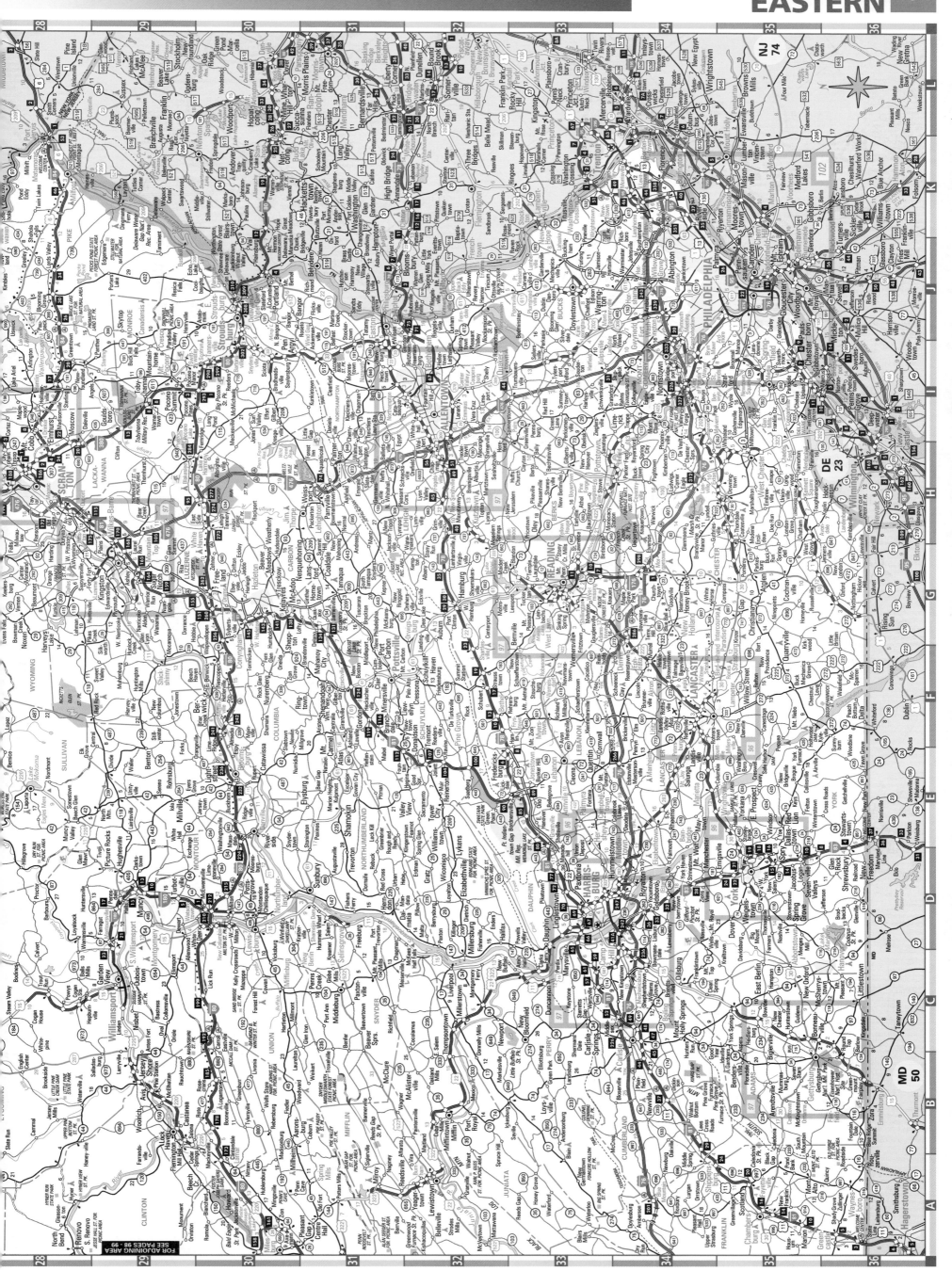

FOR ADJOINING AREA SEE PAGES 98 - 99

PHILADELPHIA-CAMDEN AREA

Scale in Miles

Scale in Kilometers

Downtown PHILADELPHIA PA

Scale in Tenths of a Mile

Scale in Tenths of a Kilometer

■ Major Points of Interest ● Other Points of Interest ■ Station ▬ Rapid Transit

PRINCIPAL POINTS OF INTEREST

Academy of Music	K-6
Academy of Natural Sciences	I-5
African American Museum of Philadelphia	J-7
Amtrak 30th St. Station	J-3
Antique Row	K-7
Arch Street Meeting House	I-9
Atwater Kent Museum	J-8
Azalea Garden	H-3
Benjamin Franklin's Grave Christ Church Bur. Grounds	J-9
Betsy Ross House	I-9
Bishop White House	J-9
The Bourse	J-8
Bus Depot	I-7
Carpenter's Hall	J-8
Cathedral Basilica of S.S. Peter and Paul	I-5
Children's Hospital of Phila.	K-2
Chinese Cultural Center	I-7
Christ Church	J-9
City Hall	J-6
Civil War Library and Museum	K-5
The College of Physicians of Philadelphia	J-5
Comm. Col. of Philadelphia	H-5
Drexel University	J-2,3
Eastern State Penitentiary	G-4
Edgar Allan Poe Nat'l Historic House	H-7
Elfreth's Alley	I-9
Fairmount Park	F-1,G-2
Fireman's Museum	I-9
First Baptist Church	J-6
First Unitarian Church	J-5
Forrest Theatre	K-6
Franklin Court	J-8
Franklin Field	K-2
Franklin Institute Science Museum & Fels Planetarium	I-4
Franklin Square	I-8
Free Quaker Meeting House	I-8
German Society of Pennsylvania	H-6
Girard College	F-6
Graduate Hospital	K-5
Great Plaza	J-9
Hahnemann University Hospital	I-6
Hayesville	A-5
Head House Sq.	J-9
Hill-Physick-Keith House	K-8
Holiday Boat Tours	J-9
Independence Hall & Congress Hall	J-8
Independence Nat'l Historical Park	J-8
Independence Seaport Museum	J-9
Institute of Contemporary Arts	J-1
Italian Market	L-7
Jefferson Medical College of Thomas Jefferson University	J-7
Lemon Hill Mans.	G-2
Liberty Bell Pavilion	J-8
Lights of Liberty Show	J-8
Merriam Theatre	K-6
Mid-Atlantic Automobile Club	J-4
Moore College of Art	I-5
Mother Bethel A.M.E. Church	K-8
Mus. of American Art of the Penn. Academy of The Fine Arts	I-6
National Archives Mid-Atlantic Region	J-7
National Guard Armory	J-2
National Park Visitor's Center	K-9
New Hall Military Museum	J-8
Norman Rockwell Museum	J-8
Old City Hall	J-8
Old Pine St. Presbyterian Church	K-8
Old St. Joseph's Church	J-8
Old St. Mary's Church	K-8
Pa. Horticulture Society	J-8
Palestra	K-2
Peirce College	K-2
Penn Center Station	J-5
Penn's Landing	J-9
Pennsylvania Hospital	K-7
Philadelphia Ethical Society	J-5
Philadelphia Inquirer Building	I-6
Philadelphia Maritime Museum	J-8
Philadelphia Museum of Art	H-4
Philadelphia Visitor's Center	J-5
Philadelphia Zoo	G-1
Please Touch Museum	I-4
Police Hdqrs.	I-8
Polish American Cultural Center	J-8
Powel House	J-8
The Presbyterian Historical Society	K-8
Presbyterian Medical Center of Philadelphia	J-1
Reading Terminal Market	J-7
Rittenhouse Square	K-5
Rodin Museum	I-4
Rosenbach Museum and Library	K-6
St. George's United Methodist Church	I-9
St. Peter's Church	J-9
Second Bank of the U.S.	J-8
Society Hill	K-9
Spirit of Philadelphia	J-9
State Office Bldg.	H-6
Thaddeus Kosciuszko National Memorial	K-9
Thomas Jefferson University Hospital	J-7
Todd House	J-8
Univ. of Penn.	J,K-2
Univ. of Pennsylvania Hospital	K-2
Univ. of the Arts	K-6
University Mus. of Archaeology & Anthropology	K-2
University Science Center	I-2
U.S. Customs House	J-9
U.S. Mint	I-8
U.S.S. Becuna	J-9
U.S.S. Olympia	J-9
Veteran Affairs Med. Cen.	K-1
Veterinary Hospital	K-2
Vietnam Veterans Memorial	K-9
Walnut Street Theatre	J-7
Washington Sq.	J-8
Waterworks	H-4
Wills Eye Hosp.	J-7
Y.M. & Y.W.H.A.	K-6
Y.M.C.A.	I-6

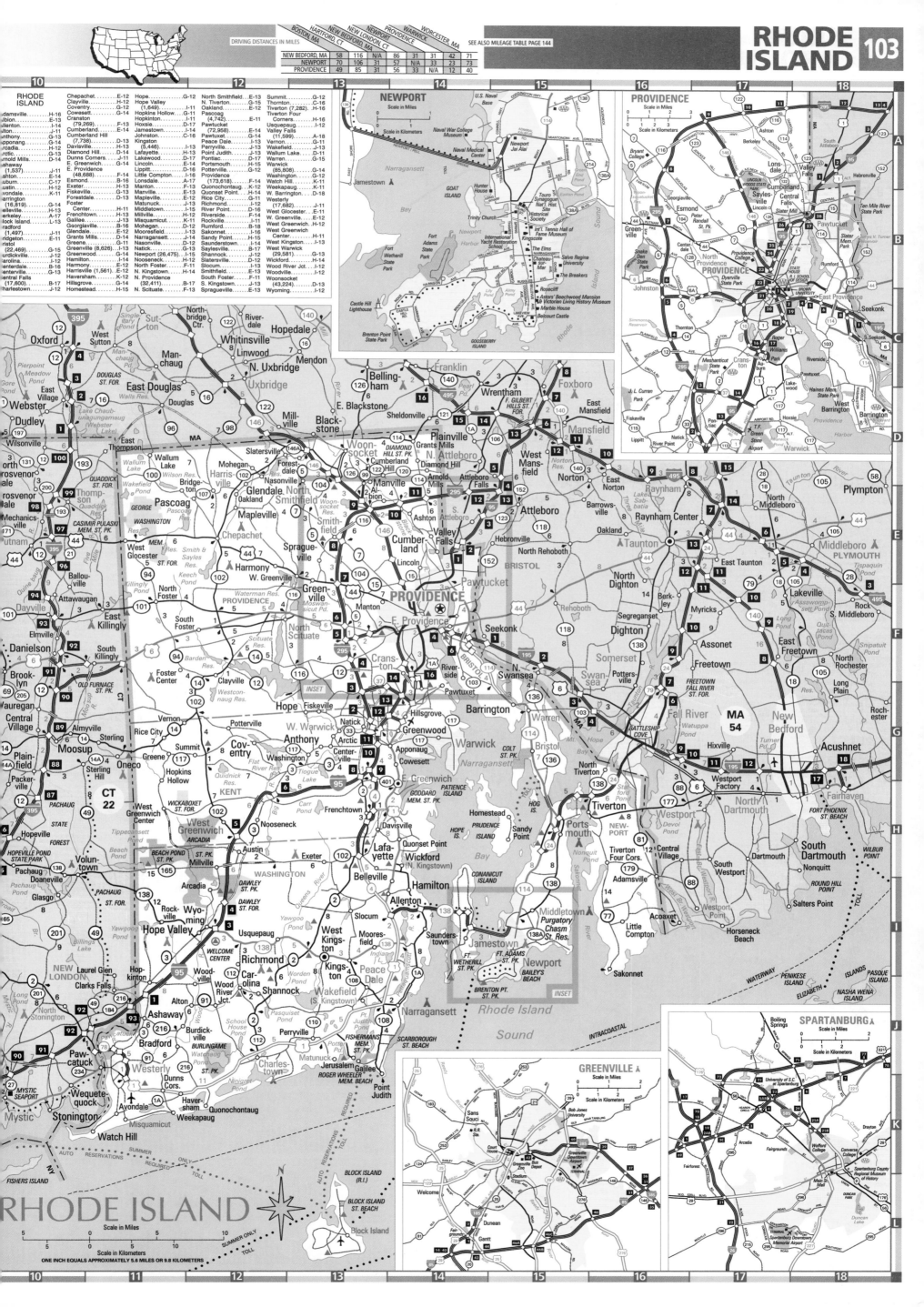

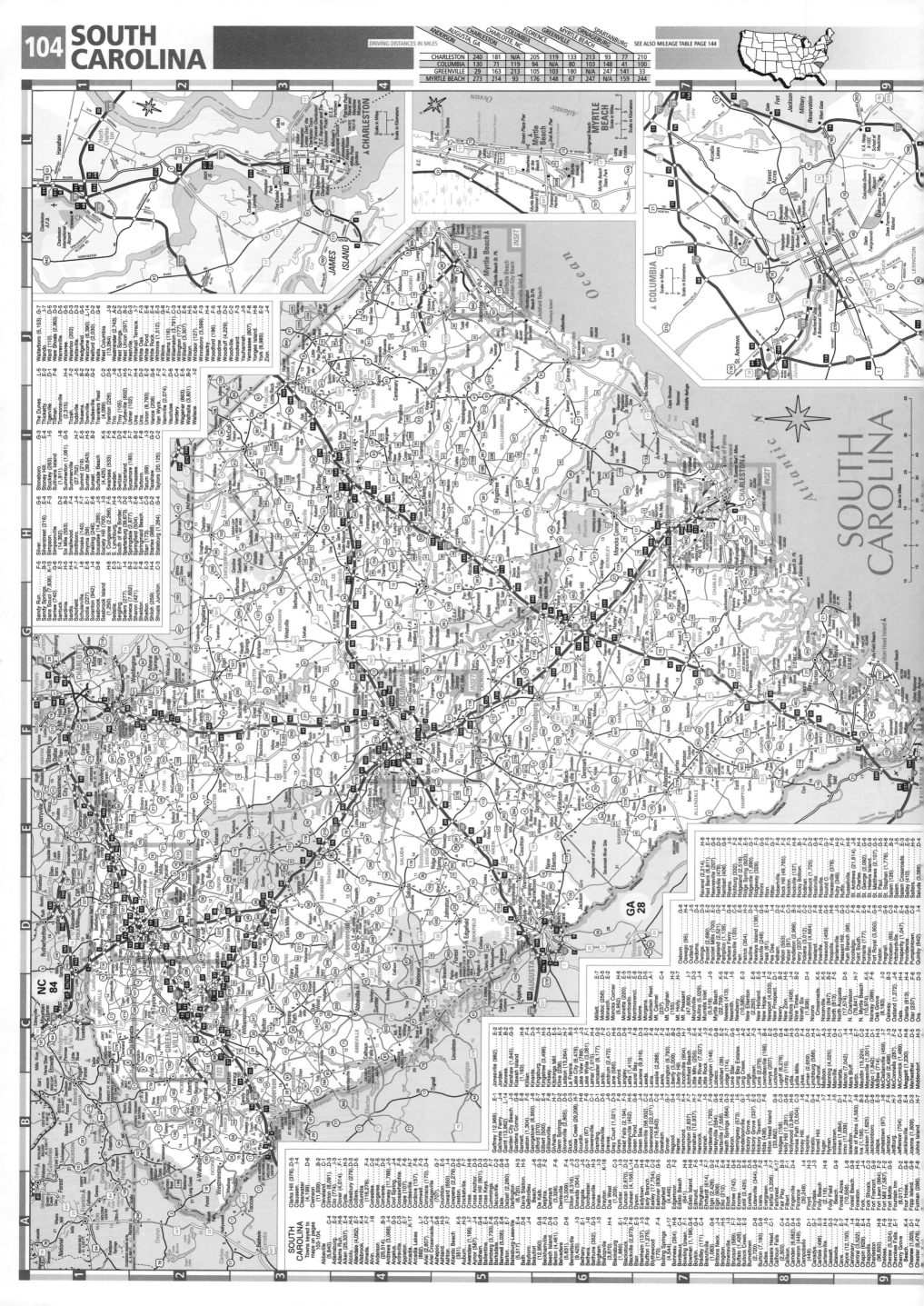

DRIVING DISTANCES IN MILES   SEE ALSO MILEAGE TABLE PAGE 144

	ANDERSON	AUGUSTA GA	CHARLESTON	CHARLOTTE, NC	COLUMBIA	FLORENCE	GREENVILLE	MYRTLE BEACH	ORANGEBURG	SPARTANBURG
CHARLESTON	240	181	N/A	205	119	133	213	93	77	210
COLUMBIA	130	71	119	94	N/A	80	103	148	41	100
GREENVILLE	29	163	213	105	103	180	N/A	247	141	33
MYRTLE BEACH	273	214	93	176	148	67	247	N/A	159	244

SOUTH CAROLINA

DRIVING DISTANCES IN MILES

SEE ALSO MILEAGE TABLE PAGE 144

	ABERDEEN	MITCHELL	PIERRE	RAPID CITY	REDFIELD	SIOUX FALLS	SPEARFISH	WATERTOWN
PIERRE	160	153	N/A	193	126	224	235	196
RAPID CITY	345	275	193	N/A	337	347	48	402
SIOUX FALLS	204	73	224	347	177	N/A	391	104

SOUTH DAKOTA

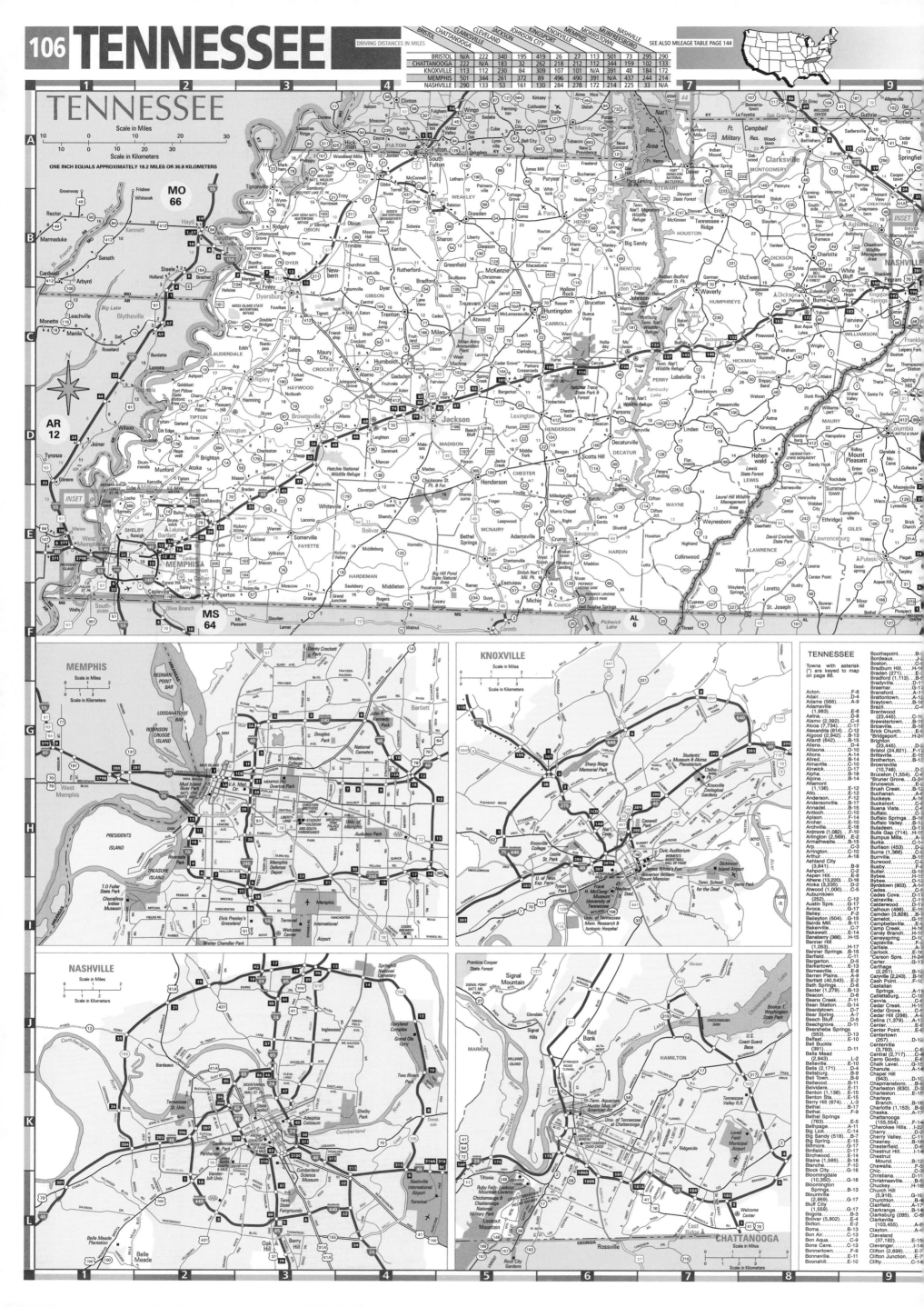

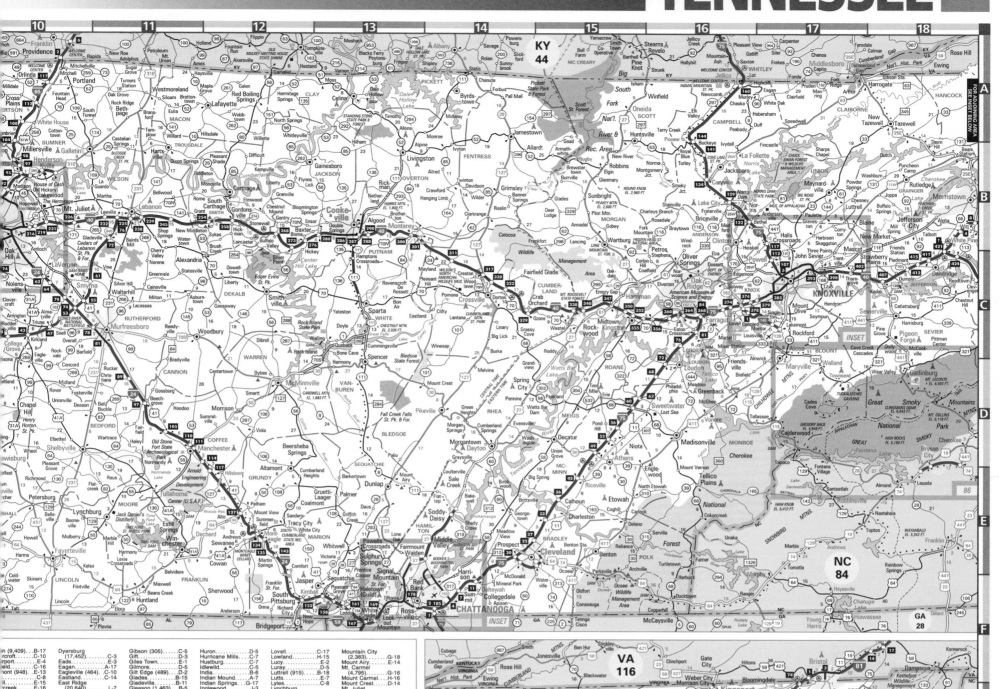

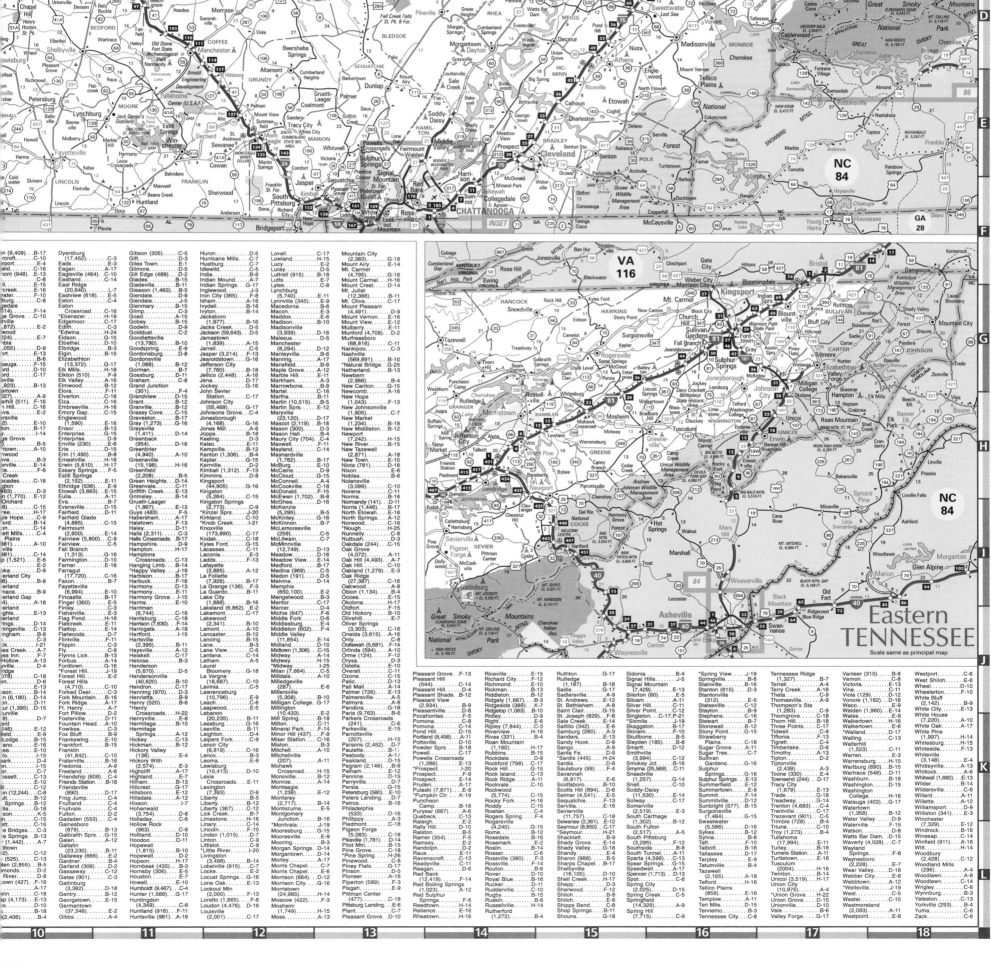

Eastern TENNESSEE

Scale same as principal map

DRIVING DISTANCES IN MILES

SEE ALSO MILEAGE TABLE PAGE 144

	AMARILLO	AUSTIN	BEAUMONT	CORPUS CHRISTI	DALLAS	EL PASO	FORT WORTH	HOUSTON	LAREDO	LUBBOCK	SAN ANTONIO	WICHITA FALLS
AUSTIN	616	N/A	247	217	194	618	188	162	232	420	79	301
DALLAS	363	194	322	409	N/A	636	31	239	425	346	272	139
EL PASO	415	618	830	695	636	N/A	601	746	702	450	545	599
HOUSTON	699	162	87	219	239	746	267	N/A	347	571	198	377
SAN ANTONIO	547	79	281	143	272	545	265	198	156	428	N/A	378

TEXAS

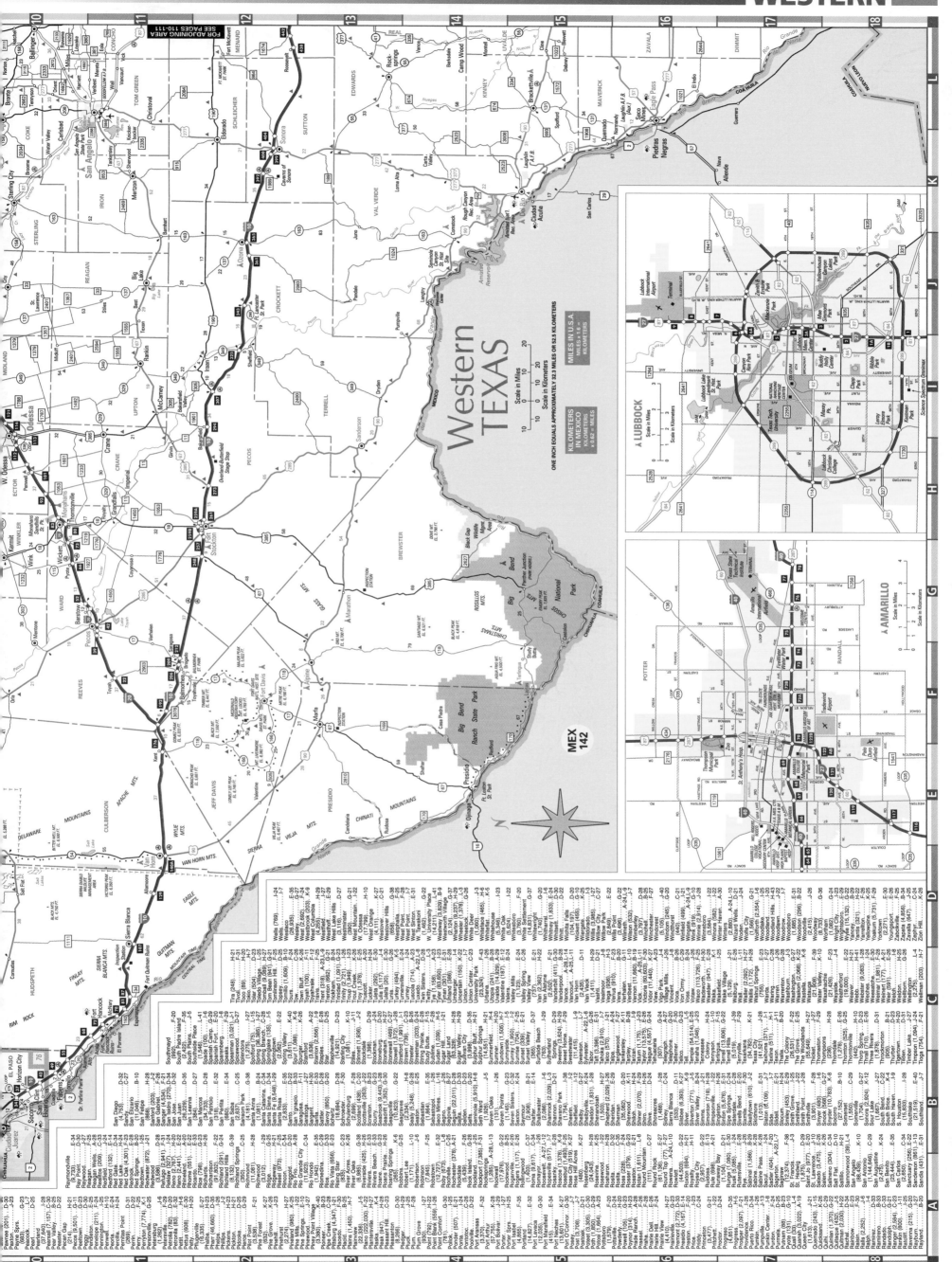

FOR ADJOINING AREA
SEE PAGES 110-111

Western TEXAS

MEX 142

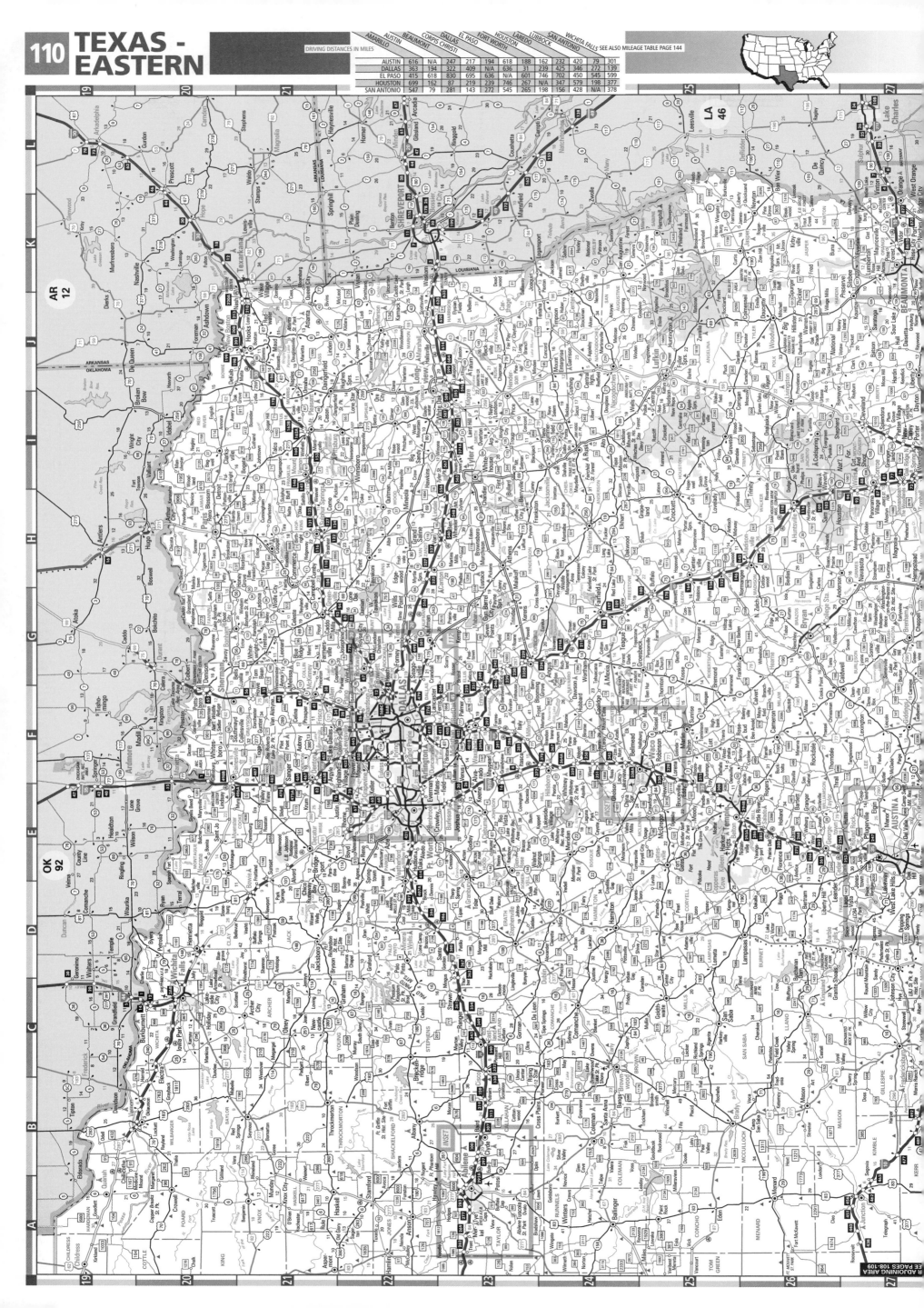

	AMARILLO	AUSTIN	BEAUMONT	CORPIS CHRISTI	DALLAS	EL PASO	FORT WORTH	HOUSTON	LAREDO	LUBBOCK	SAN ANTONIO	WICHITA FALLS
AUSTIN	616	N/A	247	217	194	618	188	162	232	420	79	301
DALLAS	363	194	322	409	N/A	636	31	239	425	346	272	139
EL PASO	415	618	830	695	636	N/A	601	746	702	450	545	599
HOUSTON	699	162	87	219	239	746	267	N/A	347	579	198	377
SAN ANTONIO	547	79	281	143	272	545	265	198	156	428	N/A	378

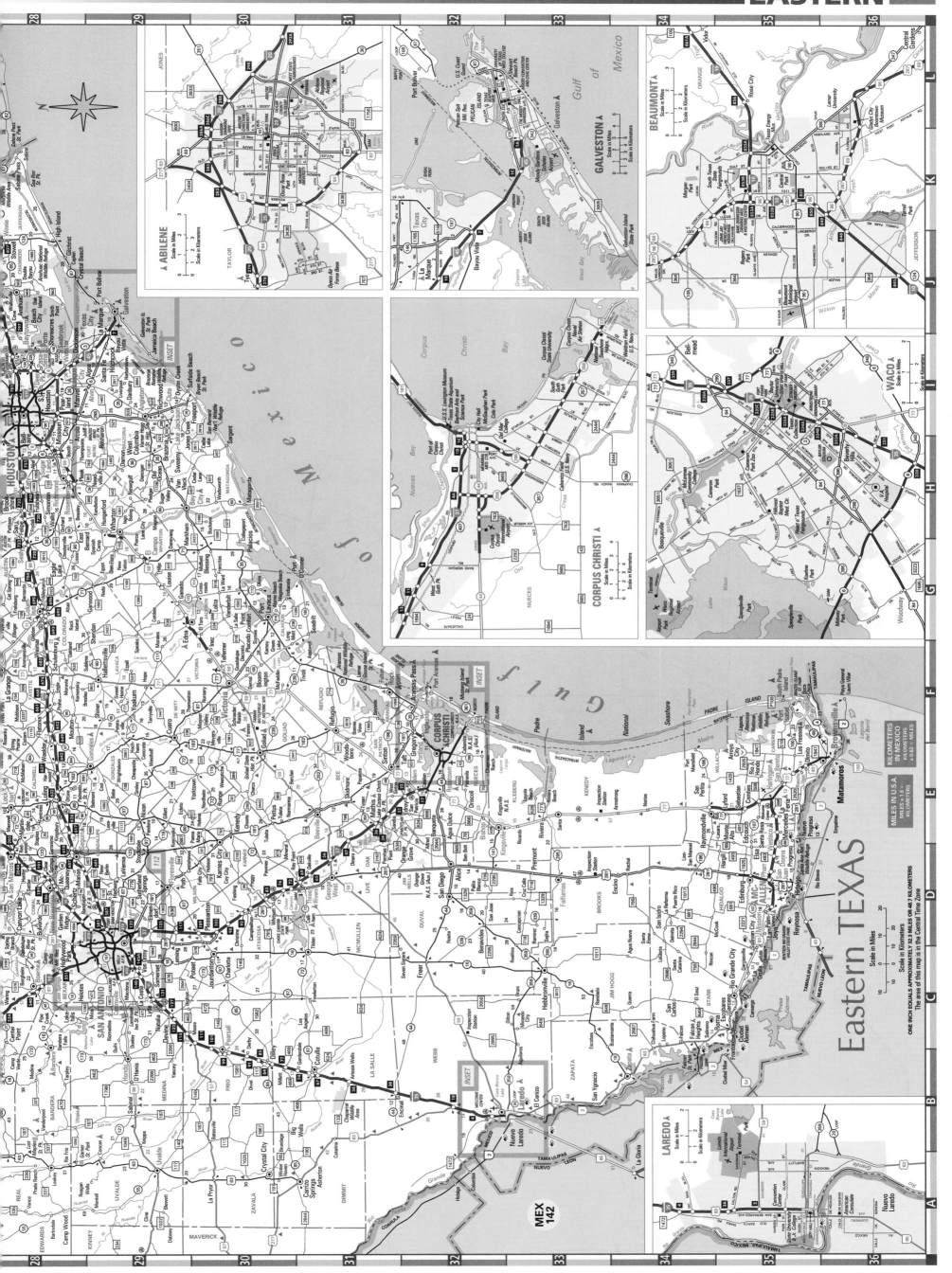

ABILENE
Scale in Miles

CORPUS CHRISTI
Scale in Miles

BEAUMONT
Scale in Miles

WACO
Scale in Miles

LAREDO
Scale in Miles

GALVESTON
Scale in Miles

Eastern TEXAS

Scale in Miles

ONE INCH EQUALS APPROXIMATELY 23.3 MILES OR 48.7 KILOMETERS
The area of this map is in the Central Time Zone

MILES IN U.S.A.

KILOMETERS IN MEXICO

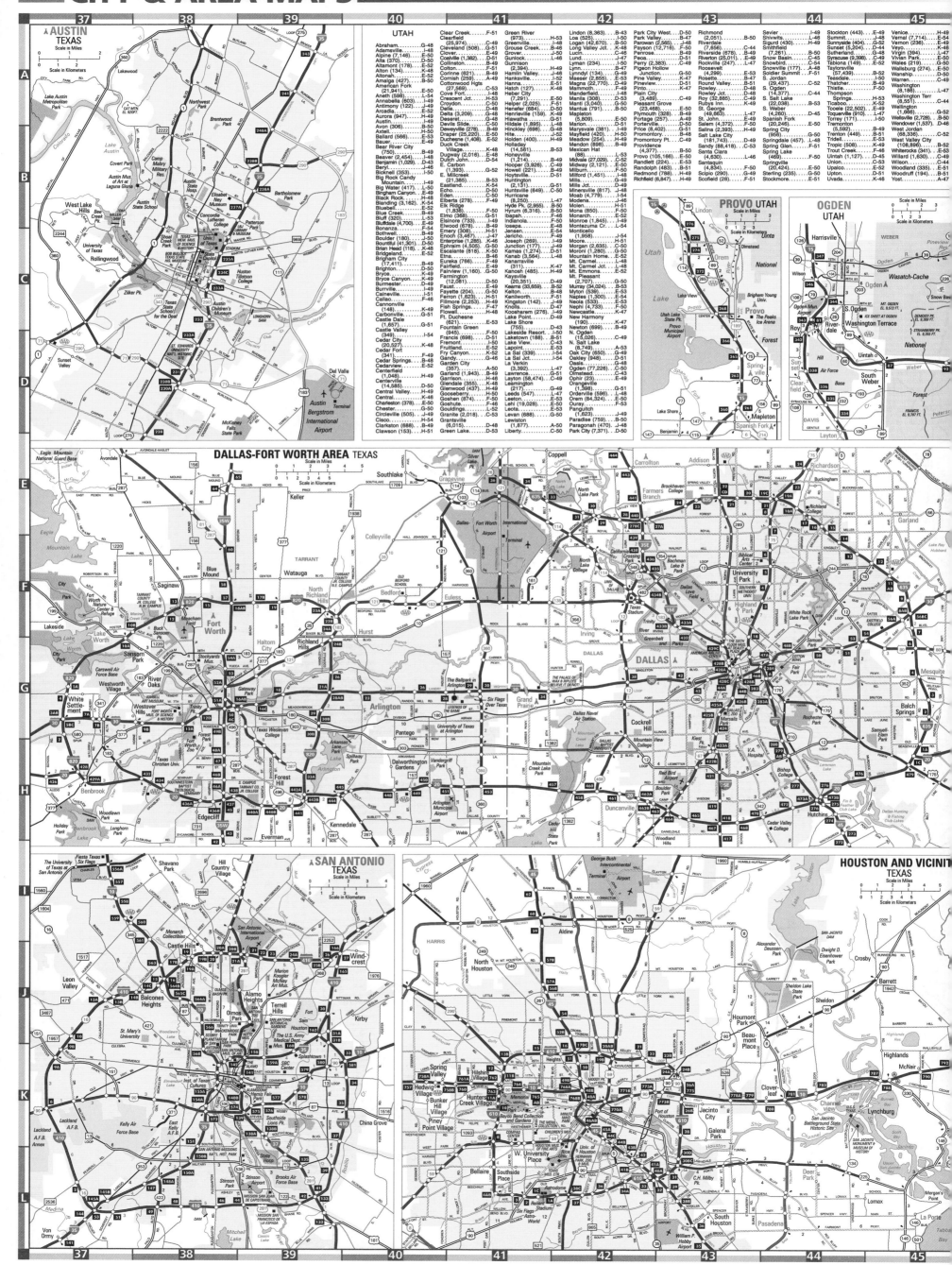

Maps include: AUSTIN TEXAS; DALLAS-FORT WORTH AREA TEXAS; SAN ANTONIO TEXAS; HOUSTON AND VICINITY TEXAS; PROVO UTAH; OGDEN UTAH; and a UTAH place-name index.

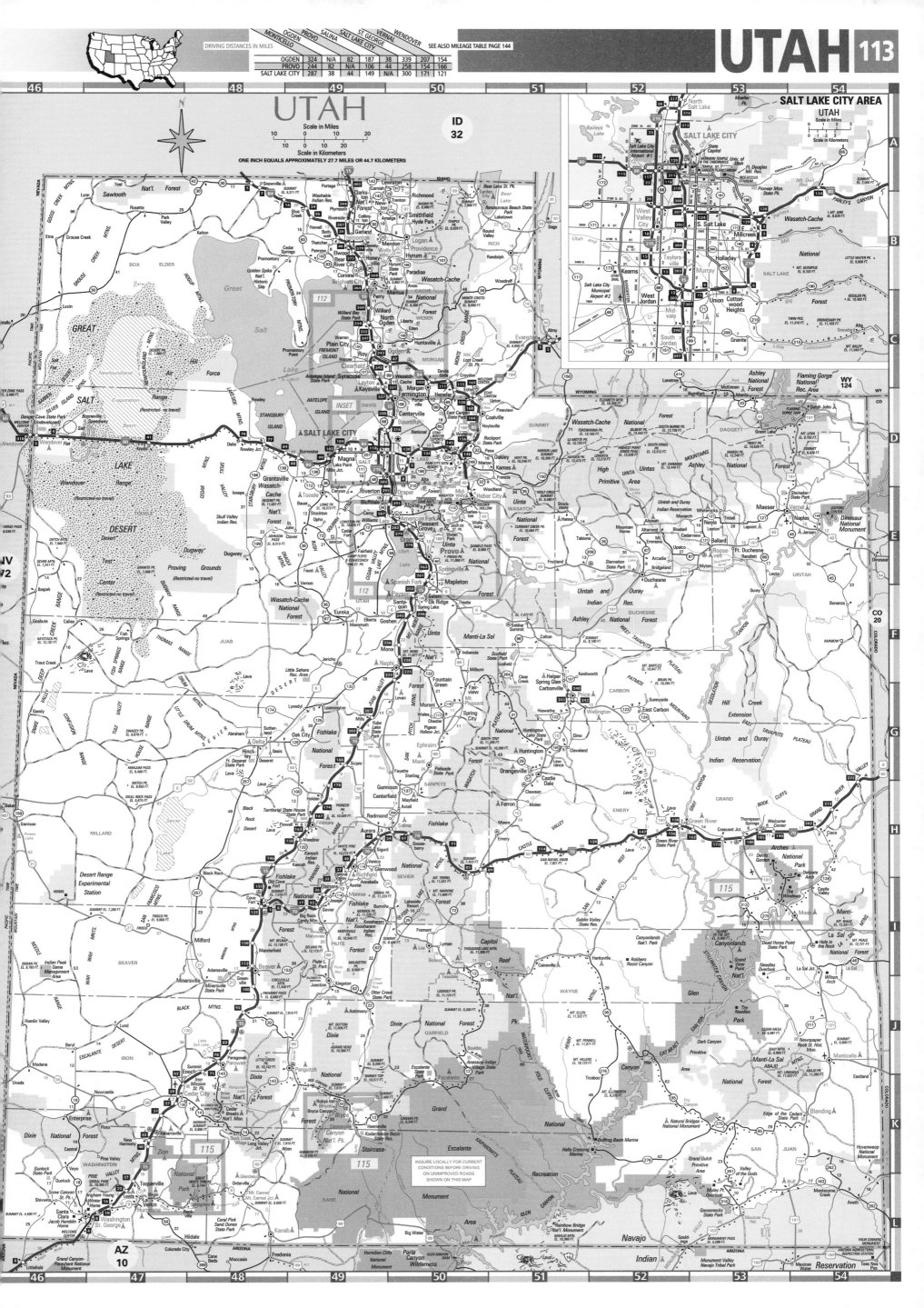

SEE ALSO MILEAGE TABLE PAGE 144

DRIVING DISTANCES IN MILES

	OGDEN			ST. GEORGE		VERNAL	WENDOVER
	MONTICELLO	PROVO	SALINA	SALT LAKE CITY			
OGDEN	324	N/A	82	187	38	339	207	154
PROVO	244	82	N/A	106	44	258	154	166
SALT LAKE CITY	287	38	44	149	N/A	300	171	121

UTAH

Scale in Miles

ONE INCH EQUALS APPROXIMATELY 27.7 MILES OR 44.7 KILOMETERS

SALT LAKE CITY AREA

UTAH

INQUIRE LOCALLY FOR CURRENT CONDITIONS BEFORE DRIVING ON UNIMPROVED ROADS SHOWN ON THIS MAP

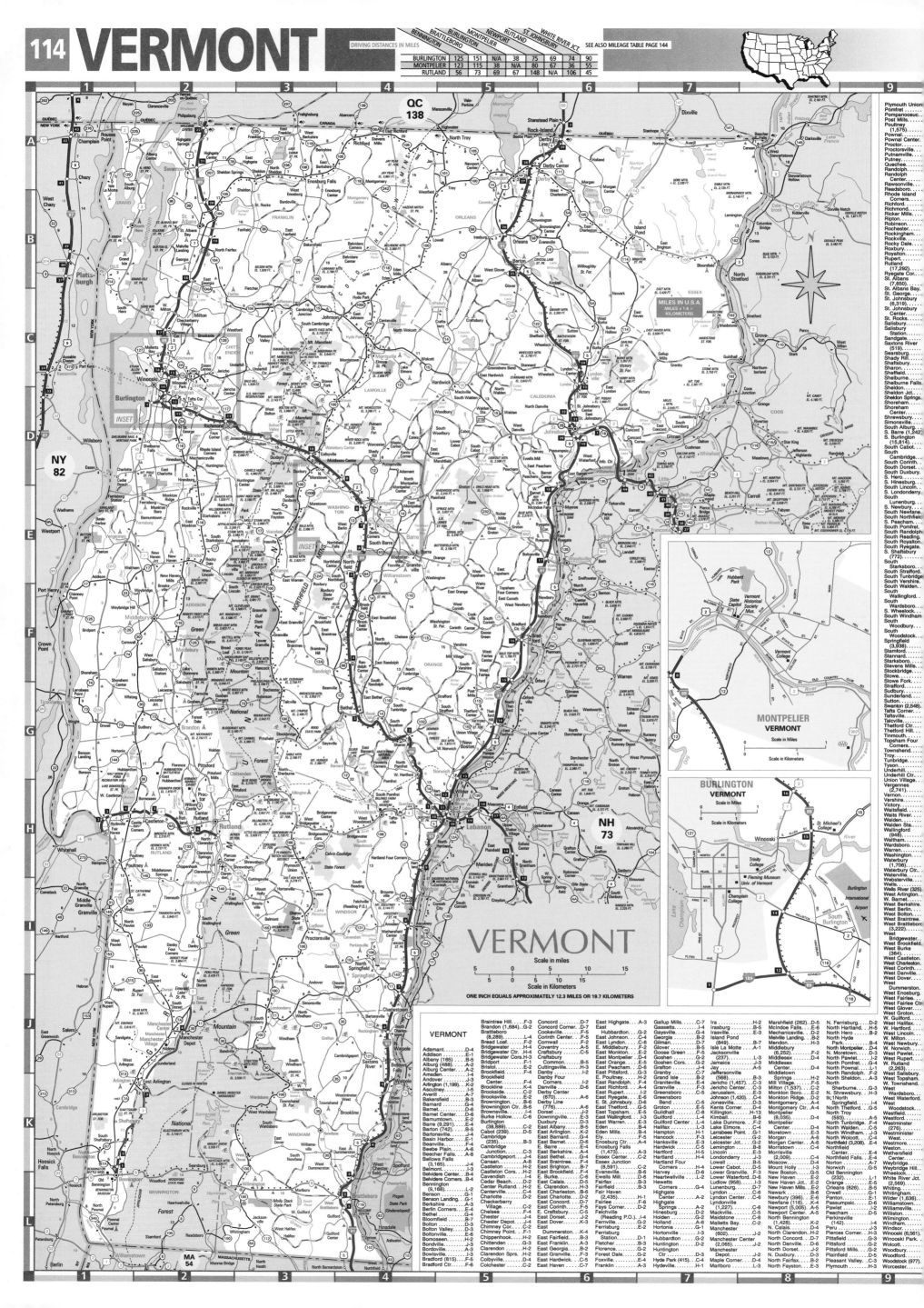

DRIVING DISTANCES IN MILES

SEE ALSO MILEAGE TABLE PAGE 144

	BENNINGTON	BRATTLEBORO	BURLINGTON	MONTPELIER	NEWPORT	RUTLAND	ST. JOHNSBURY	WHITE RIVER JCT.
BURLINGTON	125	151	N/A	38	75	69	74	90
MONTPELIER	123	115	38	N/A	80	67	36	55
RUTLAND	56	73	69	67	148	N/A	106	45

VERMONT

MONTPELIER
VERMONT
Scale in Miles
Scale in Kilometers

BURLINGTON
VERMONT
Scale in Miles
Scale in Kilometers

VERMONT
Scale in miles
Scale in Kilometers
ONE INCH EQUALS APPROXIMATELY 12.3 MILES OR 19.7 KILOMETERS

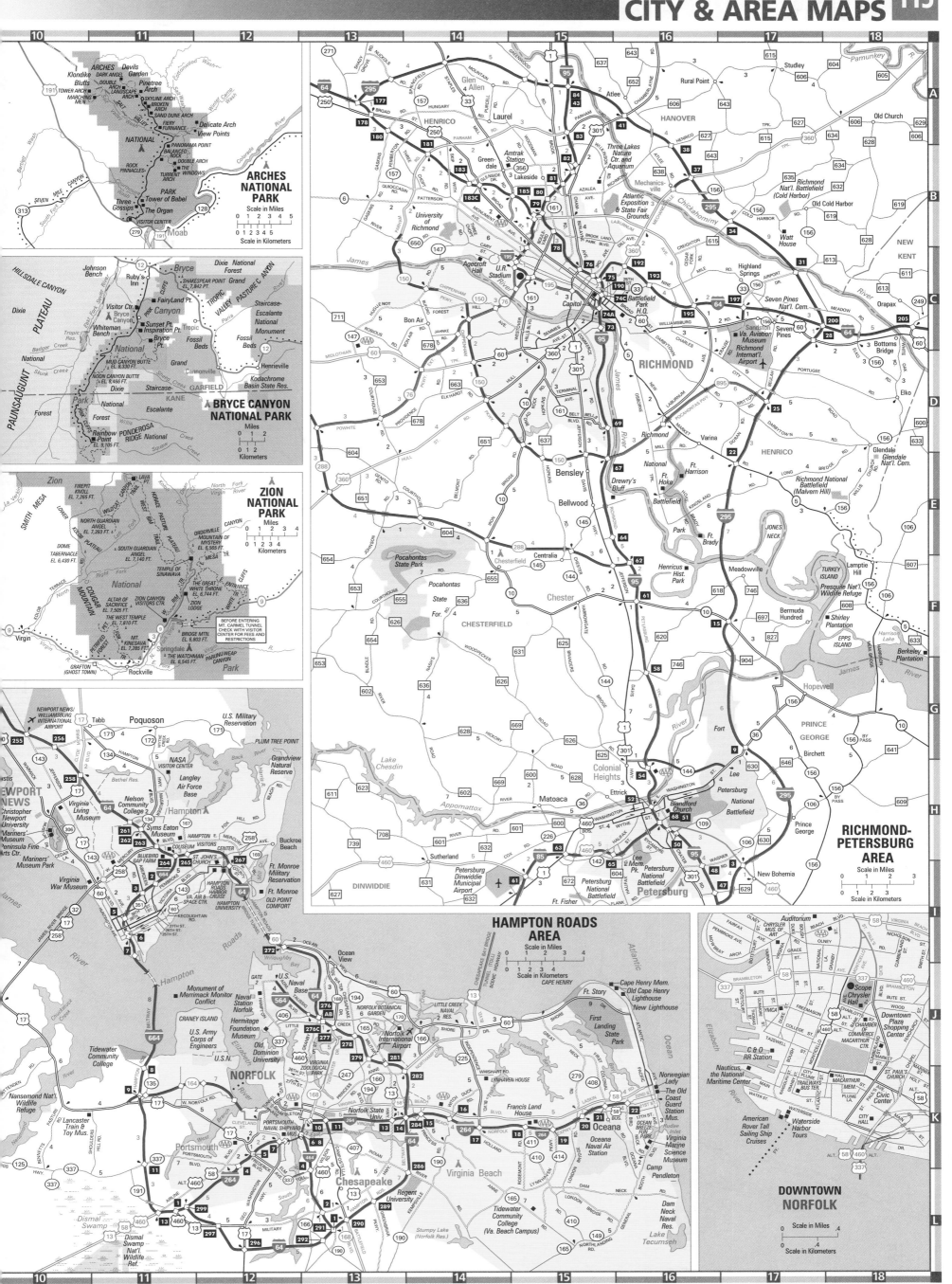

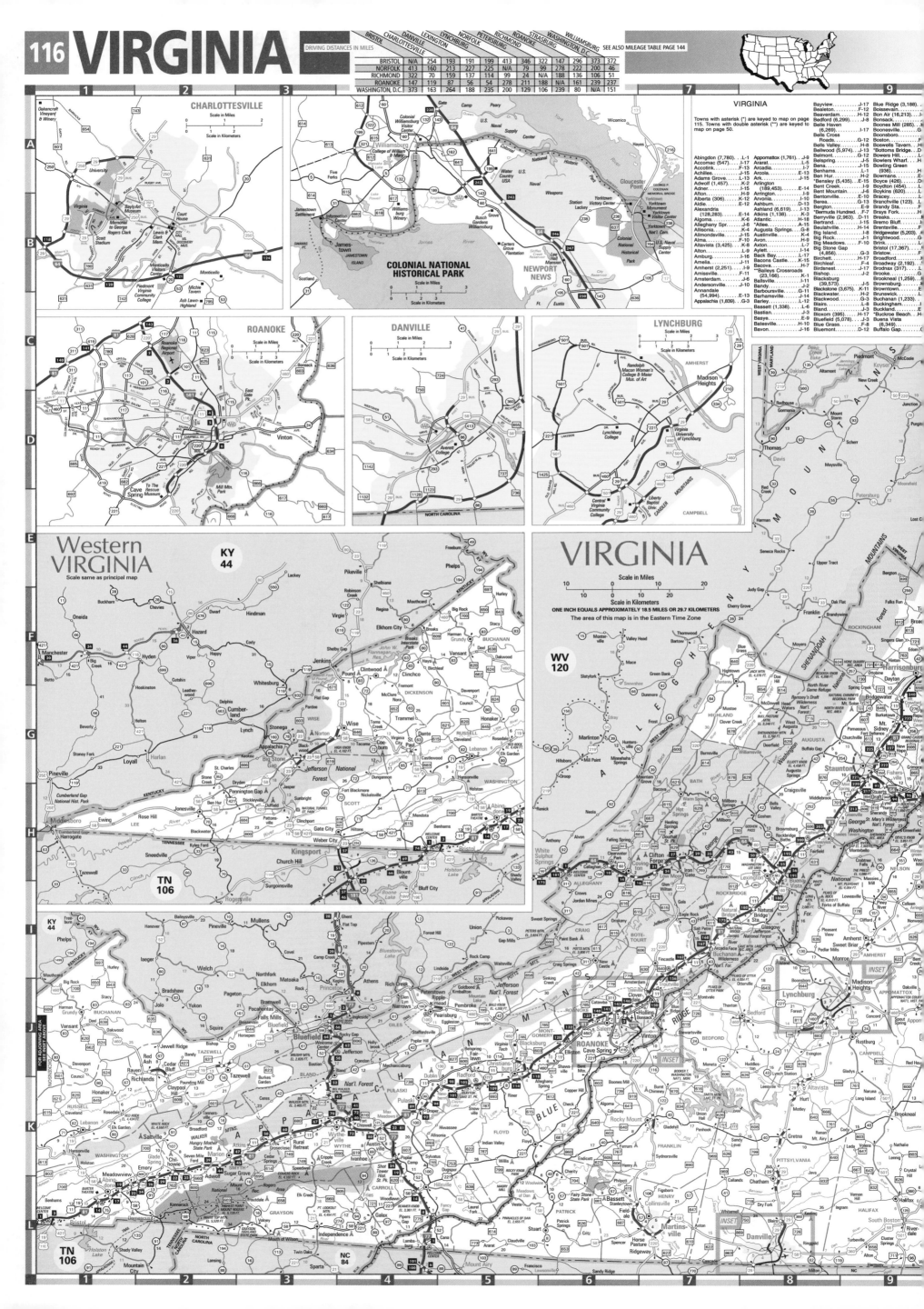

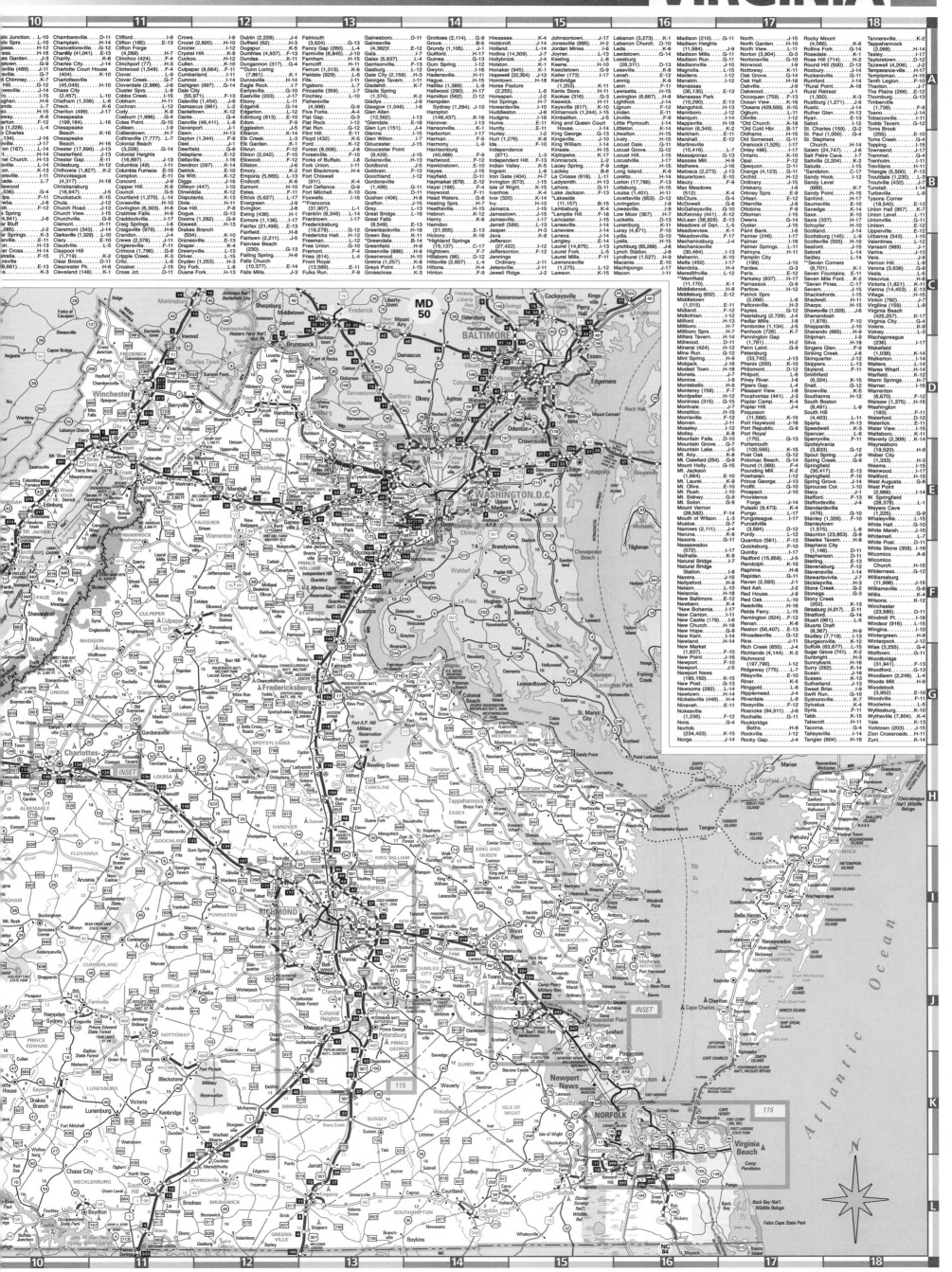

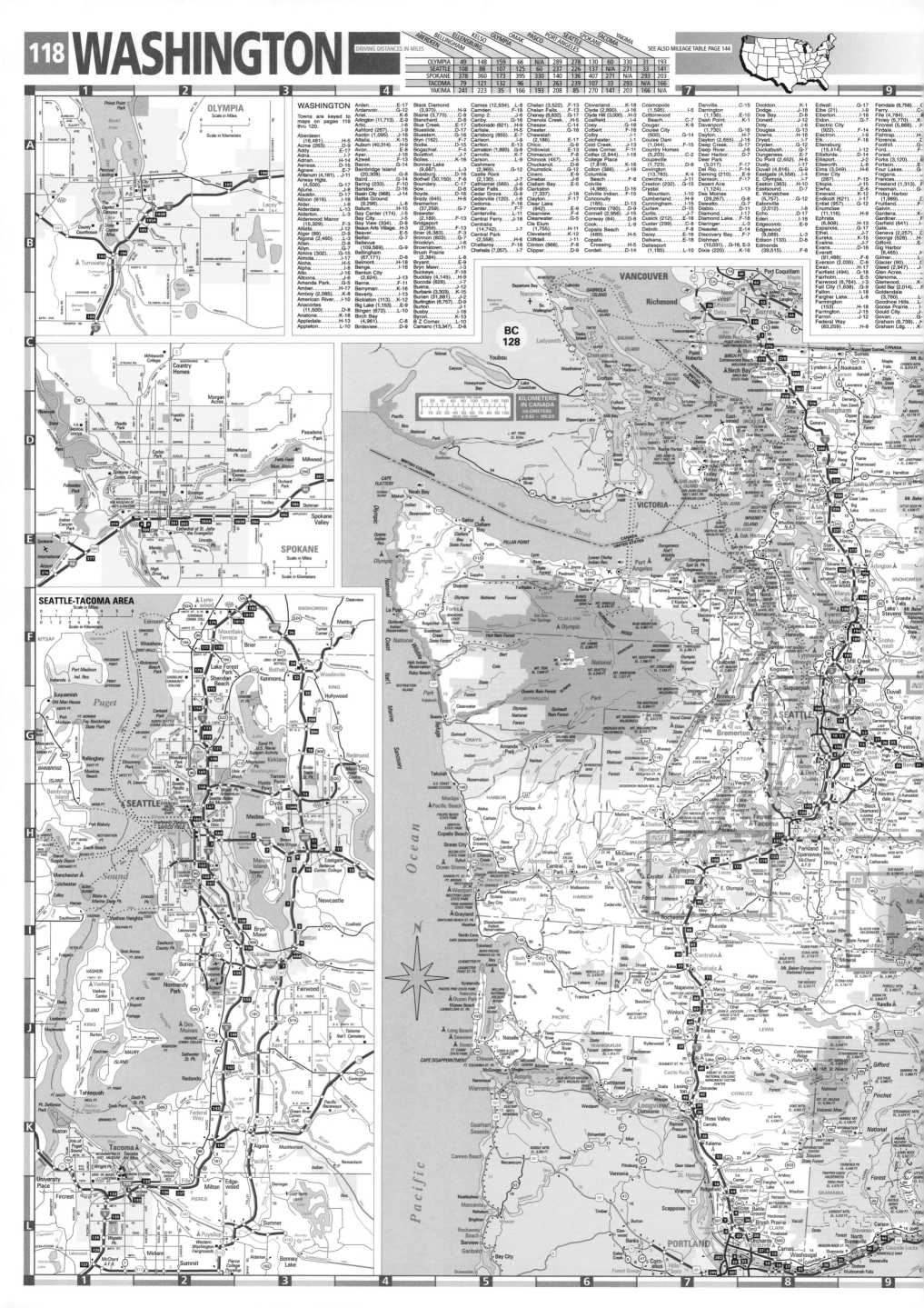

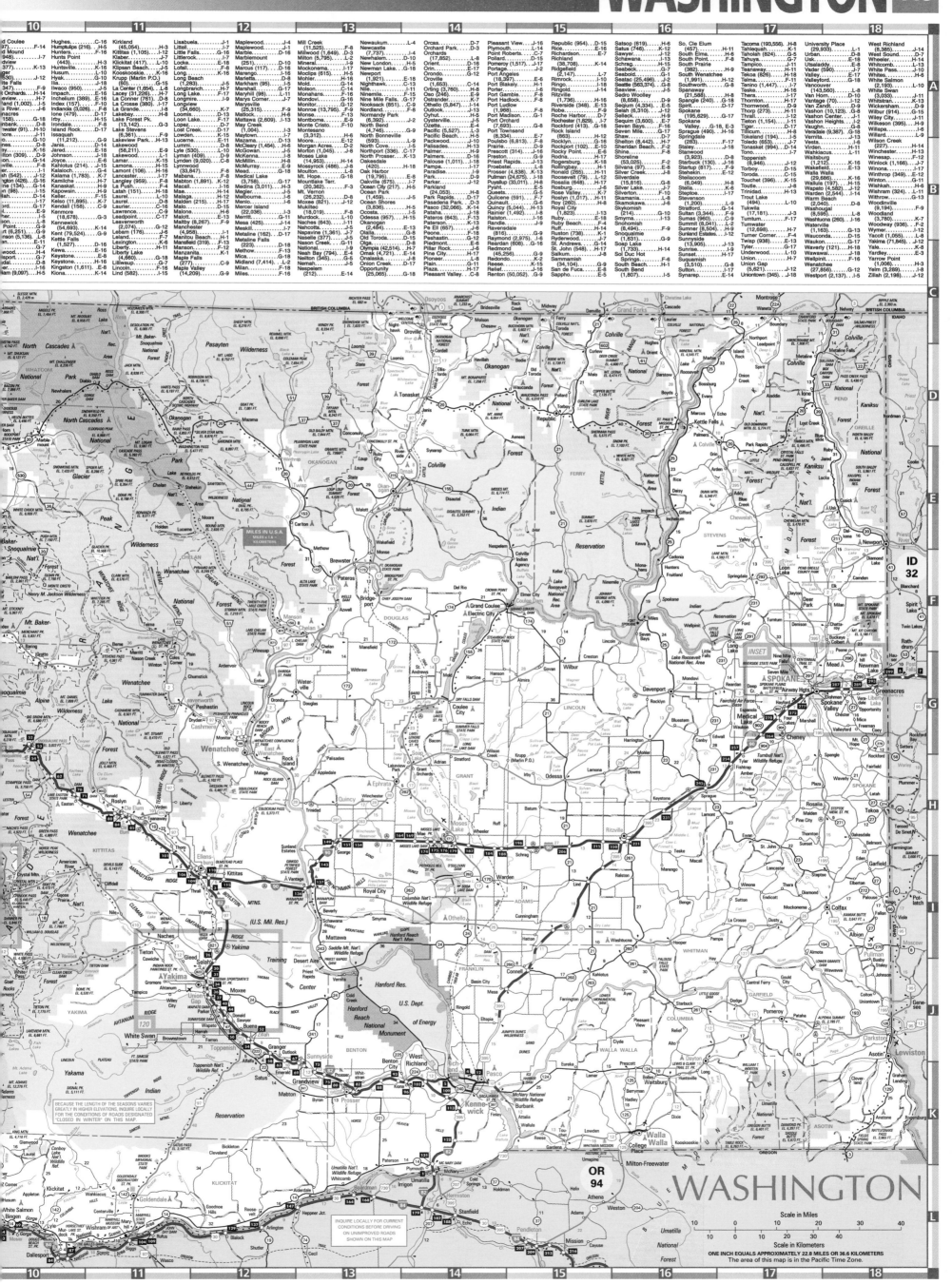

WASHINGTON

Scale in Miles

Scale in Kilometers

ONE INCH EQUALS APPROXIMATELY 22.8 MILES OR 36.6 KILOMETERS
The area of this map is in the Pacific Time Zone.

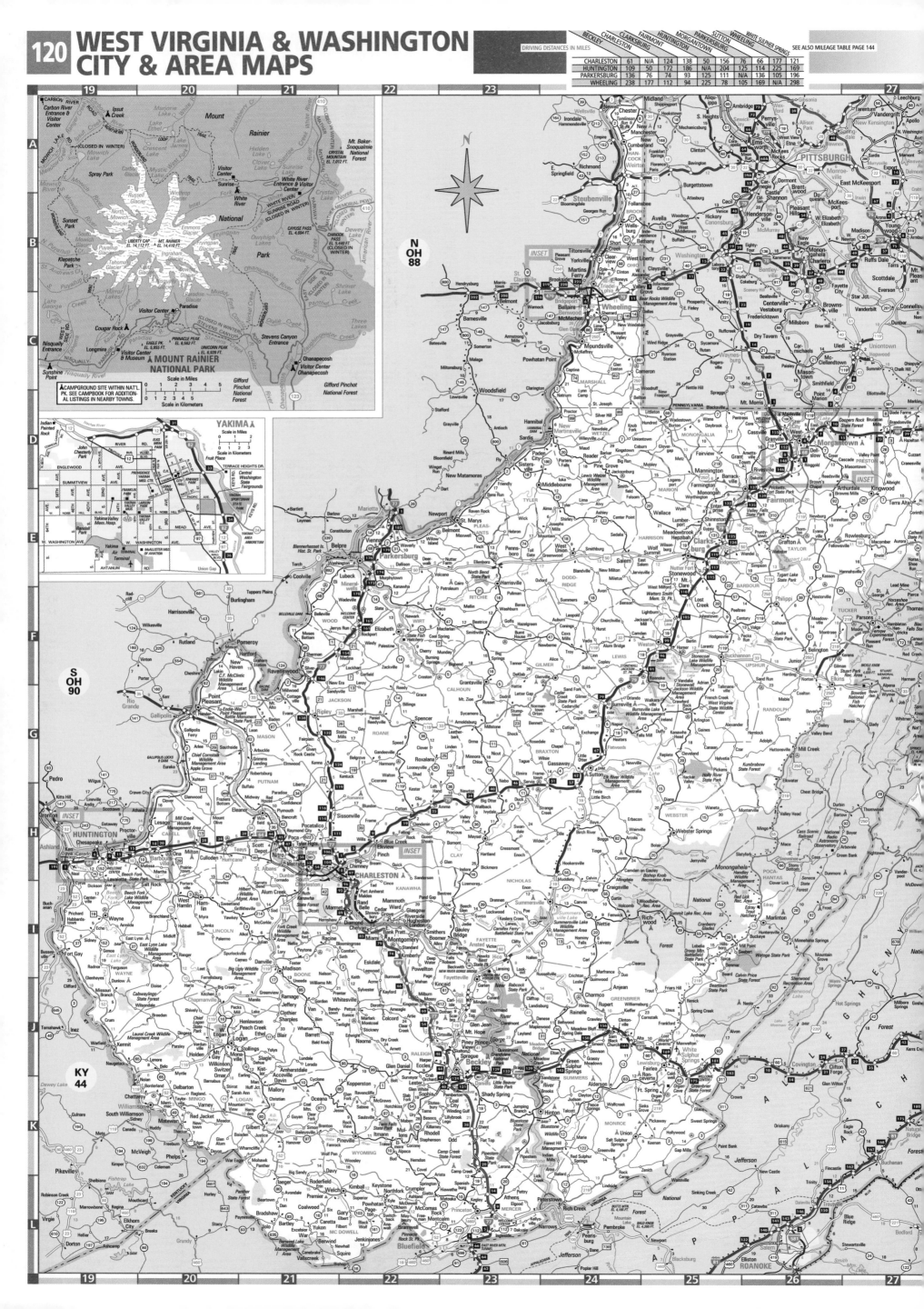

DRIVING DISTANCES IN MILES

SEE ALSO MILEAGE TABLE PAGE 144

	BECKLEY	CHARLESTON	CLARKSBURG	FAIRMONT	HUNTINGTON	MORGANTOWN	PARKERSBURG	SUTTON	WHEELING	WHITE SULPHUR SPRINGS
CHARLESTON	61	N/A	124	138	50	156	76	66	177	121
HUNTINGTON	109	50	172	186	N/A	204	125	114	225	169
PARKERSBURG	136	76	74	93	125	111	N/A	136	105	196
WHEELING	238	177	112	94	225	78	105	169	N/A	298

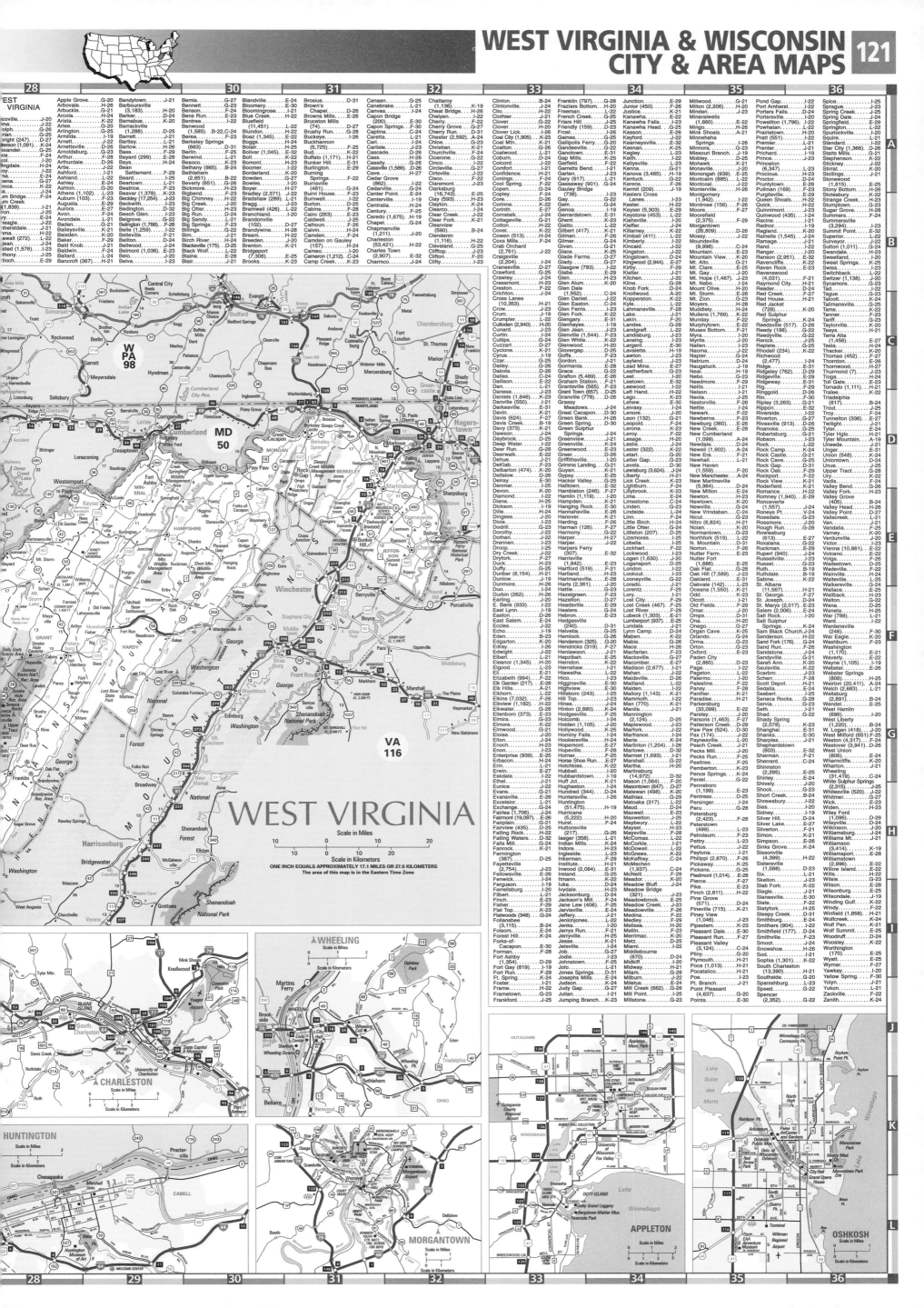

WEST VIRGINIA

Scale in Miles

Scale in Kilometers

ONE INCH EQUALS APPROXIMATELY 17.1 MILES OR 27.5 KILOMETERS
The area of this map is in the Eastern Time Zone

CHARLESTON

WHEELING

HUNTINGTON

MORGANTOWN

APPLETON

OSHKOSH

	APPLETON	BELOIT	EAU CLAIRE	GREEN BAY	KENOSHA	LA CROSSE	MADISON	MANITOWOC	MILWAUKEE	SPOONER	TOMAH	WAUSAU
EAU CLAIRE	200	224	N/A	195	279	128	177	242	246	82	81	102
GREEN BAY	31	188	195	N/A	156	203	135	39	116	254	156	96
LA CROSSE	171	189	128	203	244	N/A	141	214	210	205	44	169
MADISON	103	55	177	135	111	141	N/A	158	78	255	98	141
MILWAUKEE	107	76	246	116	38	210	78	83	N/A	324	168	210

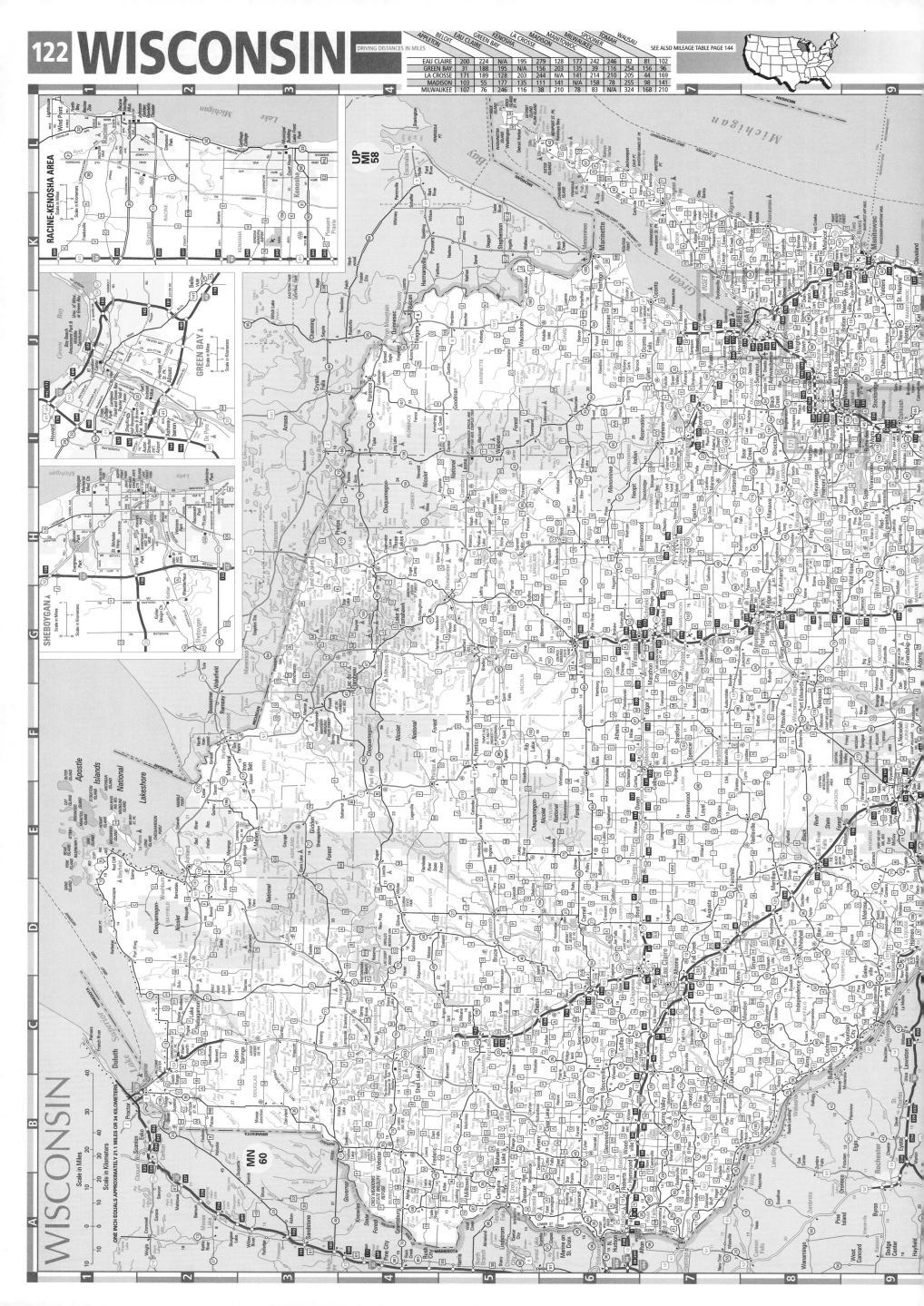

WISCONSIN

RACINE-KENOSHA AREA

GREEN BAY ▲

SHEBOYGAN ▲

UP MI 58

MN 60

ONE INCH EQUALS APPROXIMATELY 21.1 MILES OR 34 KILOMETERS

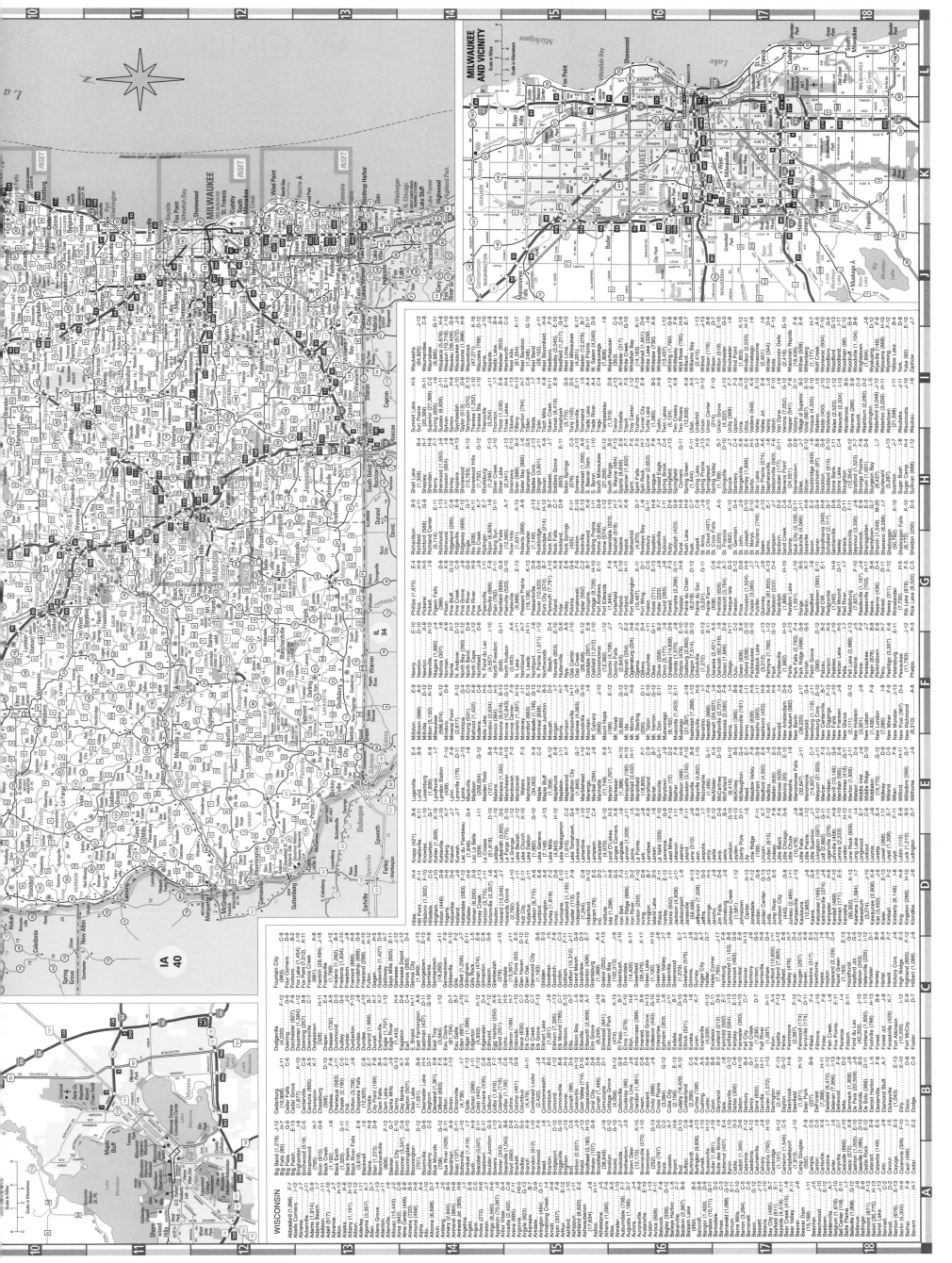

DRIVING DISTANCES IN MILES

SEE ALSO MILEAGE TABLE PAGE 144

	BUFFALO	CASPER	CHEYENNE	GILLETTE	LITTLE AMERICA	MORAN JCT.	RAWLINS	SHERIDAN
CASPER	112	N/A	180	182	263	253	117	149
CHEYENNE	291	180	N/A	247	293	402	147	326
SHERIDAN	35	149	326	104	411	352	264	N/A

WYOMING

Scale in Miles

Scale in Kilometers

ONE INCH EQUALS APPROXIMATELY 24.7 MILES OR 39.8 KILOMETERS

The area of this map is in the Mountain Time Zone.

CASPER

Scale in Miles

Scale in Kilometers

CHEYENNE

Scale in Miles

Scale in Kilometers

YELLOWSTONE and GRAND TETON NATIONAL PARKS

Scale in Miles

Scale in Kilometers

BECAUSE THE LENGTH OF THE SEASON VARIES GREATLY IN HIGHER ELEVATIONS, INQUIRE LOCALLY OR WITH THE U.S. PARK SERVICE FOR THE STATUS OF ROADS DESIGNATED "CLOSED IN WINTER" ON THIS MAP. WHEN ROADS ARE CLOSED DUE TO WINTER CONDITIONS, THE PARK IS ACCESSED BY SNOW VEHICLE OR CROSS COUNTRY SKIING.

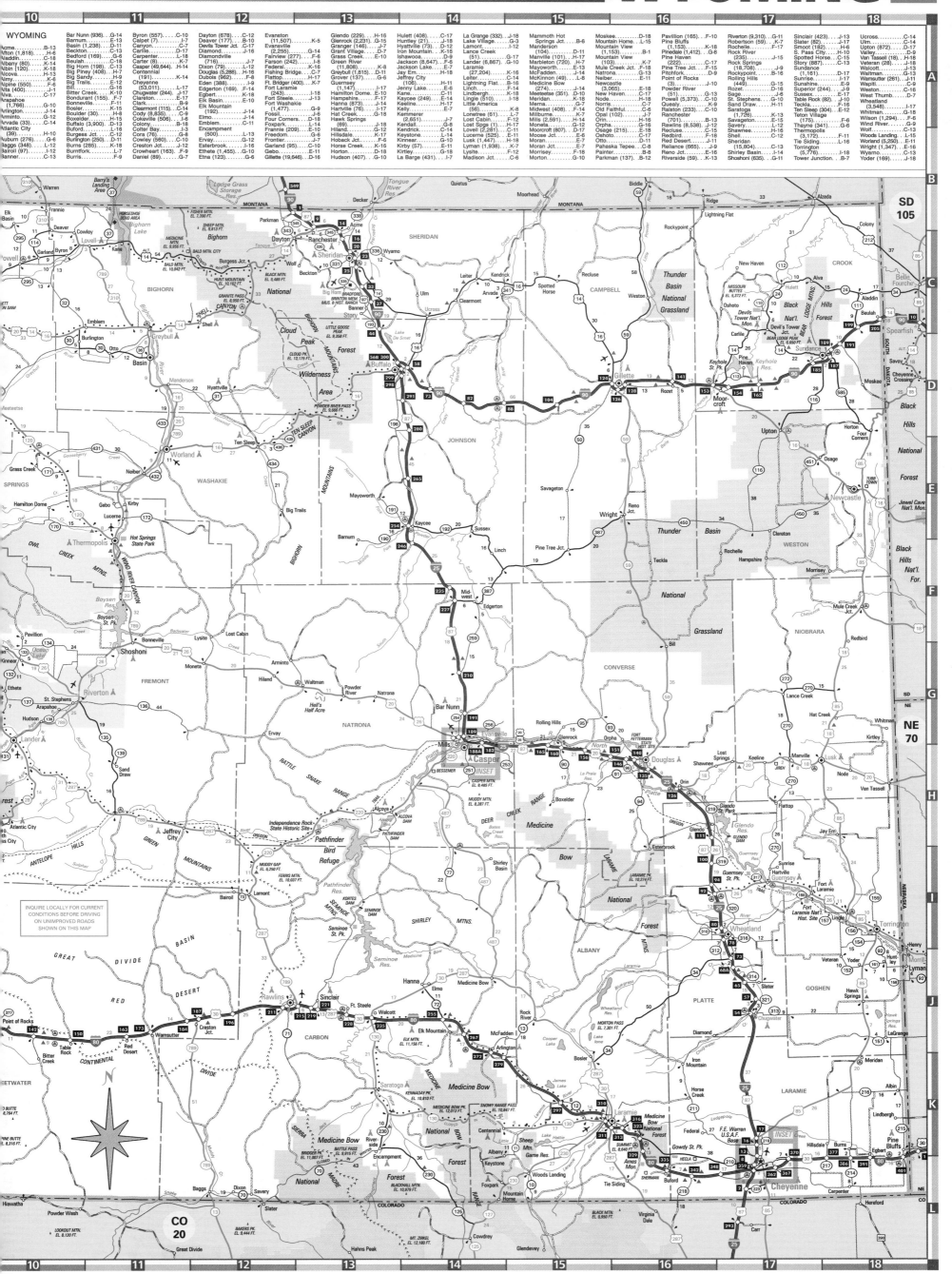

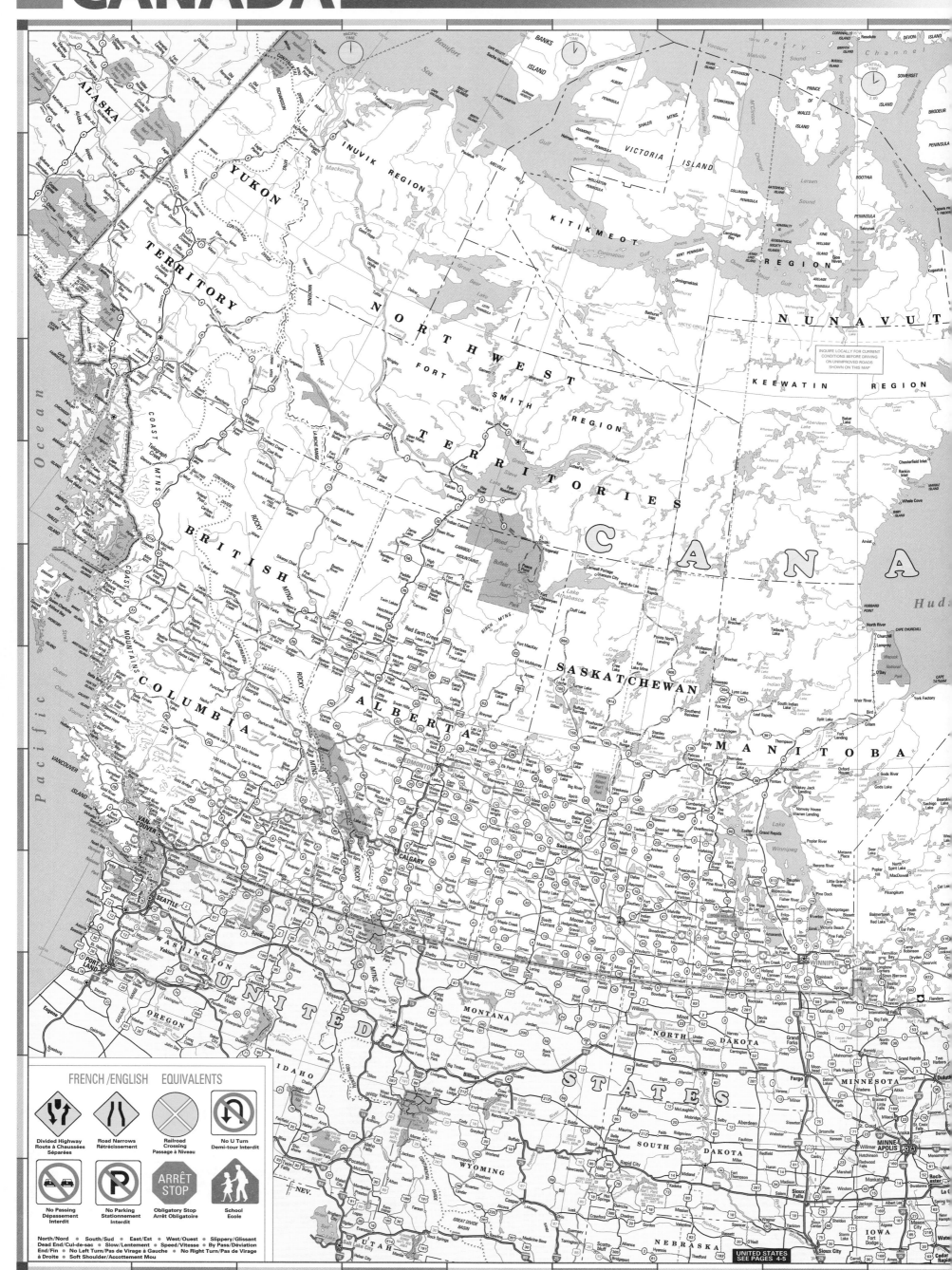

FRENCH /ENGLISH EQUIVALENTS

Divided Highway Route à Chaussées Séparées

Road Narrows Rétrécissement

Railroad Crossing Passage à Niveau

No U Turn Demi-tour Interdit

No Passing Dépassement Interdit

No Parking Stationnement Interdit

ARRÊT STOP — **Obligatory Stop** Arrêt Obligatoire

School Ecole

North/Nord • South/Sud • East/Est • West/Ouest
Dead End/Cul-de-sac • Slow/Lentement • Speed/Vitesse • By Pass/Déviation
End/Fin • No Left Turn/Pas de Virage à Gauche • No Right Turn/Pas de Virage
à Droite • Soft Shoulder/Accottement Mou

UNITED STATES
SEE PAGES 4-5

CANADA

NATIONAL PARKS, MONUMENTS AND CAPITAL NAMES
ARE SHOWN IN RED

Scale in Kilometers

Scale in Miles
ONE INCH EQUALS APPROXIMATELY 259 KILOMETERS OR 160 MILES

DRIVING DISTANCES IN KILOMETERS   SEE ALSO MILEAGE TABLE PAGE 144

	CRANBROOK	DAWSON CREEK	HOPE	KAMLOOPS	NANAIMO	OSOYOOS	PRINCE GEORGE	PRINCE RUPERT	VANCOUVER	VICTORIA
KAMLOOPS	581	867	175	N/A	822	272	504	1204	325	703
PRINCE GEORGE	862	364	595	504	1244	703	N/A	705	747	1125
VANCOUVER	943	1110	150	325	611	381	747	1446	N/A	148
VICTORIA	970	1488	529	703	119	703	1125	1826	148	N/A

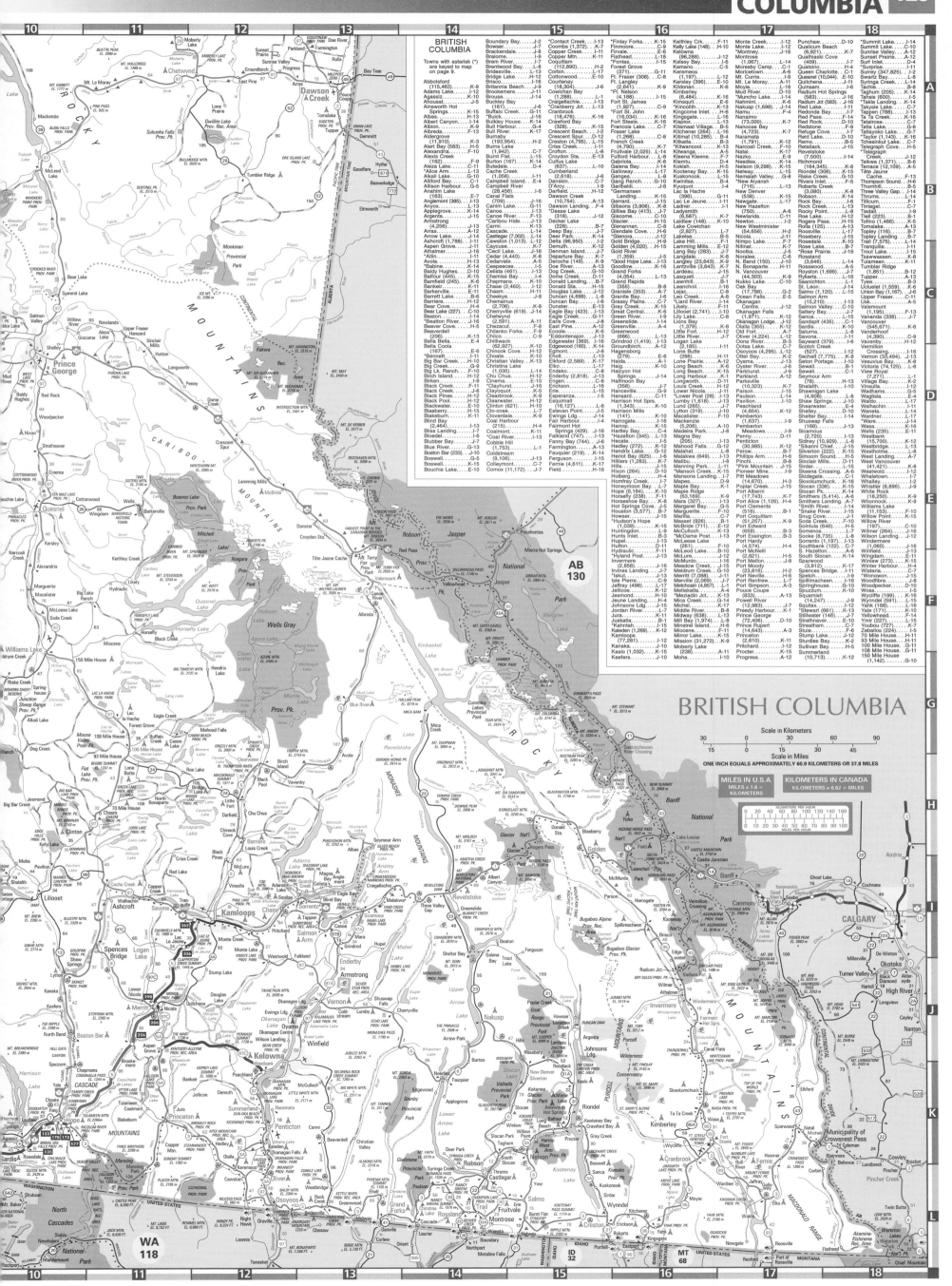

BRITISH COLUMBIA

Scale in Kilometers

Scale in Miles

ONE INCH EQUALS APPROXIMATELY 60.9 KILOMETERS OR 37.8 MILES

MILES IN U.S.A.
MILES x 1.6 = KILOMETERS

KILOMETERS IN CANADA
KILOMETERS x 0.62 = MILES

AB 130

AB 130

WA 118

WA 118

ID 32

MT 68

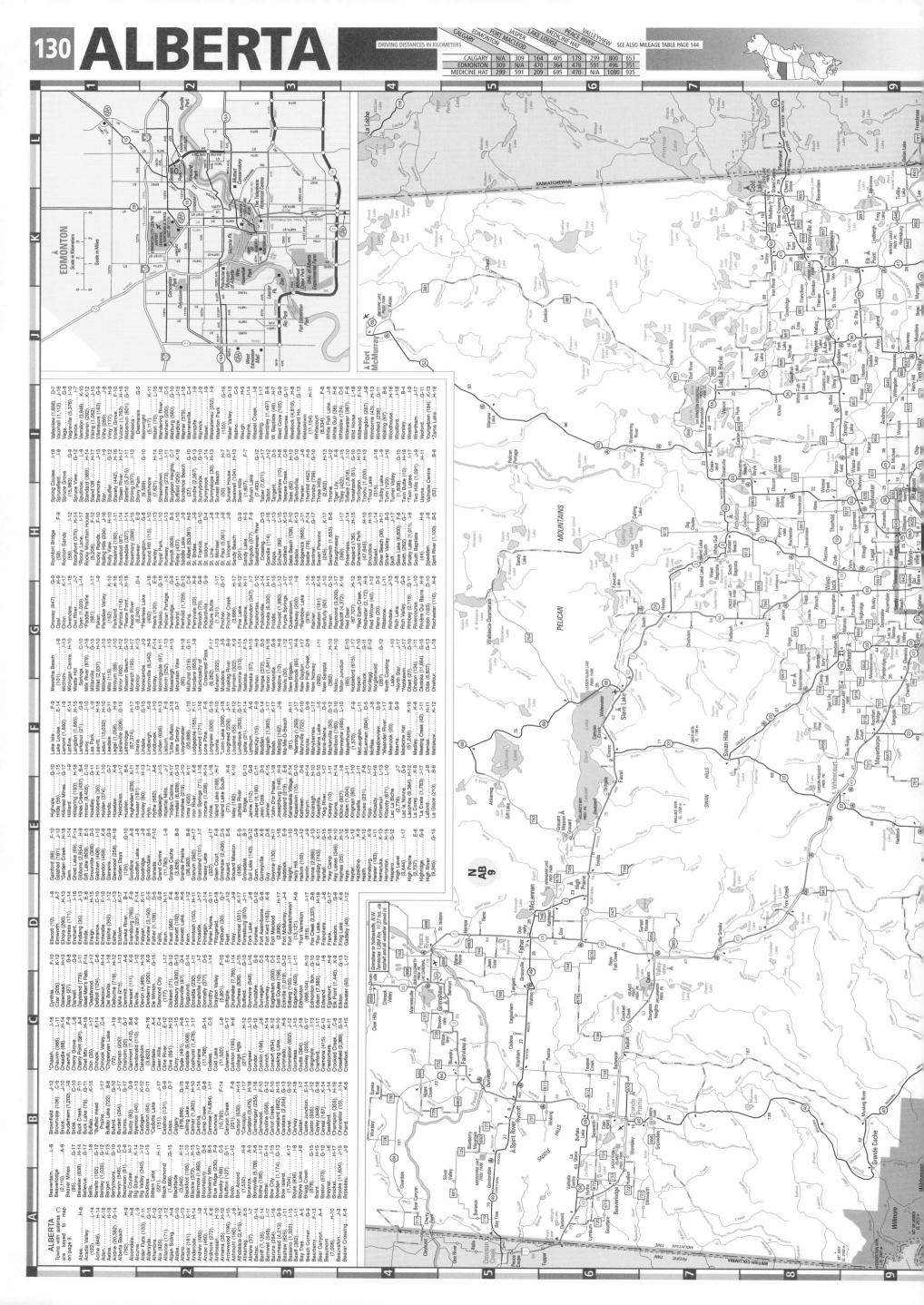

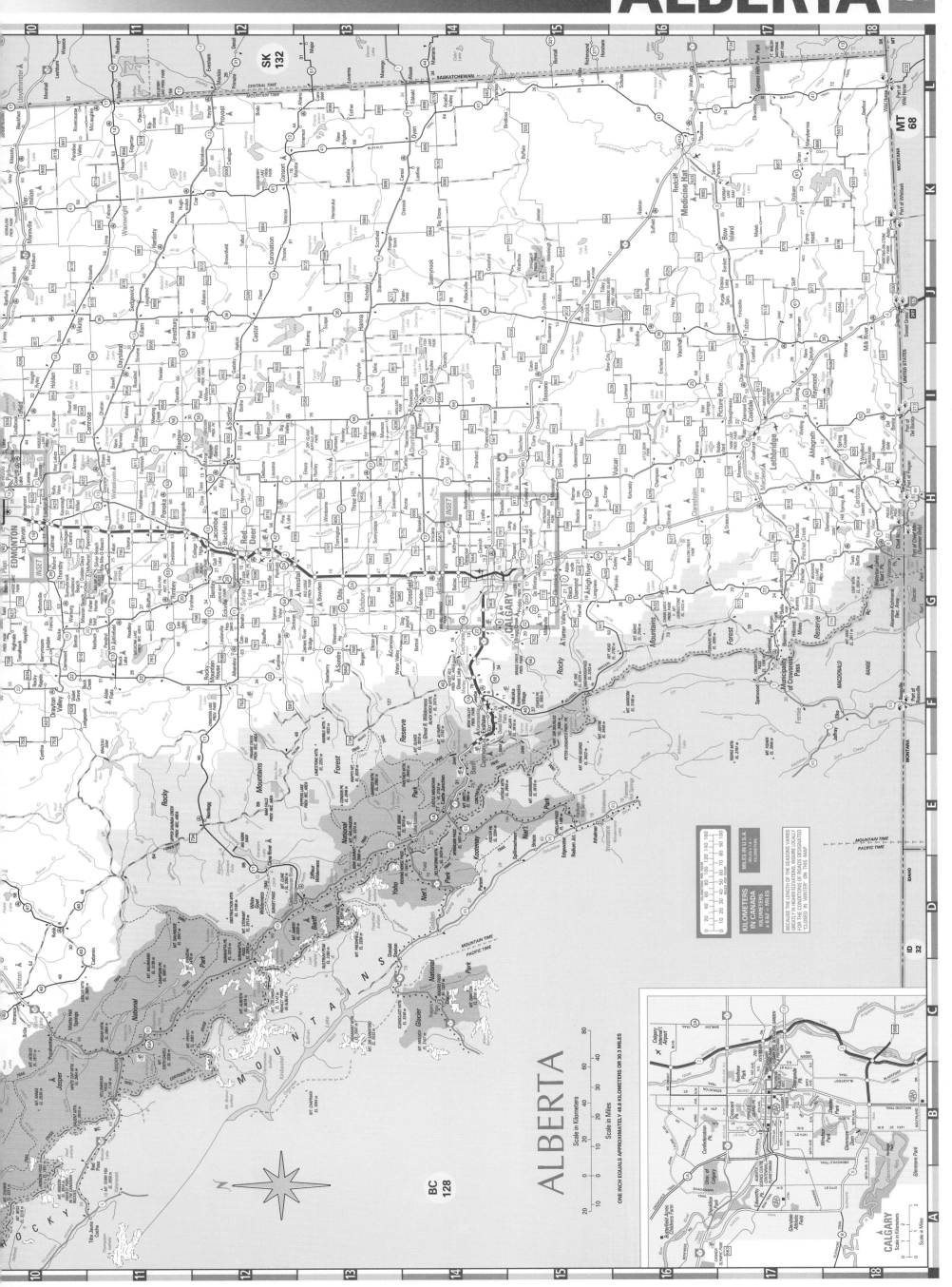

ALBERTA

Scale in Kilometers

Scale in Miles

ONE INCH EQUALS APPROXIMATELY 48.8 KILOMETERS OR 30.3 MILES

BC
128

SK
132

MT
68

BC
128

CALGARY
Scale in Miles
Scale in Kilometers

KILOMETERS IN CANADA
KILOMETERS
x 0.62 = MILES

MILES IN U.S.A.
MILES
KILOMETERS

BECAUSE THE LENGTH OF THE SEASONS VARIES GREATLY IN HIGHER ELEVATIONS, INQUIRE LOCALLY FOR THE CONDITIONS OF ROADS DESIGNATED "CLOSED IN WINTER" ON THIS MAP.

DRIVING DISTANCES IN KILOMETERS

SEE ALSO MILEAGE TABLE PAGE 144

	MOOSE JAW	NORTH BATTLEFORD	PRINCE ALBERT	REGINA	SASKATOON	SWIFT CURRENT	WHITEWOOD	YORKTON
PRINCE ALBERT	367	214	N/A	365	148	404	508	402
REGINA	74	396	365	N/A	255	240	174	191
SASKATOON	219	138	148	255	N/A	259	438	333

THE AAA STORY: 1902-2004 AND BEYOND

Americans haven't always had a love affair with their cars and the freedom of the open road. At the beginning of the 20th century, many states required that someone run ahead of an automobile to warn oncoming carriages of the car's approach! Interstate travel was no more convenient; drivers had to register and license their cars in each state they visited. The American Automobile Association was founded in 1902 when delegates from nine motor clubs, representing fewer than 1,000 members, met to combat the harsh laws being enacted against the newfangled horseless carriage. Today, one in four U.S. households is a member of AAA. The largest motoring organization in the world, AAA provides its more than 46 million members with much more than emergency road service and up-to-date travel publications. Legislative experts regularly monitor transportation issues affecting the motoring public. Travel and insurance agents provide full-service packages. New programs constantly are being developed to educate the public about traffic safety.

AAA is a fully tax-paying, not-for-profit federation with a network of offices employing more than 44,000 people. Through some 200 international affiliates in more than 110 countries, AAA members receive a wide variety of services.

AAA—headquartered just outside Orlando in the central Florida town of Heathrow—is ready for future growth and success in the 21st century.

REGINA

SASKATOON

SASKATCHEWAN

Scale in Kilometers
Scale in Miles
ONE INCH EQUALS APPROXIMATELY 46.3 KILOMETERS OR 28.1 MILES

ALBERTA

MANITOBA

CENTRAL TIME / MOUNTAIN TIME

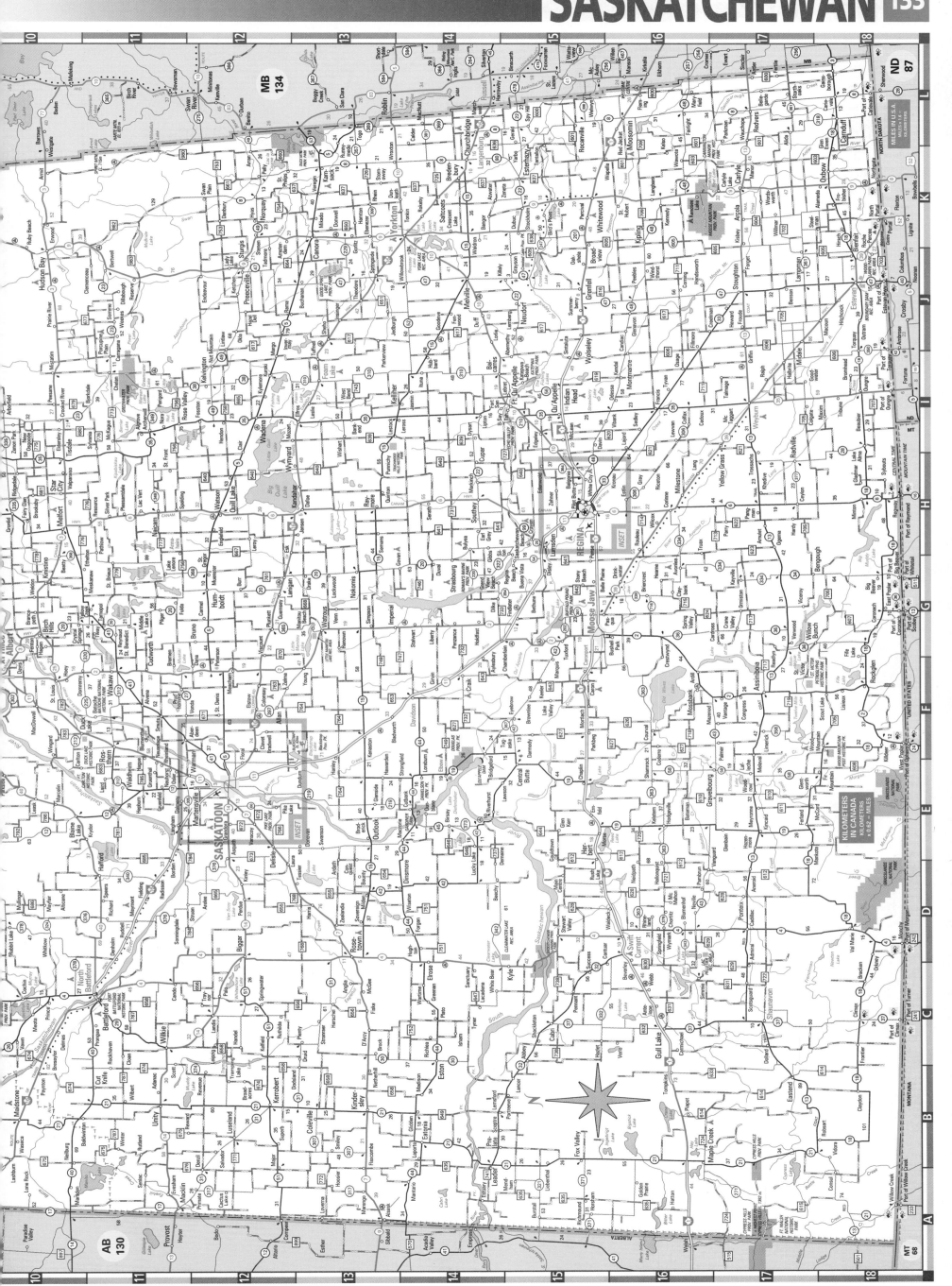

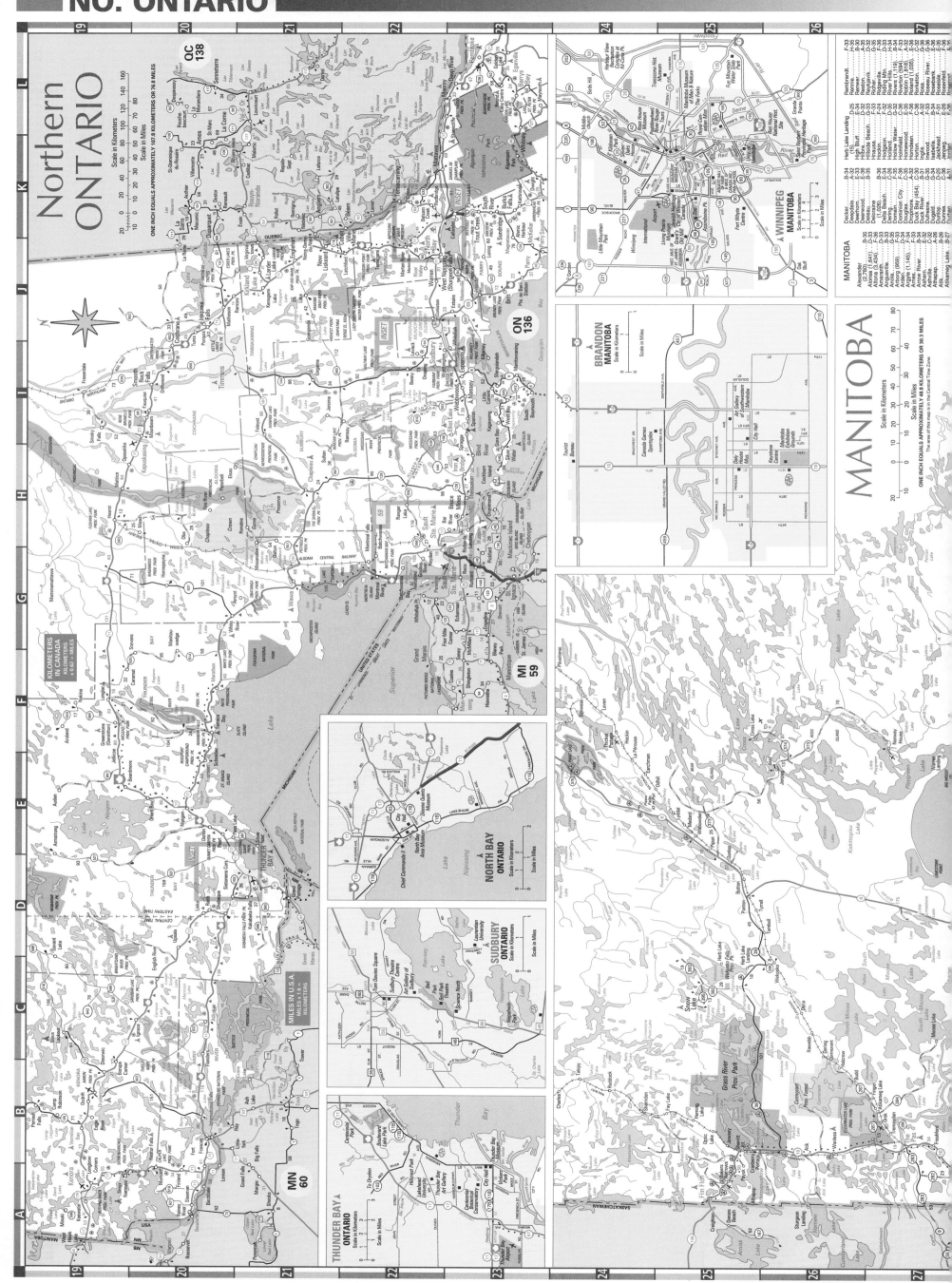

Northern ONTARIO

MANITOBA

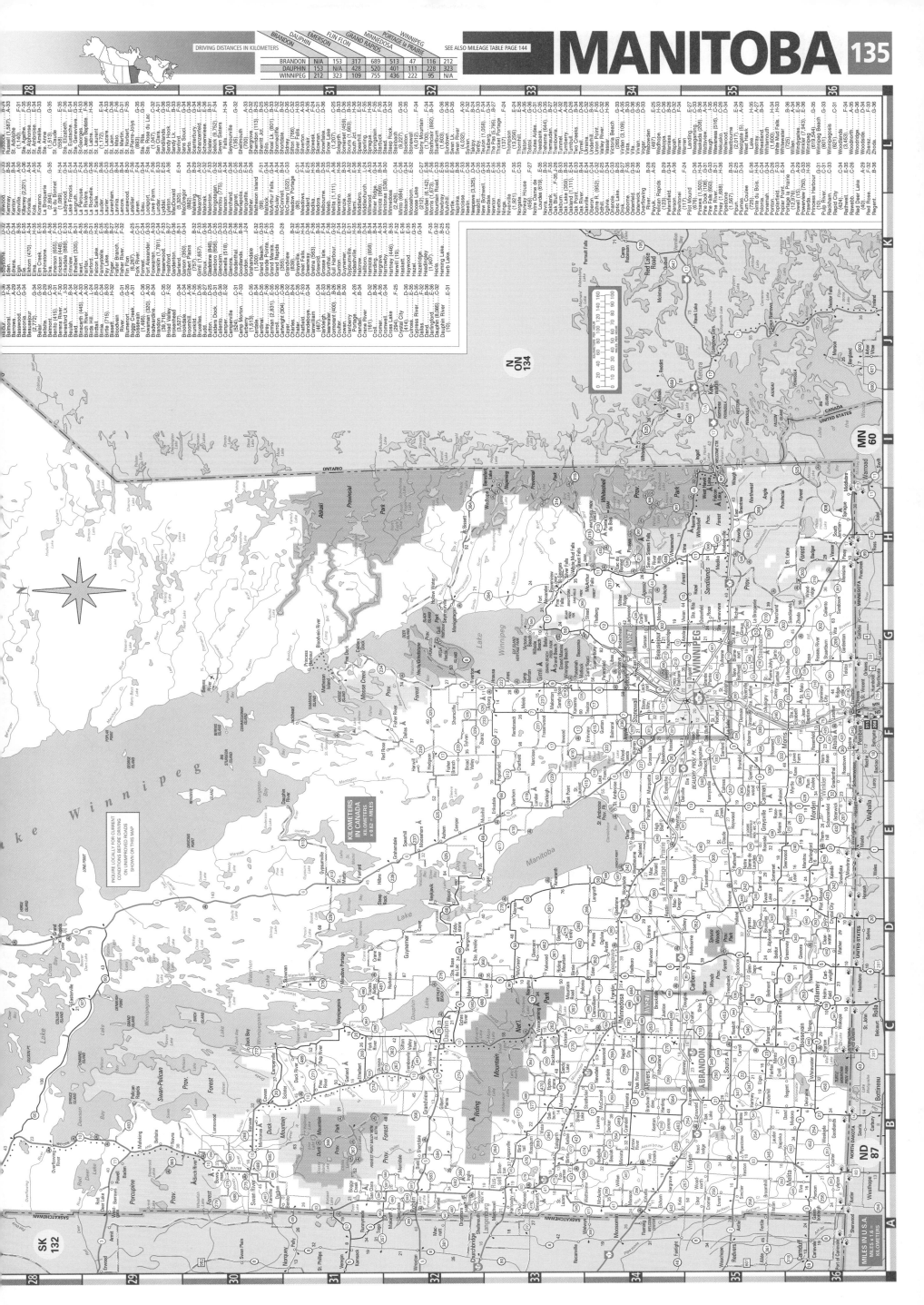

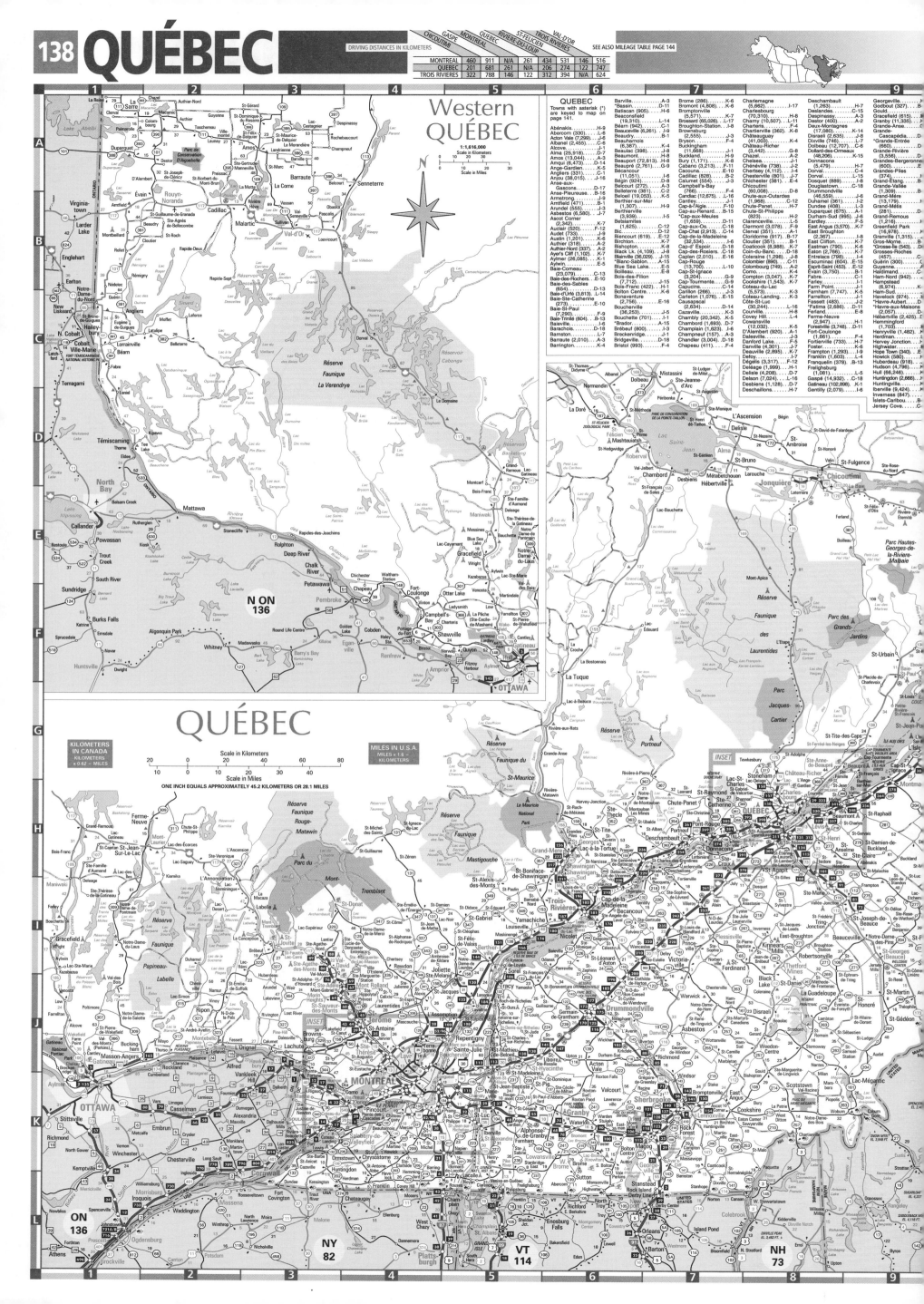

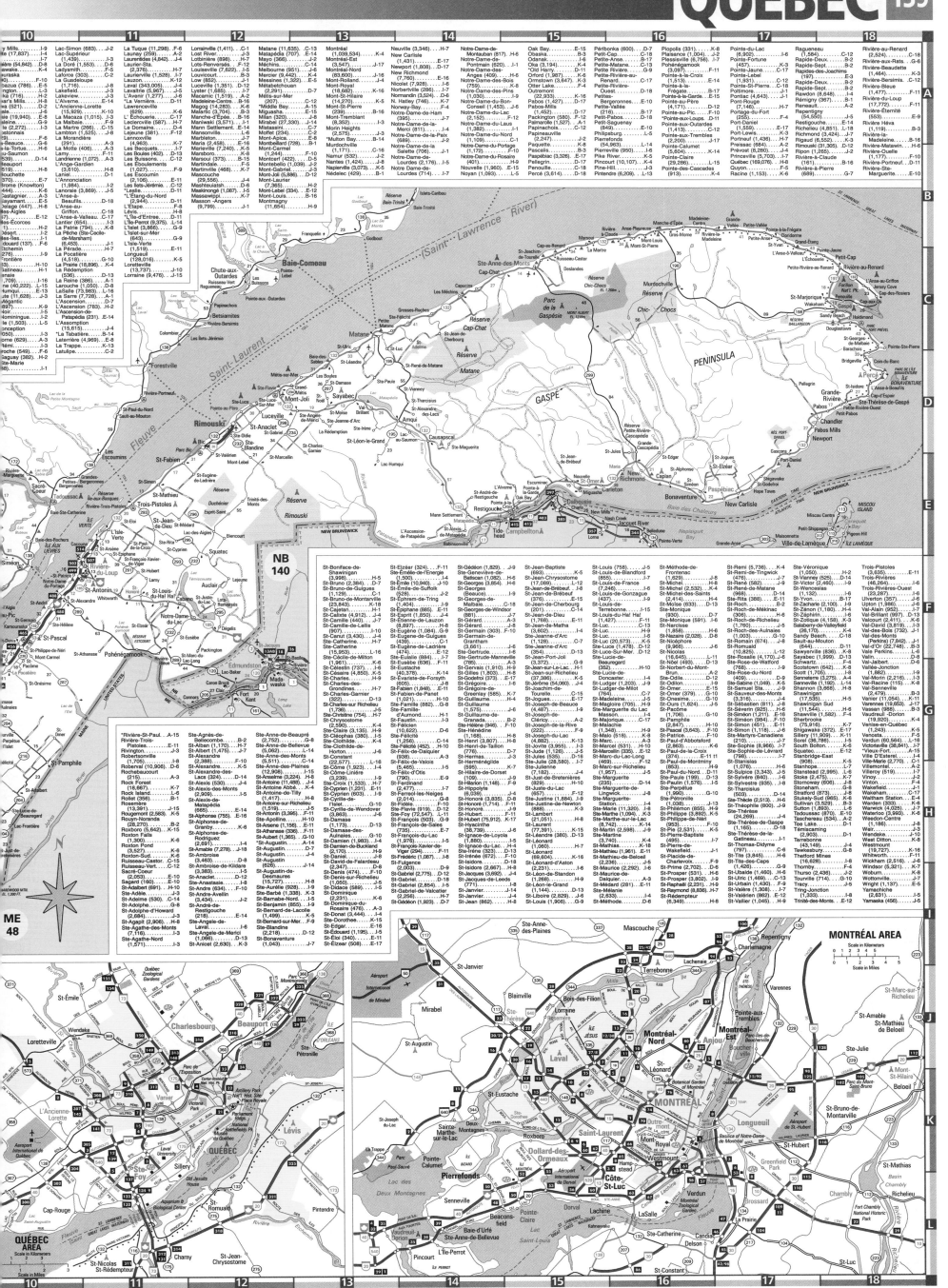

DRIVING DISTANCES IN KILOMETERS

SEE ALSO MILEAGE TABLE PAGE 144

	CAMPBELLTON, NB	CHANNEL-PORT AUX BASQUES, NF	CHARLOTTETOWN, PE	FREDERICTON, NB	HALIFAX, NS	MONCTON, NB	NEW GLASGOW, NS	PORT HASTINGS, NS	SAINT JOHN, NB	ST. JOHN'S, NF	SYDNEY, NS	YARMOUTH, NS
CHARLOTTETOWN, PE	444	706	N/A	372	327	185	293	397	322	1609	555	597
FREDERICTON, NB	372	832	372	N/A	455	180	418	521	113	1738	681	721
HALIFAX, NS	576	573	327	455	N/A	269	159	262	405	1475	420	330
SAINT JOHN, NB	484	785	322	113	405	134	372	476	N/A	1689	634	674
ST. JOHN'S, NF	1854	898	1609	1738	1475	1548	1311	1207	1689	N/A	1093	1739

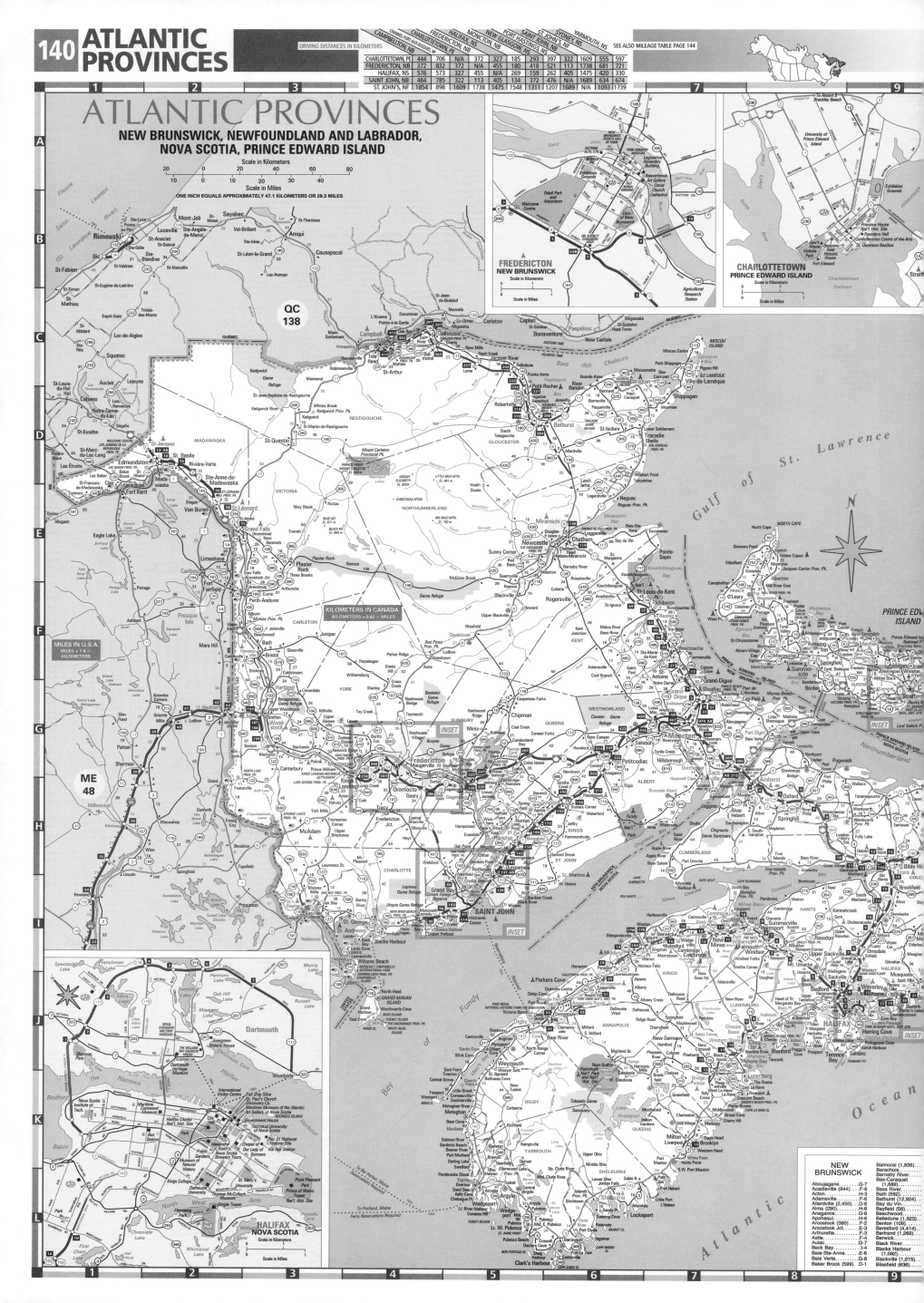

ATLANTIC PROVINCES
NEW BRUNSWICK, NEWFOUNDLAND AND LABRADOR, NOVA SCOTIA, PRINCE EDWARD ISLAND

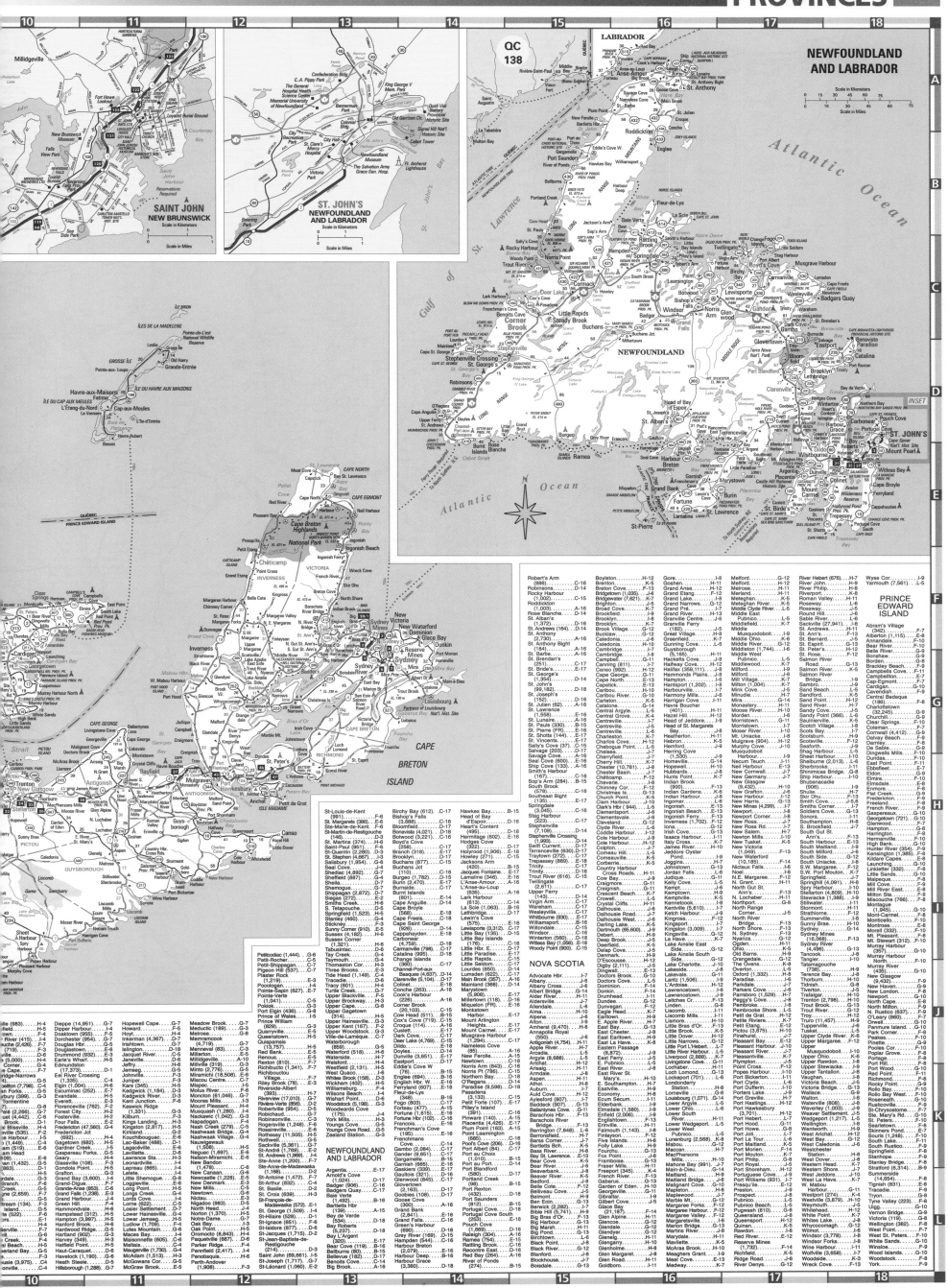

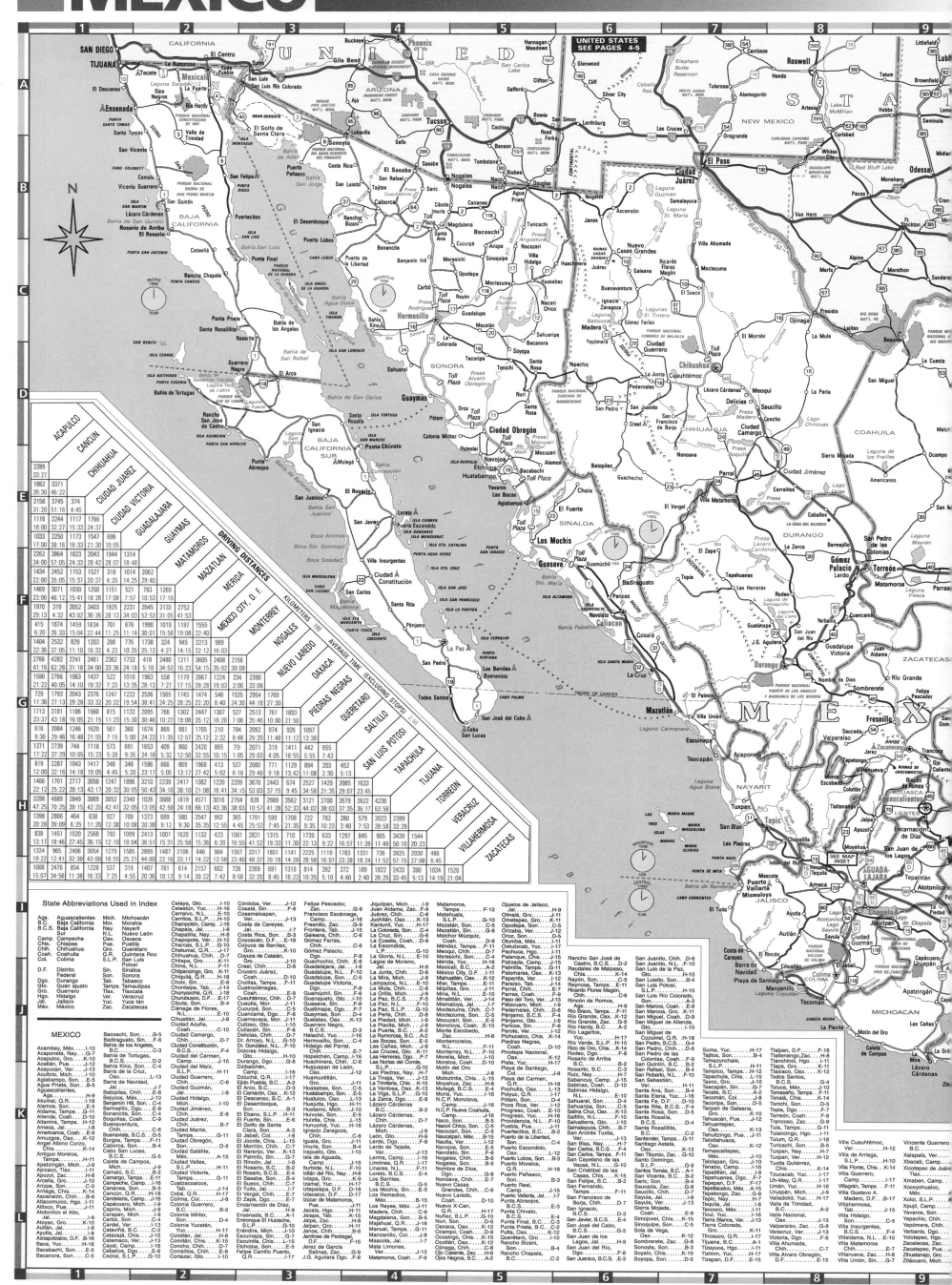

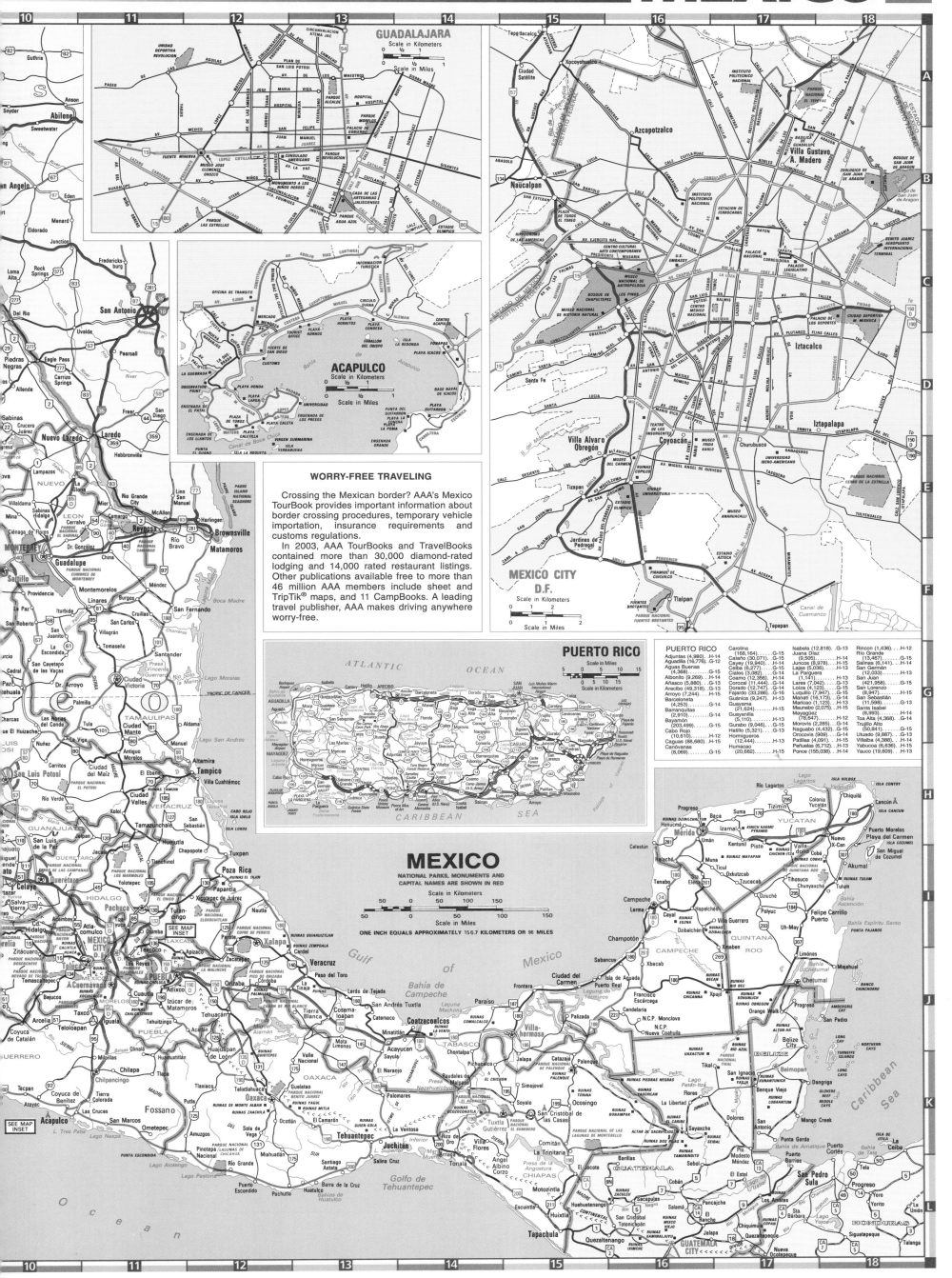

NORTH AMERICAN MILEAGE TABLE

NORTH AMERICAN MILEAGE TABLE

The routes used to determine these mileages are not necessarily the shortest distance between cities, but represent the route considered the easiest drive for general travel.

Distances are shown in miles